LAST CHIEF STANDING:

Tale of Two Cultures

Wendell George

By Wendell George

DEDICATION

I am dedicating this book to my Dad, Moses George, who was elected to the first Colville Business Council [CBC] in 1938 and to Dale Kohler who served on the CBC from 1975 to 1996. They were not only instrumental in the litigation of the Colville Confederated Tribes lower Columbia fishing case and the Wenatchee River/Icicle Creek fishing case but key resources for our tribal history. I offer this book as part of their legacy.

TABLE OF CONTENTS

Foreword
Daniel J. Evans

I grew up in the city of Seattle and had little contact with Indian tribes or customs. When I was elected to the Washington state House of Representatives I followed my interests in transportation, higher education, and the environment.

When I was elected Governor in 1965 I quickly discovered a host of new issues which demanded immediate attention. One of the most urgent was the challenge to tribal fishing rights by the State Game Department. State game agents forcibly removed tribal fishing nets from the Nisqually River and the ensuing battle made headline news both locally and nationally. I was embarrassed by the conflict and began to study the origins of tribal and US government relationships.

It was a sordid tale of forced removal of tribes from their traditional homes, forced treaties, repeated breaking of treaties by the US government, stealing of tribal natural resources, and efforts to assimilate Native Americans and eliminate reservations entirely.

I was determined to learn more and created the Governor's Indian Advisory Committee by executive order. We attempted to represent all of the tribes in the state in addition to urban Indians. The first meeting was an impressive reminder that there was much to be done. Tribal leaders from around the state, some in traditional dress, attended but it was apparent that deep skepticism ruled the day. Years of broken promises created an understandable doubt that this effort would be any different. I first met Wendell George as a representative of the Colville tribe to the Commission. He and his colleagues began the long task of educating me about the unique history and perspective of Indian people in North America.

We discussed Indian fishing rights, jurisdiction, taxation on Indian reservations, and self-governance. This new insight led me to a leadership role on the Special Committee on Indian Affairs when I joined the United States Senate. I was deeply pleased when Wendell presented the case to the Senate for the Lake Roosevelt Management Agreement. He represented the Spokane and Colville tribes and I reflected on how far we had come since the first meeting of the Governor's Indian Advisory Committee.

Now Wendell has written a fascinating history of his family and his tribe from the unique perspective of one who lived through extraordinary change and fought to retain Indian culture and traditions in a fast paced modern world. He relates that history through seven generations of his family and the tribulations and sorrow of Indians as a flood of settlers advanced westward. Manifest Destiny was the battle cry of expansion as the United States became a transcontinental nation. Indians were to be swept aside or assimilated and native culture destroyed.

This book is a fascinating story of one family's effort to maintain and build a tribal culture that fits the modern world. It is a tale of struggle and success, poignant and occasionally hilarious but always focused on strengthening the unique sovereignty that exists by treaty between Indian tribes and the United States. It ends with a message of spirituality that may be controversial but the future is unknown to us all.

EVANS, Daniel Jackson, (1925 -)

Senate Years of Service: 1983-1989
Party: Republican

EVANS, Daniel Jackson, a Senator from Washington; born in Seattle, King County, Wash., October 16, 1925; graduated, University of Washington, Seattle (civil engineering) 1948, and received a graduate degree from that university in 1949; served in the United States Navy 1943-1946; returned to duty 1951-1953; civil engineer and contractor; member, Washington State house of representatives 1956-1965; Governor 1965-1977; chairman of the National Governors Association 1973-1974; president, Evergreen State College, Olympia, Wash., 1977-1983; appointed on September 8, 1983, to the United States Senate to fill the vacancy caused by the death of Henry M. Jackson; took the oath of office on September 12, 1983; subsequently elected by special election as a Republican on November 8, 1983, to complete the term, and served from September 8, 1983, to January 3, 1989; not a candidate for reelection in 1988; chairman, Daniel J. Evans Associates 1989-; member, University of Washington Board of Regents 1993-2005, serving as president 1996-1997; is a resident of Seattle, Wash.

AUTHOR'S PREFACE

My Dad, Moses George, is responsible for me writing this book. He, along with my mother, Marie, started writing stories after Dad retired from the Washington State Highway Department in 1969. They wrote about little known episodes of our ancestors. Now I can pass this priceless information on to my family.

While I was serving on the Colville Business Council [1986-1990] we contracted with a research group to write a history of our tribe. We wanted it written so that it could be used as a textbook or reference in all our schools on or near the Colville Indian Reservation. Dale Kohler, a long-time Councilman, was the primary proponent of this. The consultants did the research but unfortunately before we could write the textbook we had to divert these resources to the Lower Columbia fishing case. This evolved into a lengthy litigation called the Wenatchee River/Icicle Creek fishing case. We won the fishing rights on August 13, 2008 but the issue of a Wenatchi reservation is still unresolved.

I have traced my ancestry back seven generations. Like most people I did this out of curiosity. But I was also interested in testing the common Indian belief that before we take any major action we should consider the impact on the following seven generations. Another belief is that we are all connected to nature including everything on the earth and in the galaxy.

The story spans seven generations of my family as they moved from a nomadic existence into the modern world and resisted extinction. Their challenges not only included physical survival but identity survival. The clash of cultures was more than just who could occupy the land. It was about freedom and what it means. The Indian form of democracy is far different than the dominant society. The question now is where the future will take both of them.

As a seventh generation I am trying to reconstruct what my ancestors did that affects my generation. From this I have identified a set of cultural traits that are useful for coping with today's world. The story is a little thin for the sixth and seventh generations back because our oral history didn't provide us with many details. Five generations back is the generation of my qqana [father's side] great-grandfather, Patwankt. He is the source of my Indian name, Potwana, given to me by my dad, Moses [Moyese] after I became of age. He said it meant "leader". I thought he made that up because he was known to embellish things where I was concerned. However, as it turned out, he was at least partially right.

The past is always intriguing to the younger generation. To them our ancestors lived in exciting times. That may be so, but more importantly we should ask: What did they leave us that will help us lead better lives and what can we leave future generations?

The underlying message sent by our ancestors was that we are all part of nature, i.e., the trees, rivers, mountains, sky, stars, etc. When we fully realize this we can do things we can't even imagine today. Small examples of this are described throughout the generations. Forward thinking people like Deepak Chopra, M.D. and Eckhart Tolle today call it living in the "NOW."

But being part of nature isn't physical like Coyote was characterized in Tony Hillerman's 1990 novel "Coyote Waits".

We aren't hungry for food. We want answers to why things are the way they are. Or are they?

Sketch by Tony Sandoval per Confederated Salish & Kootenai Tribes

ACKNOWLEDGEMENTS

I would like to thank my wife, Barbara, for her patience and encouragement while I was writing this book. I know it was hard on her at times because when I am doing something like this I am single-minded and tend to let other things slide.

My whole family encouraged me in their own way. Mike, Rick, Kerry, Matt, Kathy, and Rob were probably convinced that I would never finish it because I took so long. They eventually quit asking about it but their family members Olivia and April [Rick], Colleen and Christyna [Kerry], Jan [Matt], and Moses, Andy & Amy [Rob] would still inquire.

I was fortunate to have Mary Koch do some editing and general comments. Mary has been in the editorial business for some time and also is familiar with a lot of tribal history and is acquainted with many tribal members. She was very patient and helpful.

The book would not have been complete without former Governor/Senator Dan Evans perspective in his insightful Foreword. I appreciate his generous comments.

And lastly, I received a lot of professional help from Create Space, a subsidiary of Amazon who specializes in helping authors. They did an overall evaluation and helped format the book. I found their system for creating books covers very useful when I wrote my first book "Coyote Finishes the People".

INTRODUCTION

This is a tale of two cultures describing how one Indian family moved from a nomadic existence into the modern world and resisted extinction. The question now is where the future will take them.

The picture above is the bronze; six meter high Statue of Freedom on top of the U.S. Capitol Building. This statue was conceived in 1855, the year of the Yakama Indian War, and is a visual symbol of the evolution of America. The female body indicates justice, the military helmet is self-evident, and the eagle's head, crest of feathers, and native blanket are American Indian. And, finally, the statue faces East, the first direction of the American Indian Medicine Wheel.

In 1990 fellow councilmen Dale Kohler, Gene Joseph and I noticed this statue on top of the Capitol Dome that looks like an Indian woman in a helmet covered with feathers. I didn't realize the significance of this until I read the book by Jack Weatherford given to me by my son, Kerry, called *Indian Givers*. She is an inadvertent memorial to Indians that personifies the subtle way our culture has been infused into society. That is why I used it as a theme for this book.

Seven generations back my ancestors were faced with basic survival. As they evolved their problems became more complicated but their ability to solve them increased. What each generation learned is passed on to the next generation. The accumulation of ideas and the growth of native ability to adjust to the changes increased at a faster rate with each generation. The seventh generation is at the peak of that cycle. The eighth generation will be starting over at a new level much higher than the previous cycle.

The story begins with a vivid description of the infamous Manifest Destiny which decimated the native tribes. The story has been told before but mostly by historians, not Indians. My family lived a competitive but relatively peaceful life for untold generations before the white settlers came. When the northwest was finally discovered and opened to settlement the next few generations met and contended with the intrusion of the new immigrants. The question is always how will my family survive?

The last five generations of grandparents lived through major changes to their life style. The ways of modern civilization were not compatible to their old ways, forcing them to learn a new approach to living. But they desperately tried to merge the new with the old. They did not want to lose what had enabled their people to exist for thousands of years. In doing this they discovered themselves. It is the first time they had to look deeper for the reasons they did what they did. Before that they just did what their ancestors did, no questions asked.

Then in a more contemporary time my Great-grandfather, Chilcosahaskt, found himself in the middle of a white settlement that tried to force him to move. He refused to move and spent the remainder of his life on his ancestral grounds. As soon as he passed on the settlers used their legal means to take the land.

My grandfather, Lahompt, witnessed the signing of the Yakama treaty of 1855 and saw the one sided negotiations of an impatient governor of the Washington Territories. The governor solved the "Indian problem" by taking their aboriginal land and moving them to reservations. During the four years before Congress ratified the treaty on April 19, 1859 the Army and settlers violated or ignored the terms of the treaty. A war was started because the U.S. Army Colonel preferred to fight rather than maintain peace. Ratification of the treaty didn't change anything because the U.S. abandoned the northwest during the Civil War and the area remained in turmoil. Finally, the Colville Indian Reservation was created on July 1, 1872 and twelve tribes were forced to move there. Lahompt didn't move until the 1880's. He made the transition to a new life style in order to survive. He built a cattle ranch which fit with his love of horses.

The transition is dramatically illustrated by my dad, Moyese, who was the last of the family to be born in a tepee and the first to father a college graduate, me. This marked the change from the old ways to the new. However, he never lost sight of his Indian culture. He taught his family about their history, culture, and the lifestyle of the American Indian. He also kept the family tradition of raising horses.

American Indians are invisible to the world but they survive with their inherent tie to nature and intense concern for future generations. A lack of a written language hasn't stopped them from following Indian traditions.

Our tribe began making conscious decisions. But we never lost our desire to enable our tribe to survive as a group. So we had to carefully analyze the new way of life to see how it fit with the old way. The new immigrants tried to assimilate us into their society but it didn't take. We wanted to live in a manner totally foreign to the dominant society. Over a tumultuous period of time the smaller Indian community seemed to be destined for extinction. But gradually our modified lifestyle began influencing the communities around us. The result was a much better integrated system.

The tribe survived and thrived by developing their natural resources. I gave up a promising career in private industry to return and help my tribe develop their resources. They are now the largest employer in the area. Emphasis on training and education is preparing them for a much faster paced life. They are like the mythical Kokopelli leading us into the next world.

Although we had difficulties making this change, our tribe adjusted not only to survive but to flourish. The economy is no longer a direct line pursuit of food. Instead, it is several steps away through full-time careers and paychecks to purchase the necessities for sustaining life. Today we use jet airplanes instead of horses and legal arguments instead of guns. Battles are still fought but through negotiation and paper trails.

Now we have come full circle. Science is discovering principles that Indians have intuitively known for generations. And major religions are reconciling their dogmas to that of the American Indian.

Over the years many have encouraged me to write my story. Most recently Andy Joseph Sr. mentioned it while we were talking at the Omak Stampede Indian Encampment. He served on the Tribal Council for 14 years. We served together in 1986-87, which were his last two years on the Council. The story I offer you sends a positive message that mixes the Indian Way with the Way of the Future. A New World is emerging and, like the Hopi Kokopelli demonstrates, Indians are subtly leading the way.

ENTER THE PORTAL

Close your eyes and imagine you are resting on a rock like the mythical Coyote. The rock is on an outcropping that overlooks a large pine tree. Watch as the pinecones and needles silently sway with the gentle breeze. Feel the tranquility of the moment. The feeling permeates your mind and you don't want it to end. But you know it must.

You, like most Indians, know that the pine tree has a strong spirit. In the Northwest its spirit is second only to the cedar tree. The role of these trees is to provide people with shelter from the elements, fuel for fire, and shade from the sun, but most importantly they remind us that we are one with nature. Cedar incense is used to bring this to our attention during tribal ceremonies.

When the wind becomes stronger, listen to the unique and special song vibrating through the pines. It is haunting but simultaneously satisfying.

You are now ready to begin the journey.

Chapter One
FIRST AMERICANS

Beginning or End?

The wall clock on the Senate Interior Committee Room indicated 2:10 p.m. as Senator James Abourezk from South Dakota called the hearing to order on the bright, sunny day of July 20, 1973: "This is the second day of open public hearings on Senate Joint Resolution 133 [SJR 133], to provide for establishment of a National Indian Policy Review Commission."

The Senator, although of medium build, was big in Indian country because of his unprecedented dedication to helping Indians. Without his kind of help, we didn't have a prayer of getting any enlightened legislation through Congress. He had a unique attitude towards multiple congressional terms and seniority of legislators. He said a senator should be limited to one, six-year term. He maintained if a person couldn't accomplish anything in six years, giving him additional terms wouldn't make him any smarter. He lived up to his philosophy by retiring after one term.

I was still catching my breath after going directly to the Senate committee room from the airport, suitcase and all. I was a little light-headed but still alert. It could have been worse because I had just finished an all-night, coast-to-coast, red-eye flight from Spokane to Washington, D.C. I arrived at eight that morning.

Just the day before, Lucy Covington, a long-time member of the Colville Confederated Tribes Council, rushed a resolution through the council authorizing me to make this trip. I could still hear her words, "All tribes have similar problems. Our tribe is no exception and our problems are typical of all tribes."

"Typical" to us meant poorly developed resources and a scarcity of jobs. Since tribes couldn't solve these problems by themselves we decided to pool our efforts. Earlier that year we formed the Economic Development Committee at the National Congress of American Indians convention in San Diego. This committee became the catalyst for economic development on reservations. For over one hundred years the U.S. government had done very little. We would do what they couldn't do. It started with the timber issue when we forced the Bureau of Indian Affairs to spend their ten percent management fee for harvesting our timber locally instead of sending it to the government central office.

So my tribal council delegated me, as general manager of the Colville Indian Tribal Enterprises, to represent them at this all-important Senate hearing. After the council passed the resolution I drove a hectic eighty miles to Spokane and caught a 6:40 p.m. flight to Minneapolis, changed planes, and flew to Detroit, where I had a three-hour layover in the terminal before catching a connecting flight to D.C.

Fortunately, without realizing it, we had spent two years preparing for this moment. A small group of us provided the catalyst needed to get things started in Indian Country. We held a number of open hearings in the Pacific Northwest to review Indian problems. From there we would formulate solutions. These started out small but were so popular that we had to use the amphitheater at the University of Washington for the last one in the spring of 1973. Indians came from all over the Northwest to testify. Even U.S. Rep. Lloyd Meeds from the State of Washington participated, so our efforts paid off.

On the first day of Senator Abourezk's hearing, testimony was given by representatives of the Nixon administration and various Indian organizations and individuals who represented Indian people at the national or at least a regional level. For the second day, I was to be part of a panel of individual Indian leaders representing a broad cross section of Indian society. The senator set the stage for the panel discussion,

"Throughout the history of federal-Indian relations there has never been a comprehensive approach by the Congress and the Executive Branch that dealt effectively with Indian needs," said Abourezk. "As a result, Indian policy was shaped by a fragmented, piecemeal approach which served to inhibit, rather than promote Indian development and has directly led to the deep despair and frustration recently vented in the siege of the Bureau of Indian Affairs and the occupation of Wounded Knee, South Dakota, in February of this year."[1]

The senator looked around the room, and realized he was speaking to a predominantly Indian audience who, collectively, were more knowledgeable on the subject than he was. But he continued anyway for the record, "I firmly believe that the time has come for a thorough review of these past policies, to see where they have proved inadequate so that a more comprehensive approach can be attempted.

Senator Abourezk was proposing a bipartisan congressional commission with members from both the Senate and the House of Representatives as well as five members of the Indian community. The commission would review all of the treaties, statutes, judicial decisions and executive orders, as well as the Constitution itself, to determine the legal-historical basis for the unique relationship the Indian people have with the federal government. A goal would be to improve services to and protect Indian natural resources and strengthen tribal governments.

The senator paused to take a drink of water then announced, "Vine Deloria, noted Indian author, lawyer, and scholar will be moderator of the panel. Mr. Deloria, we are ready for you to come forward, please introduce your panel."

"Thank you, Mr. Chairman. We are very happy to be here. On my far left is Mrs. Vivian One Feather, who is representing her husband, Gerald One Feather, who is one of the leaders on the Pine Ridge Reservation. Sitting next to her is Mr. Wendell George who is General Manager of the Colville Confederated Tribes Tribal Enterprises in Nespelem, Washington. Next to Mr. George is Mr. Kenneth Smith, who is General Manager of the Tribal Enterprises of the Confederated Tribes of the Warm Springs Reservation in Oregon. To my right is John Steven, Governor of the Passomaquaddy Tribe in Maine. Next to him is Mr. Leo Vocu, who is administrative assistant to the Chairman of the Oglala Sioux Tribe, and the former Executive Director of the National Congress of American Indians [NCAI]. Next to him is Mr. Val Cordova, Chairman of the all Indian Pueblo Council from New Mexico, and finally at the end of the table is Hank Adams, Executive Director of the Survival of American Indians Association, Nisqually, Washington." Vine paused to let the panel absorb the introductions,

"We will start our presentation with Mr. Val Cordova, who represents nineteen Pueblos in New Mexico and is the major spokesman on this panel from the Southwest. So, I will turn this over to Mr. Cordova."

While Val was making his presentation, my mind reverted back to that day less than a year ago when Sherwin Broadhead, Mel Tonasket, Rudy Ryser and, my cousin, Bobbi Minnis, met at my house in Newport Hills [a suburb of Seattle]. We summarized our findings and planned for hearings of this type. Later Sherwin and tribal member Gene Joseph became part of the Senator's staff and helped implement SJR 133. I was jolted

---

[1] The town of Wounded Knee on the Pine Ridge Indian Reservation was the site of a 71-day confrontation between members of the American Indian Movement and law enforcement. The site was selected by the tribal people because it was where the U.S. Army massacred hundreds of native men, women, and children in 1890.

back to reality when Vine Deloria introduced me as the next speaker.[2]

   "Senator, the following is a chart that was presented to Representative Lloyd Meeds in Seattle this spring. We call it the Chronology of Indian Issues which traces the positive and negative impacts of federal actions over the past 200 years from the first Indian treaty in 1787 to the Homestead Act of 1887 and on to the Indian Claims Commission established in 1945. The treaties and executive orders established sovereignty, as indicated by Mr. Cordova, and the right to self-government. Initially Indians did determine their own policies such as they were   at the time. However, most of the acts of Congress since then had taken away piece by piece the right of self-government. My tribe alone lost over 300,000 acres of their prime land due to Congressional homesteading and allotment Acts.

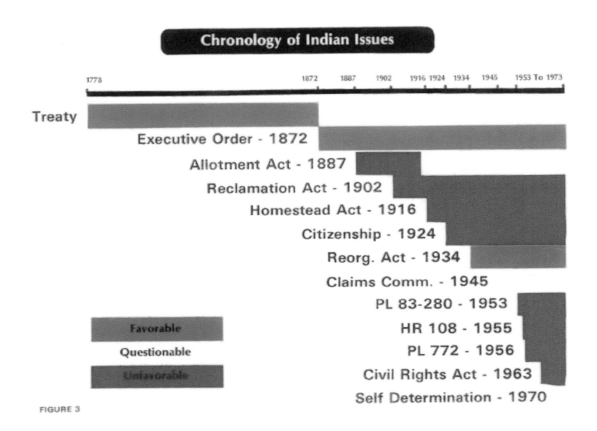

FIGURE 3

2 Congressional Record - hearings on SJR133 pgs. 50-62

Senator Abourezk's hearing would eventually lead to the creation of a commission. The commission studied all parts of Indian activity and made voluminous reports, held hearings in the field, and initiated several major pieces of legislation. The most significant was the Indian Self-Determination Act passed in 1976.

But as I sat at the Washington National [now Reagan] Airport waiting for my return flight, I thought about tribal history. We certainly didn't have the hopeful, bright future of the Suyapenex [foreigner or white man]. They viewed the Statue of Liberty from the front door where she is receiving immigrants with open arms, a benevolent smile and a promise that the United States is truly a land of equal opportunity. We see the Statue of Liberty from the back door, where she has her arms around us in a choking bear-hug, a hypocritical smile and a promise that she can do more with our natural resources than we can. All tribes seemed to have similar experiences with the Suyapenex. They were decimated in many ways. It was a true acting out of the Manifest Destiny.[3]

The government made treaties with the tribes as sovereign nations. It granted them land forever. *". As long as the grass shall grow and the waters run."* These promises were not kept. Once the notion of the American Desert was found to be largely a myth, white travelers, traders, and settlers began following the overland trails into the West. The government did not keep them out of the lands given to its Indian wards. Friction and warfare between the two civilizations followed.

Why did we allow this to happen? Did we have any control over these events? Why would anyone want to live in poverty and suffer so much? Is there something I can tell my kids or grandkids that will help them cope with life? I didn't have the answers but on the flight back I had a dream:

I was floating, weightless but fully aware of everything. I could see my family, grown children and grandchildren I was yet to know. The grandchildren were of special interest because they were a new generation. I wanted to help them understand their ancestors, to know their history. Then, as in a video, my ancestors appeared as they were in their times. They each told me stories of their lives. It all fit a pattern. They each built on each other's story.

But what could I do? A thought popped into my head that I should write what I know of our ancestors. Maybe, in time, others would add to it and we could eventually have the complete story of how we came to be.

The stories went like this....

---

3 The great American land grab.

It was late afternoon in Wenatchee, Washington one day in December 1962 and the sun became a fan-shaped arc of deep orange and yellow that spilled over from behind the higher Cascade Mountains and filled the sky with many shades of light. The shadows of the nearby trees grew larger and sharper. Their outlines would soon fade and become obscure shapes, indistinguishable in the gray darkness of early evening.

As I looked out the folks' big picture window, I noticed that a cold, bitter wind started blowing snow horizontally across the house. It was a familiar scene that probably repeated itself every winter for my ancestors and that thought caused me to remark, "I wonder how our ancestors survived the long winters."

Dad was quick to respond, "Well, son, besides having a roaring fire to keep them warm they did exactly as we're doing tonight."

"You mean the story-telling?"

"Yes, that was their biggest form of entertainment."

"Now, we have radio, television, and dozens of other things to divert our attention."

"Most of it is worthless," said Dad. Entertainment value doesn't equal quality education."

"What is worse is that we delegate education of our children to professional teachers."

"That loses a lot, especially for our Indian children because our language and culture wasn't written down and they can't teach it in school. We pass it on orally through stories, especially the Coyote stories."

"Dad, you said you wanted to come back to Wenatchee because that is the site of our ancestors."

"That's true, son. Our folks actually lived in Entiat Valley but they roamed all over this area hunting food. They were still nomads. I built this house as near as I could to the "camping spots" on the slopes between East Wenatchee and Rock Island. In 1948 I bought the old "Grant" place that was previously an apricot orchard. However, there is a big difference in the new, modern, and well-insulated house I built and the breezy pole structure covered with hides that our ancestors used. There should be a big difference, because we are living a hundred years after them in an advanced technology age."

"Why did you want to locate so close to the old camping sites?"

"It is just a feeling I have that it is a special site with a special meaning. I think I, or we, can tune in to some of the knowledge that our ancestors had." [Clovis pt. site found in 1988 is just east of our house.]

Dad stoked up the fireplace as I was contemplating the evening we were sharing with my family. The fire leaped to life and danced up into the large chimney opening. I saw glimpses of past and future in the flickering flames. Things seemed to merge together. All history and future were rolled into one. It was vague and unclear but I did get the feeling that it was symbolic of a mystery unraveling. Maybe Dad was right and we could tune in. It was eerie but fitting for an evening like this because we were doing exactly what our ancestors had done for generations. In the wintertime they would gather around the fire after dinner for the story. Each family had a storyteller trained by previous generations to hand down tribal history and customs. Our tribe, as do many others, use the Coyote as the central character. He is both a buffoon and hero. The children especially like him because they see themselves in Coyote, who is always in trouble but somehow gets out of it.

I tore my gaze from the fire and again became aware of my boys jabbering about their hero, Coyote. My wife, Barbara, was sitting next to them with a slight smile, obviously enjoying their exchange.

Dad had just finished telling our kids a Coyote story. I never tired of listening to him tell stories of the past. When he told a story it was almost as if you were there experiencing it yourself. That included the dust, the cold, and even the heartbreaks. The quiet humor and subtle morals were especially enjoyable. Like all tribes, these stories have been handed down from generation to generation. They were rich in tribal culture and hinted at deeper meanings than the surface stories. Dad would add to the story as our kids grew older. This was both to hold their interest and to reveal more esoteric aspects of our ancestors.

At the time, Barbara and I just had the four older boys, age's two to six. Up until they went to school they would always ask for the stories, sometimes the same one over and over even though they knew the ending.

After dinner, the evening started out with the kids clamoring for Dad to tell a story. Rick, our second oldest, said,

"I want the one about how Coyote brought FIRE to the People."

Kerry, number three, countered with, "No, he told that last time. How about the one where Coyote tried to change his name?" Kerry was curious about that story because, instead of a new name, Coyote was given the task to "Finish the People." What did that mean? Is the legendary Coyote really a transformer who is synonymous with the Indian Way?

Mike, the oldest, and Matt, the youngest, didn't care as long as he told a story. Barbara and I sat quietly in the background, amused at their enthusiasm.

Dad did not want to disappoint anyone so he was having trouble solving the dilemma until Mom stepped in and settled the issue by reminding everyone that Dad told the "Fire" story last so maybe it was time for the "Naming" story. To this the kids agreed.

While Dad was telling the story a strange feeling came over me. Everything was normal until Dad, with the kids enthralled and hanging on every word, said,

"One day Spirit Chief called all the Animal People together. They came from all over the world. He told them that a new kind of People was coming to live on Earth and they would change the Animal Peoples' lives forever."

NEW KIND OF PEOPLE

The new kind of People is what piqued my interest. Who and what were they? I needed to know more and I felt I wouldn't rest until I knew the answer.

According to Indian legends, Animal People existed before humans came. Throughout the Americas, not just among our tribe, the original inhabitants of the world were indeed people, but they were other-than-human and amorphous. Their essential form was that which later became restricted to the human species, with arms, legs, hands, head, and overall vulnerability. In addition, these primal people also had the attributes of spirits and of species, which were shimmering and iridescent. Through tricks of light and shadow, they could change shape and attributes as need or whim arose.

Today sightings of the descendants of these people still occur. They are called "Stick-Indians" or "Big Foot" by Indians and "Sasquatch" by others. Indians agree that these people exist today but they do not look like the shaggy, bear-like creature that is commonly described. Rather than being physical, the stick-Indians are more spiritual. They are tricksters in a playful way and never harm anyone.

After the first humans came, the Animal People coexisted with them for a long time. The first human being was essentially a higher form of animal. These first humans existed for about two million years before the humans of today arrived.

The new humans evolved from the Homo sapiens of 200,000 years ago. Their origin was in South Africa at least 120,000 years ago and they later appeared in Europe and Asia about 50,000 years ago. There is some evidence that modern humans evolved simultaneously in all major regions of the Old World. There is also evidence of migration throughout the Old World. This was intermittent enough to allow local genetic purity. The larger cranial capacities enabled the new human to become the center of the animal world because he could tune into the universe.

According to new discoveries in Baja, California, about 30,000 years ago these people migrated to North America and other places. Since then, the world population has grown exponentially to the present seven billion.

But this didn't explain how they would change the Animal People's lives forever. I had to delve further. History has shown that the Native American lives were also changed forever by the "coming of a new kind of people." The new people were Homo sapiens physically, just like Native Americans, but their mind-sets, originating in Europe, were totally different. The collective consciousness of the first Europeans called, the colonial people, became totally ethnocentric and they brought their way of living into the New World. They were blind to the ways of indigenous Indians. The settlers felt they were the ones to organize the world. They were given this mission by God. It may have been a holdover from the Crusades. The relatively small population of the Native Americans and their more simple, nature -loving ways made them vulnerable in the face of what would be called America's "Manifest Destiny."

John L. O'Sullivan co-founder and editor the *Democratic Review* coined the term, championing Andrew Jackson's belief that white Americans had a destiny to settle the American West and to expand control over all of North America from the Atlantic Ocean to the Pacific at the expense of the indigenous population. O'Sullivan wrote a column which appeared in the New York Morning News on December 27, 1845 which said:

"… and that claim is the right of our manifest destiny to over spread and to possess the whole of the continent which Providence has given us for the development of the great experiment of liberty and federated development of self-government entrusted to us."

O'Sullivan was explaining America's need for expansion, and to present a defense for America's claim to new territories such as Texas, Oregon, New Mexico, and California. The philosophy behind Manifest Destiny permeates American history. Jackson ruthlessly decimated the Seminoles in Florida because they were friendly with the Spanish. The new Americans didn't want competition in claiming the Florida territory. Theodore Roosevelt did the same in the Spanish American War for Cuba.

They had the majority of public support because it was the political and philosophical belief that it was American's divinely assigned mission to expand westward across the North American continent and to establish democratic Protestant ideals [ironically the principle of democracy mirrored many tribes who were self-governed]. Even arguments from such notables as Andrew Carnegie and Mark Twain couldn't turn the tide. Both were members of the Anti-Imperialist League [1898]. Sam Clemens [Mark Twain] was vice-president of the organization. Carnegie opposed the annexation of Cuba by the United States. Mark Twain didn't become active until the U.S. conquered the Philippines. He wrote in the *New York Herald* on October 15, 1900:"We do not intend to free but to subjugate the people of the Philippines. We have gone there to conquer, not to redeem. It should, it seems to me, be our pleasure and duty to make those people free, and let them deal with their domestic questions in their own way and so I am an anti-imperialist. I am opposed to having the eagle put its talons on any other land."

However, most Americans agreed that, "It was white man's burden to conquer and Christianize the land," to quote O'Sullivan.

With this surge of enthusiasm and energy for pushing West, they believed that the white man had the right to destroy anything and anyone [namely Indians] who got in the way. The white man of that time felt justified because he was preordained to settle the land and civilize the Indians. This resulted in mass destruction of tribal organizations, confinement of Indians to reservations, and full-blown genocide.

The American Revolution was started in part because Britain tried to prevent colonists from settling beyond the Appalachians, presumably because it was Indian Country. The British issued the Royal Proclamation of October 7, 1763, which was intended to protect the Indians from further encroachment by the colonists. It said great frauds and abuses were committed in purchasing lands of the Indians. It established a western boundary for colonial settlement along the Appalachian Mountains. To the west the lands were reserved for the Indians. After they won the war the new American government passed the Northwest Ordinance of 1787 which made provisions for forming new states and initiated a policy of land-acquisitions [read stealing] and organization that the U.S. followed until they reached the Pacific Coast.

Western territories promised the American Dream: the freedom and independence of a seemingly limitless land coupled with the agrarian spirit. Therefore nothing was to stand in the way of progress. Americans took whatever they wanted like the Cherokee plantations in Georgia. Their Manifest Destiny gave them this right and power.

The movement hit its peak in the late 19th century. The U.S. government destroyed tribal governments and broke up Indian reservations by implementing the "progressive" Manifest Destiny Doctrine. Arrogance that flowed from the Manifest Destiny philosophy was exemplified by Albert J. Beveridge on January 9, 1900.[1]

Although his speech was directed at the Philippines it applied equally to how the American Indians were treated. The newly elected senator from Indiana rose to make his first speech before the U.S. Senate and announced:

"Mr. President, this question is deeper than any question of party politics; deeper than any question of the isolated policy of our country even; deeper even than any question of constitutional power. It is elemental. It is racial. God has not been preparing the English-speaking and Teutonic peoples for a thousand years for nothing but vain and idle self-contemplation and self-admiration. No! He has made us the master organizers of the world to establish system where chaos reigns. He has given us the spirit of progress to overwhelm the forces of reaction throughout the earth. He has made us adepts in government that we may administer government among savage and senile peoples. Were it not for such a force as this the world would relapse into barbarism and night. And of all races He has marked the American people as His chosen nation to finally lead in the regeneration of the world. This is the divine mission of America, and it holds for us all the profit, all the glory, all the happiness possible to man. We are trustees of the world's progress, guardians of its righteous peace. The judgment of the Master is upon us: "Ye have been faithful over a few things I will make you ruler over many things."

---

1 Congressional Record pages 704-712

Despite all this there was no rush of settlers to the Far West for many years because of the opinion of the time that farmers could not succeed in the country west of the Mississippi. Schoolbooks even called it the Great American Desert. But missionaries and traders did explore the Far West. From 1812 to 1846 fur trade was the chief resource of the Far Northwest. The U.S. Congress decided to use the land as the basis of a permanent Indian policy. They enacted the Removal Act of 1830 in which Congress offered to buy the lands of tribes living in the settled states east of the Mississippi and to give them new land in the West. The Indians of the Plains were persuaded [read coerced] to accept tribes that were moved from the East. To assure a smooth transition, the government established a bureau to look after the needs of the Indians. When settlers continued to infringe on Indian land, troops were sent supposedly to protect Indians and their rights.

The government made treaties with the tribes as sovereign nations. It granted them land forever...**"so long as the grass shall grow and the waters run."** These promises were soon broken. At first a few fur traders and adventurers made the trip west and discovered vast areas of fertile farmland. Then other white travelers, traders, and settlers began following the overland trails into the West. The government did not keep them out of the lands given to its Indian wards. Friction and warfare between the two civilizations followed.

Later, when Dad had finished the Coyote story and the boys had gone to bed, I asked Dad if he knew about the Indian Commerce clause of the U.S. Constitution

"No, tell me about it," he said.

"It was passed in 1789 at the same time the Constitution was ratified by the states. Article I, Section eight, Clause three states 'The Congress shall have Power.. to regulate Commerce with foreign Nations, and among the several States, and with the Indian Tribes.' This clause is the principal basis for the federal government's broad power over Indians."

"At least they recognized that tribes existed. That clause means we are equal to the states," said Dad.

"That's been our argument all along. About the same time, they assigned Indian Agents ironically under the War Department to be liaison with tribes. They were empowered to negotiate treaties with the tribes."

"When was the first treaty?"

"Oddly enough the first treaty was completed before the states ratified the Constitution. It was in 1787 that the U.S. signed their first treaty and that was with the Delaware tribe. Before that 175 treaties had been negotiated by Indian tribes with either the British or Colonial governments. From 1787 to 1868, three-hundred and seventy-one treaties with Indian tribes were ratified by the Congress."

"Son, it seems to me with all these treaties we should be in pretty good shape."

I was somewhat surprised at Dad's comment. We weren't in good shape at all. The difference in opinion was obviously due to our backgrounds. He was the expert in Coyote stories, native spirituality, and lived the tribal history on the ground level. I was the expert in political history and the overall big picture. I explained some of the politics to Dad.

"Before the Revolutionary War there weren't any formal agreements nation to nation. The British in their own way tried to work with Indians. But they were worlds apart in their thinking. The British were from an area that had to divide up their land a long time ago because they had too many people for the limited space. They developed laws to control land ownership.

Indians did not have a need for land ownership. Their population was small and land was plentiful. They had no concept of land ownership; it just wasn't in their culture. They could live together peaceably without formal laws to control them. This worked for a while even with the Europeans when there weren't very many of them. But as their populations grew they started fighting over the most desirable land.

When they entered into negotiations for land rights with the Europeans the Indians were at an extreme disadvantage. They were playing under the Europeans' rules, which they didn't understand. Under contract law each party entering into the contract has to be equally competent or the contract is invalid. In today's environment these contracts would be invalid. Of course, at that time there wasn't anyone to enforce this or any other action of the ruling culture. It was essentially an invasion and takeover.

The Revolutionary War provided motivation for both the British and Colonies to develop more formal agreements with the tribes in order to make them allies. Also takeover of the land became more forceful."

"So the federals took the land anyway?" Dad asked.

"One way or another. And then the fledging United States got lucky."

I reminded Dad of the Louisiana Purchase. France needed money and wanted to upstage the Spanish so they offered the U.S. a deal.

On April 30, 1803, the U.S. purchased from France for $15 million the Louisiana Territory of 800,000 square miles from the Mississippi to the Rocky Mountains. The deal provided provide free navigation of the Mississippi and would enable settlement by the Suyapenex [foreigners]. Of course this was without consideration of the many Indians who were already living in the region. France did not own the land, but usurped it.

The Constitution did not specifically empower the federal government to acquire new territory by treaty but the Senate ratified the purchase anyway on October 20, 1803.

This may have been the beginning of the Manifest Destiny which was to come later.

In 1823 a landmark Supreme Court decision in Johnson v. McIntosh involved the validity of land sold by tribal Chiefs to private persons in 1773 and 1775. Ironically these sales were before the Revolutionary War and before the creation of the U.S. which was also the genesis of the U.S. Supreme Court.

The court held that Indian tribes had no power to grant lands to anyone other than the federal government. The federal government, in turn, held title to all Indian lands based on the "doctrine of discovery" – the belief that initial "discovery" of lands gave title to the government responsible for the discovery. Thus, "Indian" rights to complete sovereignty, as independent nations, were necessarily diminished, and their power to dispose of the land, at their own will, to whomsoever they pleased, was denied by the original fundamental principle that discovery gave exclusive title to those who made it.

That wasn't enough, so Congress passed the Indian Removal Act in 1830 which mandated the removal of American Indians from east of the Mississippi River to territory west of the Mississippi.

In 1831 and 1832 two more Supreme Court cases changed the nature of tribal sovereignty by ruling the Indian tribes were not foreign nations, but rather were "domestic dependent nations." As such, both cases provided the basis for the federal protection of Indian tribes or the birth of federal trust responsibility [virtual imprisonment].

In 1831 the Cherokee Nation sued the state of Georgia because it passed laws and enacted policies that violated the U.S. Constitution and limited Indian sovereignty. In 1832 a missionary from Vermont named Worcester, who was working in Cherokee territory, sued the state of Georgia, which had arrested him, claiming that the state had no authority over him within the boundaries of the Cherokee Nation. The court ruled in Worcester's favor and held that the state laws did not extend to Indian Country. Such a ruling clarified that Indian tribes were under protection of the federal government.

The only problem was that President Andrew Jackson refused to enforce the ruling. He said,

"[Chief Justice] John Marshal has made his decision; let him enforce it now if he can."

Jackson then sent federal troops to forcibly remove 16,000 Cherokee from Georgia where they had developed plantations. The Suyapenex took over the plantations and 4,000 Cherokee died during the removal process."

Dad thought that over for a little while and then said, "Then they moved west and began taking our land away."

"Right. Unfortunately none of our people here in the West knew what was happening back east so we were not prepared for whatever was to happen here."

"Son, you've studied this so give me a rundown on how this affected our reservation."

"Well, because we were so remote from the 'civilized' world it took a while for our ancestors to be noticed. But eventually we did feel the impact of the Manifest Destiny."

Until the mid-1800s the tribes of what is now north central Washington were nomadic, following the seasons and sources of food and moving from place to place to fishing sites and to harvest berries and native plants. They also moved from summer to winter camps. They did little farming because of this constant movement.

The first trading post was established at the confluence of the Okanogan and Columbia rivers in 1807 by the Hudson Bay Company of Canada. Both Americans and Canadians claimed the Oregon Territory [which included Washington State] until the Treaty of 1846 which established U.S. ownership south of the 49th Parallel. The indigenous native people were ignored and not part of the treaty.

On March 2, 1853, President Fillmore signed a bill creating the Washington Territory, which included today's state of Washington, northern Idaho, and western Montana.

Major Isaac Stevens of the U.S. Corps of Engineers was appointed governor of the new territory and he reported to the Commissioner of Indian Affairs on "Indian" issues within his new domain.

On May 3, 1853, Commissioner George W. Manypenny of Indian Affairs expressed a concern that the U.S. was only considering giving Indians lands that were smaller than their natural habitat. They used much more land than what was to become the reservation. Manypenny felt then the U.S. should purchase the land not included in the reservation.

In 1854, Governor Stevens was directed by the commissioner to negotiate with the Indians, "particularly in the vicinity of white settlements, toward extinguishment of the Indian claims to the lands and the concentration of the tribes and fragments of tribes on a few reservations naturally suited to the requirement of the Indians, and located, so far as practicable, so as not to interfere with the settlement of the country."

Late in 1854, a historical five-day "council" took place with nearly every tribe from present-day eastern Washington State participating so that each tribal leader or chief could mark and claim specific reservation boundaries for the individual tribes.

The council gathering and division of the land was done purposefully by the federal government so that no land would be for sale and no payments would be made to any Indians. Governor Stevens carried out his duties by successfully negotiating the Point Elliot Treaty in January, 1855; the Yakama Treaty in June, 1855; and the Hells Gate Treaty in July, 1855.

The indigenous native peoples who would later become the Colville Confederated Tribes were not forgotten. In a December 22, 1855, letter to the Commissioner of Indian Affairs, Governor Stevens told of meeting with some Indians, as he had promised during the Yakama Treaty negotiations, but "they did not sign a treaty although they pledged to take no part in the Yakama War which broke out that year".

The Yakama War lasted until 1859 and involved tribes located in todays southern Washington State and Oregon. At the same time, Indian people and gold miners were involved in altercations in the Wenatchee and Okanogan valleys. From 1859 until 1865, the federal government allowed [more than likely due to their preoccupation with the Civil War] the Indians of north central Washington State to live without a treaty or an "Indian Agent" to oversee them. That changed in 1865 when George A. Paige was sent to the area as the first Indian Agent. He traveled and visited tribes through 1868 and made periodic reports to the Superintendent of Indian Affairs. He died in 1868 at Fort Colville.

Superintendent Thomas L. McKenny, who replaced Stevens and oversaw the entire Washington Territory, commented on Paige's May 9, 1867 written report as follows: "From this report, the necessity of trading with these Indians can scarcely fail to be obvious. They now occupy the best agricultural lands in the whole country and they claim an undisputed right to these lands. White squatters are constantly making claims in their territory and not infrequently invading the actual improvements of the Indians. The state of things cannot but prove disastrous to the peace of the country unless forestalled by a treaty fixing the rights of the Indians and limiting the aggressions of the white man. The fact that a portion of the Indians refused all gratuitous presents shows a determination to hold possession of the country here until the government makes satisfactory overtures to open the way of actual purchase." He felt there should be negotiations of determine which and how much land would be set aside for the reservation.

President Ulysses Grant's Executive Order on April 4, 1872, established the original reservation which was to include all the lands from the Columbia River on the west and south to the Idaho border on the east and north to the Canadian border. A key point to remember is the boundary line was the "middle" of the Okanogan and Columbia Rivers.

The aboriginal tribes of the Methow, Okanagan, San Poil, Lake, Colville, Kalispel, Spokane, Coeur d'Alene, and other scattered tribes who were not parties to any treaty were confined to the original reservation. Three months later, due to opposition from non-Indian settlers in the east side of the reservation, another presidential executive order issued on July 1, 1872, moved the Colville Indian Reservation to its present location on the west side of the Columbia River and diminished its size to 2,825,000 acres. The areas between the Okanogan River and the crest of the Cascade Mountain Range in the Methow Valley and between the Columbia and Pend Oreille rivers and the Colville Valley were excluded from the second and final reservation.

None of the tribes affected by the presidential order were consulted. The areas deleted from the original reservation were rich in minerals. For thirty-five years the gold mine in Republic was one of the biggest in the world. Thomas Ryan and Phillip Creasor [non-Indians] discovered gold on Granite Creek on March 5, 1896. The Knob Hill mine was opened in 1896 when the North Half of the Colville Indian Reservation was opened to mining by the U.S. Congress. The mine was in full production by 1902 and closed in 1998. Some 2.4 million ounces of gold have been removed since 1941.

On April 19, 1879, and March 6, 1880, two tracts of land where the present day city of Wenatchee lies, north to the Canadian border between the crest of the Cascades and the Okanogan River, were established by another presidential executive order for the Chief Moses tribes consisting of the Columbia, Chelan, Entiat and Wenatchi.

Three years later, on July 7, 1883, Chief Moses and his people agreed to either move to the Colville Indian Reservation or accept an allotment of 640 acres for the head of each family.

Some tribal families took the allotment of 640 acres and remained in their ancestral homelands along the Columbia River and at majestic Lake Chelan outside the established boundaries of the reservation.

In 1885, Chief Moses, who had moved to the Colville Indian Reservation, invited Chief Joseph and his tribe of Nez Perce, to live on the reservation. Chief Joseph and his people were never allowed to return to their former homeland in the Oregon Territory. Joseph died at Nespelem, Washington, in 1904. Many descendants of his band reside on the Colville Indian Reservation today and still belong to the Confederated Tribes of the Colville Reservation.

Twenty years after the Colville Indian Reservation was moved to its present location, the north half of the reservation was ceded to the United States by an act of Congress [27 Stat. 62]. At that time 660 Colville Indians were allotted 51,653 acres located in the ceded area.

In that same year, the United States negotiated an agreement with the Colville Confederated tribes for the purchase of the unalloted acreage located in the north half and paid them $1.5 million dollars for 1.5 million acres, priced at one dollar an acre. No evaluation was made for the minerals, timber or other natural resource located there which were significant.

The Colville tribal leaders of 1892 were able to reserve the right for members of their tribes to hunt and fish on the former north half of the reservation for time immemorial.

Later, a presidential proclamation on October 10, 1900, opened the south half of the Colville Indian Reservation, totaling 1,449,268 acres, to homesteading, which began sixteen years later.

The Reservation Allotment Act of 1887 was finally implemented on December 1, 1905, when two-thirds of the estimated number of Colville Indians available on that date signed the McLaughlin Agreement that ceded the south half of the Colville Indian Reservation for an 80-acre allotment to each Indian. By 1914, 2,505 Colville Indians had been allotted 333,275 acres of reservation lands.

A presidential proclamation of May 3, 1916, opened the remaining 417,841 acres of unalloted and unreserved reservation lands to settlement. An article in the July 5, 1916 issue of the Wenatchee Daily World summarized this situation:

"Registration for the drawing for lands in the south half of the Colville Indian Reservation, waited for more than two years, is on. It began simultaneously at midnight last night at Wenatchee and five other points including Omak. Wenatchee is thronged with people of all classes, laborers, clerks, stenographers and farmers, all after free lands, practically the last the United States has. The first train from the west this morning brought 150. The second discharged a like number. No. 44, east-bound, arrived six hours late, bringing 400. Another train carried 300. As early as 9 o'clock a crowd began to gather around the entrance of the Western Building, the registration office. Shortly before midnight it numbered 250. When the doors were opened promptly at midnight, the people pushed forward almost breaking the doors off their hinges. This morning the registration office registered 30 in one hour, an average of more than six a minute."

After July 22, the applications were drawn by lot, the first one having the pick of the entire reservation, the others coming in the order in which the names are drawn.

As I finished my account, Dad commented, "Well, son, it looks like we're lucky to have any reservation left after all that activity."

"That's right Dad, but our tribe is resilient and we'll make do with what we have as we always have."

THE NEW INDIAN AGENT

My mother, Marie, had been sitting and listening to us philosophize until she became impatient and said, "Why don't you tell son about when Chief Moses adopted my dad into the tribe and he promptly got himself in trouble and kicked off the Reservation?"

"OK, Mom, I will. I know how hard it is to make somebody understand when you don't speak their language. I speak Wenatchee fluently but Yakama less so and Spokane even less. The Wenatchee Salish language changes as you go upstream on the Columbia River. English is a world away from any Indian language. So Chief Moses and Chief Joseph spoke through interpreters on complicated matters. That is very awkward. Even if the interpreter is fluent in both languages, a rarity at best, there is a lot of error. The interpreter many times missed the nuances of either language and changed the entire meaning.

"After some futile attempts Moses and Joseph were desperately looking for someone they could trust that knew their languages. At the very meeting where this all happened …

Moses stood up and looked at his tribesmen. They were sitting around him in several loose circles. It was early morning at the Moses Crossing near the future site of the Grand Coulee Dam. The air was cool but not chilly, a perfect early spring day in 1891.

"I called you together today to discuss a matter of importance to us all. We have many problems with the Suyapenex. The Indian Agent stays in Fort Spokane and very seldom comes to visit us. We can tell him our problems only if we go see him which takes several days. When we send a messenger he doesn't always get the story straight. Language is a problem because we don't speak theirs and they do not speak ours. We can use the Suyapenex way of writing letters but we need to get someone we trust to write it for us. Language is still a problem because those who write usually can't understand what we want. Chinook is spoken by few but not by many of those who can write."

A young Indian next to Moses spoke up, "We know all that, Uncle ["Wasen" in the Wenatchee dialect used not as a relative but to show respect]. What we need is a way to solve it. I've heard you've asked someone to be here that may be able to solve our problem for us. Is that right?"

"Yes, son, you are right. And thank you for getting me back on track. I tend to wander at times. Sitting beside me is Louis Picard, a young man I asked to come up from the Oregon country. I met him on one of my trips there, and was very impressed with him. When I first saw him he said, "Hi you, Skookum… which you know is the Chinook language of us River People. We had a nice long conversation and I found out he not only spoke Chinook but French and English too! Then he told me he can write in English. My first thought was that we can use him up here."

"He should tell us a little about himself."

The young man next to Moses stood up but the top of his head only came up to Moses' chest. He said mostly in Chinook in a loud voice,

"My name is Louis Picard. I am 25 years old and have a wife Eliza. We've lived in Oregon until now. I have brothers, John and George, living up here near the Okanogan River. They have been asking me to come up for some time. I would like to settle down here. We are all ranchers. We farm and raise stock."

"Can you run some of the equipment the government has left with us? None of us know how."

"Yes, I have used some of the same type equipment. Farming is well established in Oregon."

"Are you Indian? You don't look it with your big moustache."

"The moustache is French but from both sides of my family I have Okanogan, Molalla and Iroquois blood. Some of my family was fur traders in this area early in this century."

They discussed this at some length and finally Moses said, "I've asked Louis to be my special interpreter and informant of the latest news and gossip. He can do this by hanging around the Suyapenex and observing what they are saying. But I think it would be a stronger tie if he became one of us. So, I would like you to consider adopting him and welcoming him into our tribe.

"I agree with you, Moses. He will be useful to us. Your father not only was adopted into the Sinkiuse but later made Chief."

"Any other comments?"

"Yes, there are a few of us who question his Indian blood. If he remains he should see to it that his children marry into our tribe."

"My children are infants now but when they grow up I'm sure they'll marry other Indians. I'll encourage it."

"OK, everybody agree then? Louis is one of us from this day on. I'll inform the authorities."

So Louis began serving as their interpreter using mostly Chinook to talk and English to write. He and Moses spent many long winter nights together discussing how to improve conditions on the Rez [Reservation].

And they had a lot to discuss. The north half of the Reservation was opened for mining on February 23, 1896. Miners, gamblers, liquor peddlers and others of questionable character rampaged the South Half on their way to the mines.

In 1891 the Feds also gave allotments in the ceded tract to 660 tribal members who received a total of 51,653 acres leaving 1,449,268 acres for Suyapenex settlers. Indians didn't understand the concept of land ownership. They had roamed all this land in search for food. It didn't belong to anyone. It was there to help everyone and anyone who needed it. Most of the Indians didn't take to farming. It was too limiting because they were used to roaming up and down the river.

In 1900 they suffered another blow. The North Half was then opened for homesteading. The tribes were compensated for none of this.

As part of Moses' negotiations the government did assign Henry Steele, designated as The Farmer, to the Colville Indian Reservation. Steele was to teach Indians how to farm. He wasn't too successful as farm equipment, such as the wheat thresher, was always broken down. Since Louis had experience farming he tried to help with the project. This didn't go over too well with Steele and created some resentment towards Louis.

It was at least a two-day trip to Fort Spokane for Moses to meet with the Indian agent. At that time Captain John W. Bubb was temporarily assigned from the Army Unit as the Indian agent. He obviously was unfit for the assignment as were most of the Indian agents because they were not trained or screened for that type of work. Moses brought serious complaints of miners passing through the reservation and ravaging his people. Bubb was replaced by George B. Newman in June 1896 but the situation didn't improve.

Moses repeatedly asked Agent Newman for help without success. This made Moses resentful.

Then he learned of McKinley's election and thought he could take advantage of the change. He knew a change of administration would mean a change in Indian Affairs. President Harrison let the 1892 bill that removed the north half become law, so he was not a friend of Indians.

So, on Inauguration day, Moses asked Louis to write a letter [printed exactly as written] to the new President. On March 4, 1897, Louis offered the following letter for Moses to sign:

"Dear Fried this day I understand you are going to take your position. I know that you folks have don more for me than any other kind of people in Washington. My reservation is rich with gold and the white are try to take it away from me without pay me for it and I had an understanding with the department that I would lette them have a part of my reservation for cash money and today they want it all and I haven't received a cent yet. Please tell what you are going to do. About twenty years ago when I agreed to give my home to come here I also promest you to cause no more trouble so I will not do so but I wish for you to see that the whites do not robe me my people are very poor. If you want my land and gold please give me something for it. This is all I have to support my people for a life time. The republican is my fried they have dun justes with me always. Please send me the exactly law so I will know wright. I remaine respectfully Chief Moses."

Moses nodded his head slowly and exhaled a soft, deep-tone "aah" indicating his approval of the letter that Louis had written and read to him. The Chief, although growing old, was still the statesman with an everlasting concern for his people. He was a big man with a stocky, powerful build and his piercing, brown eyes seemed to look right through you.

He said in the common-language Chinook,

"I want to add: "Please send us a new agent at once!"

Louis was in total sympathy with Moses but he felt the need to offer a warning,

"Agent Newman won't like this and there is no telling what he will do."

Moses grunted his agreement and resolutely added,

"If we do nothing, he will do nothing; so we have to make something happen!'

Louis made the addition and the letter was sent to President William McKinley on March 4, 1897. It reflected the general feeling of the Indians because they were virtually starving, with little hope for improvement. They were trying to rebuild a society demolished by the forced move of the Sinkiuse, Chelan, Entiat, and Wenatchee tribes, among others, to the Colville Reservation where they had never lived before.

The move disrupted both the economy and the tribal governments. Without leadership tribal members were powerless to help themselves. This made them easy prey to manipulations of unethical federal employees and those hungry for the rich tribal natural resources. Although the Reservation was created on July 1, 1872, it wasn't until almost 66 years later on February 26, 1938, that the tribal constitution was approved. During this time there was very little formal organization to the collective body of twelve tribes.

The President never saw the letter. Instead, it was routed directly to the Indian Office and down to Agent Newman at Fort Spokane.

Newman sent it to Henry Steele, the Farmer in charge at Nespelem, who called in Moses and Louis to discuss it.

Steele opened the meeting by asking,

"Moses, did you really dictate the request for a new agent?"

Moses answered,

"Yes, I did and I expect some action."

"Did Mr. Picard put the idea in your head?"

"No, I can think for myself and this is my idea and my idea alone.

Steele wasn't satisfied. He later wrote Newman,

"Mr. Picard's conduct, I assure you, is important, haughty and arrogant and his air of independence and defiance I would say demands severe censure."

Newman agreed and they sent Indian police to escort Louis off the reservation. He was banned for an undetermined amount of time.

Louis and his wife, Eliza, were living in a small log cabin at the mouth of the Nespelem River where it emptied into the Columbia River. The road to it was not much more than a horse trail although a buckboard wagon could wind its way through the steep and rocky terrain. Eliza's biggest problem was that she had three children Lula [6], Bert [4], and Bill [2]. They had a few head of cattle including a milk cow and the normal array of farm animals like horses, chickens and pigs. They had been there long enough to establish a vegetable garden, but it would be a couple of months before it produced.

Louis had been looking for a place to grow wheat, but Indian allotments were not yet available so they were just camped at that location.

When the Indian police came to get him he told Eliza he would be back as soon as he could. Her only response was that he always spoke his mind even when he knew it would get him into trouble. He couldn't disagree but knew he couldn't change.

Louis asked Moses and Joseph for help and they immediately began organizing it. The Indian women brought as much food as they could spare which wasn't a lot because it was the end of winter and their stores were nearly depleted.

Luckily, Louis was brought back to the Reservation before the weather turned that fall. Louis later was able to file for allotments on the Owhi Flat for himself and his family. Louis and his family moved to Owhi Flats and built a very successful cattle and wheat ranch. He stayed active in tribal politics even after the passing of his friends Chief Moses and Chief Joseph.

REFLECTIONS

My grandfather wrote another letter of interest summarizing the problems in the early days of the Reservation.

INDIAN OFFICE FILE 46189-35 August 16, 1935
To the Office of Indian Affairs, Box 126 Nespelem, Washington
Dear Sir:

40 years ago I was adopted by Chief Masses [Moses] and Chief Joseph and the Indian department for the sole purpose of helping Masses take care of him and his people, keep them at peace. He agree to mind me and he did. About one year before he died he held a war council. They agree to drive all the minner off the Reservation or kill em all. I call him to my home with 12 of his nearest warerer [warrior]. We agree to write the Indian department. We was promist to settle for all damage the miner would do. I kept them at peace in a year or two after Masses died and Joseph died. He had also appointed me his secretary. Then I left in charge of all their people. Then appointed another chief to help me, Joe Masses. He died then we name Quiltena [Quiltenenock] as chief. He died I still left alone at the age of 69. I was to report to the Indian Office of all bad conduct so I reported on an agent Newman of being to high temper and rull with the Indians that he would cause the Indians in trouble. The Government put him out in 30 days later. I find that the whole sub agency at Nespelem was in very bad conduct. I reported Governor send in a secret service man in 30 days. He had the hole sub agency discharge. When the Governor helps me like this I can still keep the Reservation at peace. It must be borne in mind that the Government must do their part or I can't do anything.
Very respectfully Louis Picard

The passing of our chiefs was a major obstacle we had to overcome. There was a lull from when my grandfather wrote the letter in 1935 to when the tribal constitution was approved in 1938 just a year before he passed away. From that point on the tribe slowly picked itself up and moved into the new era.

Chapter Two

WAPITI

Datuk-tuk [Fawn]

Wapiti sees a doe as she carefully makes her way through the creek bed. The doe senses she is being watched but cannot detect by whom or from what direction. She constantly moves her head, covering all directions, stopping occasionally to observe something that may have been out of place. Finally, she moves on.

Wapiti is not interested in her as game meat. He is waiting for her mate. He has been taught to leave a doe alone if a buck is available. The buck offers more of a challenge. It is male to male. Stalker and the stalked. Native ability against native ability. Survival of the fittest.

Wapiti has the advantage of a bow and arrow if he can get close enough and shoot accurately. The buck has superior speed and alertness. Hunter and hunted are almost evenly matched. They both have detailed knowledge of the forest. Wapiti knows the deer trails, feeding habits, and watering holes. The buck senses this and sends his doe out to scout. He knows she is safe under ordinary conditions.

Before the hunt, Wapiti spends a full day in preparation. He always has his weapons ready so his final act is to put his mind in order. It is not exactly a purification process, but much simpler and straightforward. It is more to clear his mind of other thoughts and worries so he could concentrate on the hunt.

He begins in the sweathouse. The sweathouse is used for many reasons such as hunting preparation, petitions for others, and giving thanks for a good life. Special rocks that won't explode when heated are warmed in a fire outside the sweathouse. When sufficiently hot, they are brought in and deposited in a shallow hole. Rose water is poured onto the rocks to make steam and heat up the interior. As sweat pours from his body, Wapiti prays: "Creator-God, How-we-en-chuten, please allow me to take enough food to feed my family."

He follows this with a few minutes of meditation, visualizing himself quietly moving through the trees and situating himself to take his share of food. He ends with a prayer of thanks and then jumps into the nearby stream, cooling himself off and giving a yell that indicates acceptance of what he is given. He then lays down and sleeps soundly until just before daybreak. He arises and, looking east, makes his final petition to his Creator to enable him to be quick and accurate with his shot so the target animal will not feel much pain. He has been taught this from an early age, sitting around the campfire as his Sxxapa [Papa] told the story of the Creation of the Animal People:

"Everything comes from the same source. You are made from the same things as the Earth. That ties us together as one. When you do something to hurt yourself you hurt everything else." His people always reminded the younger ones of this.

Just as Wapiti had anticipated, the buck appears out of the brush just minutes behind the doe, slowly and carefully. Every sense is alert; his nostrils flaring, his eyes sweeping the area, his ears listening for the slightest noise. He knows something is different but can't decide what. Wapiti already has his arrow loaded and bow aimed at the buck, now easily within range.

In his mind's eye, he glimpses the young ones of his tribe crying because they are hungry. They are depending on him. He feels a flash of desperation. He calms himself and slowly pulls the bowstring back as he envisions the path of his arrow straight to the buck's heart. When everything is right, he releases the arrow quickly and it smoothly slips out of his grasp. The arrow strikes hard and fast. The buck leaps forward in a split-second effort to escape but it is too late. He falls and dies instantly.

Wapiti raises his arms to the Creator and then salutes the buck with his hand over his heart. He thanks the buck for giving up his life so Wapiti's family can live. Everything is balanced. As Wapiti dresses out the carcass and readies it to transport back to his family, his thoughts return to the miracle of life. The spiral symbol the women bead on their bags represents the miracle of life and is the same as that painted on the rocks in the middle of the big river. For untold generations his people painted figures on the big rocks telling about the miracle of life and go there to speak with their Creator-God. They believe that we all receive our physical and spiritual power from the sun. It comes to us in the form of spirals. We know this because nature is full of examples, such as the sunflower. The rose is another symbol. The sunflower is especially revered maybe because of its dual and opposing spirals. These designs have been used as far back as anyone can remember. The spirals were painted a long time ago on the rocks near the river by ancestors.

When Wapiti first learned about the grounding pole at the tribes' winter dance, he realized it had something to do with explaining the miracle of life. There was no doubt about feeling closer to nature after a dance, a sweat, or any ceremony he took part in. He could see things more clearly and felt he understood his place in the world. The smoke from cedar branches, rose water, and the color red all helped remind him of his tie to earth.

He finishes the carcass and loads it on his packhorse. With a running jump he leaps on his horse and starts for home, satisfied with his effort. As black clouds form over Badger Mountain he knows he better hurry if he doesn't want to get wet. He nudges his horse into a fast walk. He is trailing his packhorse with the deer and he can't go much faster because of the steep grade. He doesn't want to lose his load.

Before long it begins drizzling and he quickly is soaked. He pulls his buffalo robe tighter around his shoulders. He is warmed by the thought that he will soon be back with his bride of two weeks. He smiles to himself as he thinks of the happy pleasure she will show when he returns. She will run, fast and graceful as the deer she is named after, squealing all the way down the path to meet him.

The trail grows rougher and he slows down to pick his way through rocks and fallen trees. He reflects on their courtship. Tribal tradition dictates that he could not speak to a young maiden. He could only observe and admire her from a distance. Then one day he happened to surprise her alone as she dipped a lined cedar basket into the cool, fresh spring water. She retreated like a frightened little rabbit, until, at a safe distance, she turned to stare at him with large, dark brown eyes like the animal for which she is named Datuk-tuk, or Fawn. Her shining black hair hung in two neat braids, interwoven with delicate, pink petals of wild roses. He looked into those luminous eyes and was lost forever. Soon after that, early one morning, he tied three of his best mares in front of her fathers' lodge. This was his offer of marriage.

He then had to wait for her father's answer. He spent the rest of the day in misery. His fear of refusal was so great that he was almost overcome with nausea. He couldn't believe that such a weak, dainty little girl could reduce him, a big, strong warrior of his tribe, to such weakness. But he need not worry. His uncle Schmowh, who was Chief of the Peshastin tribe, had pleaded his case to her father.

"My tunx [nephew, his sisters' son] is one of the best hunters of our tribe. Wapiti's family always has meat to eat. In addition, he has a spacious, warm pole lodge with many robes and furs for comfort in the winter.

Although he is only twenty years old he has killed many buffalo and deer and he has counted coup four times with the Xeman [pronounced "haman" meaning enemy]. He will be a good addition to your family."

The old Chiefs' eloquent praise of his prowess as a hunter did have an effect. Wapiti's reputation started the day he was born because his dad took a big elk, an unusual and great day for the tribe. He was given the name Wapiti [Chinook for elk] to make that day special and to give him a name everyone would respect.

Wapiti again thinks of his uncle gratefully as he urges his horse into a brisk gallop. He is now on a good trail, the rain has quit, and he can't wait to see Datuk-tuk. He rides for several miles before he notices his horses' ears twitching, its head moving back and forth. His sure-footed horse is giving him notice that something is different ahead. As they come over the last ridge, Wapiti jerks the animal to a sliding halt.

His pole lodge is gone! All that remains are a few burning embers with thin, gray smoke spiraling into the sky. He kicks his horse into a run and rides to the middle of the camp in a fury. He dismounts and runs around looking for his wife. He finds nothing. That gives him courage, because at least there is some hope. It doesn't take him long to read the signs. There were at least five riders and their horses. They had burned or destroyed everything they couldn't carry with them. He picks up their trail outside of his camp heading straight for the big river at Rock Island. Then he notices one horse must have had two riders because of the deeper imprints. She is alive but a captive.

He quickly heads for Rock Island, the home campsite of his tribe, the Ka-wa-chin. He is in a daze as he approaches the campsite fearing what he will find. Reaching the campsite, his worst fears materialize. The entire camp is destroyed. Everything was either burnt or torn apart. There were at least twenty-five pole lodges there the day before.

As he looks closer Wapiti sees dead bodies scattered in grotesque positions. He searches until he finds his parents and lets out a cry of anguish. They were both elderly and didn't deserve to die like this. It was grossly disrespectful. To make up for the disrespect he raises his arms upward toward the sky and calls out:

"Creator-God [How-we-en-chuten] please bring into balance these two honorable people who did nothing wrong and should be treated with dignity."

Then he resumes his search for his wife and realizes he must also find his younger brother, Dee-ee-ik. Yet he doesn't find either, and the eighty head of horses are also gone, either stolen or let loose.

He knows if Datuk-tuk is captured she will first be a slave to the enemy women and then be chosen by one of the men in the tribe to be their wife. The chief would have first choice and then down the line of seniority. Sometimes, if someone had a need, such as having lost their wife, they would be given special consideration. Others could defer their rights and let him have her. The thought horrifies him.

His uncle, Chief Schmowh, lives about twenty miles away, near their annual salmon fishing area. Wapiti heads that way, still leading the packhorse. When he enters the chief's lodge, the first thing he sees is his fourteen-year-old brother, Dee-ee-ik, who is visiting his uncle, oblivious of the disaster.

Wapiti has the difficult task of telling his uncle and brother about the carnage. The old chief takes it all in and then asks for Nantook whose leather-lunged voice could be heard miles away and sends him out to relay the news and tell everyone to prepare for a council and a war dance that evening. He also dispatches a crew to go to the other campsite and prepare the bodies for burial.

As preparations for the ceremonial dance get underway, the elders and warriors gather in Chief Schmowh's pole lodge, which is the largest. They convene a council to determine what action to take.

The younger men call for immediate revenge: "We have been insulted and our relatives desecrated. We need to act now. We will follow them and destroy them no matter how long it takes!" At first this seems to be the consensus but as each man takes a turn to speak some of the cooler heads caution against such action: "There is no doubt this is serious and some action should be taken. But to take on such a long journey we need food and supplies. We do not have enough stored to last so we first have to gather and prepare food. That will take time. It would give the Xeman even more of a head start than they already have. We would not catch up with them until they reach their home grounds. Their advantage would be tremendous because they would have the rest of their tribe to back them up."

The discussion goes back and forth far into the night until everyone has his say. The chief guides the discussion, making sure everyone has a turn, but doesn't voice his opinion. Finally, Wapiti stands up to speak. He is one of the better warriors but not the most senior. He has waited his turn. He first walks around the lodge looking into each of the council member's eyes before he begins to speak. He wants to connect with each one. He begins softly but gradually his voice builds in a crescendo.

"I thank you for your offer to help, but it would be a hardship on your tribe because we are in our season of food gathering. If that is interrupted it could be a hard winter for you. In addition to that, such a large war party would be too easily noticed by the Xeman and would put my nuxnux [wife] in danger. In light of all this, I believe it would best if I went after her alone. I could move around undetected and have a reasonable chance of rescuing her. All I would need is a few provisions to take with me. I already have a deer on my packhorse outside. I could trade it for jerky already prepared."

His words cause uproar. Each of the young men protest, saying it is his duty to go. After much debate, Chief Schmowh makes the final statement: "It is Wapiti's right to choose what we do because he is the one most directly affected. We will defer to him to make the right decision."

Outside the lodge Dee-ee-ik makes a last plea to go with Wapiti.

"Big brother, it is a long ways to go alone. I could be a lot of help. Please let me go."

Wapiti feels sympathy for his younger brother, knowing he is grieving, too, and wants to do something. He answers: "We are the last of our tribe, little brother. If we both were lost our tribe, the Ka-wa-chin, would be gone. You have to stay to make sure that doesn't happen. It is your duty."

The warriors dance well into the night. Several honor songs are sung, some for those fallen in previous battles and others for the present mission. Wapiti pantomimes his coming battle. Then everyone rests.

The next day the entire tribe goes to bury and mourn the dead. Many stories are told about those who died, some funny and some serious. Each person who feels motivated tells a story. Some stories include morals to be learned and others talk about warning signs for the tribe to heed. Some speakers are very eloquent; others very emotional. At the close of the ceremony everyone sits down to eat.

Wapiti gives special friends and relatives keepsakes for them to remember his parents. He says: "Since everything was burned or destroyed these are only tokens that I wish to pass on. In about a year we will have a dinner in memory of my parents and I will give away more items. These will be more substantial and worthy of them. At that point my time of grieving will be complete."

A group of volunteers had been delegated by the chief to prepare food and provisions for Wapiti to take on his trip. They help him load his packhorse and he leaves on the fourth day after the disaster.

The trail of the Xeman is easy to follow. There were at least fifty in the war party and they are herding additional horses. Wapiti follows them to the Lobo trail and over the Bitterroot Mountains. It takes several weeks at the steady pace he uses to conserve his horses. When he can, he travels at night too to make up for lost time. By the time he catches up with the war party, the warriors are already with the main part of their tribe. As he watches them from a high ridge a few miles away he can see there were dozens of what the Xeman called tepees. He has heard of this different kind of lodge, but this was the first time he has seen them.

It looks impossible to rescue his wife against such odds. He needs a plan; something that would give him the advantage. For several nights he reconnoiters the Xeman's camp being careful not to be seen. Luck is in his favor. The Xeman feel so secure, they do not post sentries. On the third night, Wapiti spots a lodge made of logs, some distance from the Xeman encampment. Another first! He has never seen a log house either. He is curious, so he creeps up closer to get a better look. As he approaches, he smells buffalo meat cooking in a pot hanging over a fire burning in a stone structure. He is reminded of his hunger. In his anxiety, he hasn't taken time to eat.

As he nears the door, he hears a voice from inside: "*Klahowa, Sikhs.*" Wapiti instantly recognizes "good friend" in Chinook. A strange man with hair on his face and blue eyes comes out the door. This is the first Suyapenex [white man pronounced "shooyapee" or sh-yo-yap-pen-oo-ch] Wapiti has ever seen. They speak to each other in Chinook. The hairy man offers Wapiti some stew. After some reluctance, Wapiti finally accepts the bowl and gulps it down hungrily. As he eats, the Suyapenex continues to talk: "I want to be your friend. I am a French-Canadian fur trader. I am called Andre. I offer Indians blankets, knives, pots, cloth, beads and tobacco for their furs."

When Wapiti does not respond he continues: "I know you're not from this tribe. I saw the war party leave this camp and come back with many horses and one young woman. My guess is the woman is why you're here, right?"

Wapiti looks at Andre, a question in his eyes.

"Yes, she is doing fine," Andre answers, "but she is watched carefully by the women. She is a prisoner."

Wapiti blurts: "She is my wife, and I come to take her back."

Andre sympathetically offers: "I don't believe in stealing someone else's wife or taking a woman as prisoner."

Wapiti finds himself defending the Indian custom.

"Both tribes do it. We have done it as long as anyone can remember. Sometimes it is the only practical way to grow a family without becoming inbred. That does not mean I have to let it happen with my woman. And I won't. It is my responsibility to rescue her."

As the men continue to talk, Andre reveals that he has a special woman friend of his own in the camp. Her name is Matike and she is one of Datuk-tuk's guards. Andre is convinced Matike will help Wapiti see his wife in secret and make plans for her escape. They can arrange it for the next morning, when Matike and Datuk-tuk will go to a nearby stream for water.

"Do you trust me on this?" Andre asks.

Wapiti has no choice but to accept the offer. The Suyapenex called Andre already knows he is there and what his mission is. He could alert the Xeman anytime he wishes, but Wapiti is still cautious. He doesn't understand Andre's motive for helping him. Andre is taking a great risk, for if he is caught, it will cost him his life.

"I have nothing to offer you." Says Wapiti. "I lost everything when they burned my pole lodge. How can I repay you?"

Andre smiles.

"I've been around Indians long enough to know that you are usually very generous." He says: "When someone is in trouble you help them. If you, in turn, get in trouble then they help you. That's what friends are for, right?'

Wapiti solemnly nods.

Andre continues to explain that the resources for fur trading in this area are diminishing. He and other traders will be moving further west, to Wapiti's territory.

"When we do, I want you to remember me as the one who helped you," says Andre. "Then it will be your turn to help me."

Again, Wapiti nods.

"You're offering something that we will need or want. There is no reason not to trade with you," he says. "You are proving you are someone to be trusted."

With that they shook hands, although each in his own way. Andre grips Wapiti's hand hard. Wapiti lightly touches Andre's.

Early the next morning, Wapiti is waiting in the bushes near the water. It is cold, and he shivers both from being cold and in anticipation of seeing Datuk-tuk.

When the young women finally arrive, Wapiti calls softly: "Datuk-tuk?"

"Wai, Wapiti!" she replies with a gasp of surprise. They eagerly embrace.

"Meet me here tomorrow night and I will have everything ready to escape," he says, looking to Matike to determine if she will cooperate. Matike nods in support.

When Wapiti returns to the log cabin Andre gives him pemmican, jerky, and smoked trout for his return trip. He also tells Wapiti that the Xeman chief has two prize horses that look to be bigger, stronger and faster than any in the herd. The chief is careful to tie them to a rope he keeps inside his tepee so he can constantly be assured the horses are still there.

Wapiti knows the answer to that. He cuts two long willow poles. When evening comes and he is sure the chief is asleep, he carefully unties the horses and reties the chiefs' rope to the willows he has firmly planted into the ground. The poles will bend just enough to give the feel of a horse being tied on the other end. He is good with horses and these two allow him to lead them away without making a sound.

As they had arranged, Datuk-tuk appears at the edge of the camp. They walk the horses until they are out of earshot. For emergency backup, Wapiti also brings his other two horses. They mount and gallop for most of the night. They want to put as much distance between themselves and the Xeman as they can. They have the fastest horses but the Xeman have the numbers. They can ride in relays, change horses, and also maintain a fast pace.

After sleeping while hidden in the brush, the next day they start on a prescribed pace of galloping, walking, and trotting for several weeks, resting only when they are too exhausted to go on. They decide to stay away from the main trail, which means they must travel more slowly, but if their trail is not picked up, they will be safer.

By the time they reach the rolling hills of the Palouse country, their clothes are worn out, they have no food and are exhausted from mental strain and physical exertion. Their horses are thin and footsore from the constant travel. They stop long enough to let the horses graze on the plentiful bunch grass and rest, while they collect food, mostly birds or small animals.

They sense that the Xeman have given up. They detect no sign of pursuit. They are still cautious and begin a slower pace to keep their horses fresh in case they are suddenly chased. As they keep moving nearer to their home country, each day they see a cloud, standing as still as a sentry, just north of the Peshastin campsite.

On the third morning after their rest in the Palouse, they round a bend in the river where they can see Rock Island. They are greeted by Dee-ee-ik, who has been looking out for them. Dee-ee-ik signals the tribe with three puffs of smoke from the fire he is maintaining. Their people send out a welcoming party and escort the weary travelers home.

After they have settled in for a while at the Peshastin camp Wapiti and Datuk-Tuk talk about the cloud that guided them home. Datuk-Tuk wonders if it could be a sign.

"It is unusual that a cloud would stay in the same place for several days. It must mean something." Wapiti agrees.

"Maybe it is like a rainbow which points to a place that is, or will be, blessed with good luck," Datuk-tuk suggests. Wapiti nods thoughtfully.

"The cloud is directly over Entiat Valley where we go every summer to pick berries and get away from the heat in the lower valleys," he says.

It becomes obvious to them that they are meant to move to the Entiat Valley and start over. They plan to build a new tribe, the Entiat, with Wapiti's sole surviving brother, Dee-ee-ik. They already have a good start with the baby who Datuk-tuk knows will arrive next year. They agree the baby's name will be Chilco-sa-haskt, which means Standing Cloud.

With that settled, they think about what it means to start over. They feel unprepared because they have lost their elders who would teach them the Indian Way. They begin by asking each other what they remember of their teachings.

Wapiti remembers being taught that we are all one with nature. The Earth is their mother, the sun their father; that this is true of every plant and animal, therefore everything is connected.

Datuk-tuk remembers being taught to be careful not to harm friends and relatives either verbally or physically, and to give everyone privacy when they need it.

They were taught, too, to share, especially with young ones and elders. They recall that chiefs are sometimes the poorest in the tribe, because they give everything away and depend on the help of others for survival.

They have been taught to make unselfish decisions, based on what is best for the tribe. Together, they resolve to begin again, teaching their children all these things and their story will be told by generations to come.

REFLECTIONS

My Dad worked twenty-three years for the State Highway Department in Wenatchee as an engineer. He was proud of being a licensed professional Land Surveyor. After his retirement my folks sold their house in Wenatchee and moved back to the Rez, a hundred miles north. Like homing pigeons Indians always want to return home. Some of them make it and others don't. My folks were among the lucky ones. They still had their Indian allotments and had someplace to go, Kartar Valley. So like the early settlers they "homesteaded" on their own land.

This brought back a lot of memories. They wanted to record some of their stories- our family history that had been handed down for generations - but couldn't discipline themselves to do it. Finally, they decided to take a writing course at Wenatchee Valley College in Omak.

Dad would tell the story and Mom would record it. From that they developed an essay for their writing course. One of those was "Wapiti." I have since refined it by adding details and clarifications that were necessary. I was curious about the source of the Wapiti story so I asked, "Dad, who was Wapiti? Was he one of our relatives?"

"I think so, but it was told so many times over several generations that the real name was lost. I had to give him a name so I chose 'Wapiti.' Wapiti in the Chinook hybrid language means elk and is an honorable name.

"When did he live?" I asked.

"Sometime before Chilcosahaskt so I would guess the early 1700s or late 1600s. The tribes who lived in the Wenatchee area were pure Indian, untainted by the Suyapenex [foreigner]".

That was a period when major changes began in the Northwest. When our ancestors first saw the horse about 1740 they said it looked something like an elk without the horns. Horses found their way through trade with tribes in what is now California. This greatly improved the economy of the Northwest tribes. But soon after, fur traders came and the subtle invasion of the Suyapenex began. My folks' story describes this time of transition. Wapiti was from the Ka-wa-chin, one of the small bands that occupied the Rock Island area on the Columbia River. The name defines the area.

Dad liked to describe the area:

"About 13,000 years ago the glaciers receded and formed the terrain in North Central Washington. The country is the result of slow evolution of an environment that included gigantic uncut trees, roaring rivers and streams full of trout and salmon, and plentiful wildlife such as deer, bear, coyotes, and beaver.

Archaeologists are studying the two hundred-plus sites and caves in Baja, California, that are 30,000 years old. The indigenous tribe, Pericu, inhabited the area but vanished 200 years ago. Their skulls are more like the aborigines, native to southeast Asia and the Pacific. The theory now is the Pericu tribe navigated from island to island in canoes, parting from Polynesia and Asia in times when the sea level was lower.

During the Ice Age a long tongue of ice ground down the Okanogan Valley blocked the Columbia channel and pushed up over what is now the apex of the triangular Columbia Basin. There it stagnated long enough to leave a short moraine, a ridge of unsorted rock and soil laid down along its melting edge. Receding, it left the once buried plain strewn with "haystacks" of enormous boulders, which it had ripped and transported from the Okanogan country to the north. The stream of melting water issuing from the stationary edge of that ice lobe flowed southward and etched a canyon into the plains surface, which today, as Moses Coulee [named after Chief Moses whose people roamed that area], is a great trench with a small stream draining the countryside.

Today the land lies open and barren because the Cascade mountain range blocks moisture coming from the Pacific Ocean, Rainfall changes from 100 annual inches in the mountains to 10 inches in the plains. Temperatures reach 114 degrees Fahrenheit in the summer and up to 30 degrees below zero in the winter.

The whole landscape was clothed with bunch grass in the plains with pine and fir trees in the mountains. Indian population varied according to the availability of food. Then, like now, more people lived along the Pacific Coast because of the available salmon, oysters, and other seafood.

Inland from the coast the people lived along the large rivers, such as the one now called the Columbia, for the same reason: availability of food. They migrated to the mountains in the summer to get away from the oppressive heat and dust storms of the lowlands and to follow the ripening of the berries, camas and other plant foods. The Columbia attracted the natives because of the salmon and moderate winter weather. In aboriginal north central Washington the confluence of the Wenatchee and Columbia rivers became a gathering place for the tribes. From Rock Island to East Wenatchee were the campgrounds and meeting places of our ancestors."

Chapter Three
TAWAKA

The big river is at its peak flood stage. I know better than to try to run the rapids at this time of year. But we are late for our rendezvous at Fort Okanogan. We do not want to miss the trip down the Columbia in the much-talked-about bateaux, heavily loaded with fur.

We have traveled this way before, but the water was calmer. Now the river is raging and around every bend, a whirlpool threatens. We enter a large canyon and the inevitable whirlpool rapids.[1] Here the river drops a distance of five men's height in a very short distance. Water sprays over our canoe and the river roars.

I look at my partner and wonder if he feels the same as I do. I am not one to scare easily; I have been over many rapids in my time. I fought the upper reaches of the Peace River with Alexander Mackenzie, one of the first fur traders to explore northern Canada. On those trips, there were times when I was too tired to care if I survived. Other times too thrilled with the excitement from shooting the rapids to notice. But this time is different. The river is bigger, faster, and more treacherous than any I have ever seen. The whirlpools are dark and threatening with their spirals sinking into nothingness. No use pretending; I am worried. For the first time in my life I can feel the presence of death, and I want to live. I want to see the offspring that I don't have yet. I want to grow old and live with my memories of a good life.

We round a bend in the river and find ourselves on the same side as the whirlpools. The spiral current quickly catches our boat and starts pulling us toward the center, a dark threatening hole. I shout over the roar of the river to my partner, a fellow Iroquois: "Put your paddle on this side!"

To explain my intent I point to the other side of the river. Luckily, the shoreline is only a stone's throw away, much closer than normal for this river. Maybe we still have a chance. We both row furiously, as hard as we can. At first, the canoe does not respond. Gradually we start moving outwardly toward the center of the river. We are careful not to get sideways with the current because we could quickly capsize. Both of us are silently praying as we slowly negotiate the boat through the swirling whitecaps of the most dangerous and treacherous rapids of the Big River. Although we are good swimmers, we know that in this current, we don't have a chance.

---

1 Box Canyon, below the current site of Grand Coulee Dam

Sweating more from tension than exertion, we paddle together with a precision achieved from years of practice. Finally, we pass the center of the river and it becomes easier to move toward the shore. After beaching the canoe and securing it, we both collapse on the sand between large boulders. It is several minutes before Tanaka, my partner, speaks.

"I never want to go through that again!"

"Once is enough," I agree. We decide to make camp and rest. There is still some daylight left, but we have traveled a long distance this day and that is good enough for us. I am exhausted, but before going to sleep I meditate while watching the river flow by.

I remember my first fur-trading expedition from Fort Astoria, up the fast-flowing river with its many rapids that we were forced to portage around. We saw much beauty all the way along the river. We were exploring this land just like the other fur traders, many of them Iroquois like us. We love to travel. Happiness is going somewhere, anywhere. We don't care. We have to be on the move.

Not quite conscious, not quite dreaming, I see that people of the future will use water in many ways. They will create barriers across the river and because of that they will capture a strange new power to make them warm in winter, to enjoy light in the deepest dark of night. They will create the Fire of the Coyote stories in ways that are beyond my vision. My vision tells me this power can lead the people to a good life, but it also presents a dangerous threat if used in the wrong way. I hope and pray that the people of the future will be careful.

As I travel up the river, I wonder at the solitary, towering rock pillars that rise from the rolling plains. I am intrigued by the hundreds of drawings on rock cliffs, especially one of a person with the sun's rays around his head. What stories are those pictures telling me?[2]

I am from the Iroquois tribe of the Great Lakes region. I spent most of my life in Canada, first with my tribe around the Lakes and then for a while in Montreal. My first taste of the fur trade was bringing loads of fur from the York Factory on Hudson Bay to Montreal. I soon grew tired of the monotony of the slow, big fifty-foot boats and longed for more action. I then really learned the trade on the Peace River as far as the Athabascan Pass.

We were recruited by the Hudson Bay Fur Trading Company because there are no better boatmen in the rapids and dangerous waters than the Iroquois. The English and French-Canadians consider us moody. Sometimes we sing while rowing, and other times we are silent for long periods. Most of us are very strong because of our constant rowing, and the Europeans keep a wary eye on us.

I speak Iroquois, French and Chinook, and I probably am better educated than the rest of the men in my party except for maybe the clerks, who can read and write. My education comes from my tribes' traditions. Everyone in my tribe has a role. The tribal system requires that each tribal member learn about his tribe and then be trained for his role through apprenticeship.

The day after our close escape from the whirlpools, Tanaka and I easily reach Fort Okanogan. Here we wait for the fur to be transported by mule train and boat from the Thompson River and She-Whaps area in Canada. My company chose to locate the Fort Okanogan trading post where two rivers meet, a gathering place for members of all tribes. The Indians meet there for salmon fishing on the Big River and celebration with old friends and relatives. They compete in horse racing and stick games. Tribal leaders discuss hunting and fishing. The women trade stories about root-gathering trips, their men and children. They have a good time and spend many weeks there during the different seasons.

When the fur arrives, we help gather it into bales to fit the large bateaux, which will be used to transport the fur down the Columbia River to Fort Vancouver [Astoria]. The bateaux are double-ended, made of long, sturdy cedar planks caulked with pine pitch. They measure twenty-five to forty feet long and five feet wide in

---

2 Petroglyphs along the Columbia were numerous at Vantage, Buffalo Cave, Crescent Bar, Spanish Castle, and Rock Island Rapids. At Rock Island alone there were at least 350-500 petroglyphs. At least a fourth of the human forms had lines radiating out from their heads. The concentric circles are actually spirals which indicate the interchange between the physical and spiritual. Plates 55, 56, and 57 at the Wenatchee Valley Museum are typical. These are the very few that were saved before the dams were built.

the middle, tapering to points at each end. Each bateau is capable of carrying from one to two tons of cargo and supplies. With eight of us rowing, the bateau can be steered from either end, usually by the boss or his helper. We crew members are short – five-foot-six or less – which allows as much room for furs as possible, but we are very strong.

Two bateaux are finally ready to go, and we are scheduled to leave at daybreak the next morning. Tanaka and I tell our crew mates of our experience with the whirlpools upstream. They already know about the whirlpools at Ribbon Cliff downstream where, according to stories of local Indians, monsters reach up to pull down the canoes. The French-Canadians ridicule the stories, claiming it's a ruse to keep us out of the territory. We aren't so sure. There is truth in all stories. A story may be retold many times and details may change or become richer in the retelling, but the main point is always there. After our experience we are not taking any chances. We express our concern to the rest of our crew, which consists of five French-Canadians and one strange-looking boy who says he is from Hawaii. Although the crew members discount the part about the monsters, they agree the waters could be dangerous.

We consult the boss and his clerk, who man the steering oars on each end of the double-bowed boats. They have been up and down the river several times and know about the rapids at Ribbon Cliff. They agree we should stay on the opposite bank when we pass the rapids. They do not want to risk their precious load.

We talk of our concern to the crew of the other bateau, but they don't seem to take us seriously. They tease us about our lack of courage. They carry on well into the night until everyone starts shouting at each other, and the crew boss has to break it up and tell everyone to go to bed.

The next day is uneventful until we near Chelan Falls, a day's travel downstream. I notice a small leak in our bateau and alert the boss, who is observing from the bow while his clerk steers from the stern. He decides to stop at Chelan Falls to re-caulk. There is no convenient place for many miles beyond that. He signals the other bateau and both pull over. It has taken us almost ten hours to reach this point, and since it is early fall it is nearing darkness. So we prepare to stay the night and will resume our trip early the next day.

The Indians at Chelan Falls always want to trade something for tobacco or maybe cooking utensils. I have saved some tobacco as a special item to trade. I'm not interested in trading for fur, because that is my boss's job. These local Indians usually don't have fur to trade anyway, because they use all that they are able to trap.

But I am interested in trading for some of the berry picking baskets woven by the tribal women. The designs intrigue me. They usually have elaborate roses and leaves beaded on the side in various arrangements. One beaded buckskin shirt interests me the most. It is very elaborate, showing a deer in the forest and a spiral in the center.

When I ask what the spiral means, the woman who made the shirt said it is a symbol for the source of life, a symbol that has been used for many generations. She hangs the shirt in the center of her lodge for all to see. It is beautiful.

I ask if she will trade for it and she answers without hesitation, probably not. We speak in a combination of sign language and the Chelan version of the Chinook language. I don't press the issue. I know I probably don't have enough tobacco for the trade. Even if I made the trade I wouldn't know what to do with the shirt. I carry only a small sack of belongings with me, and the risk of losing or damaging the shirt is too great. But maybe someday I will be able to trade for it.

Every time I look at the design on the shirt, it seems to take on new meaning. I can imagine the deer moving through the forest freely and without any danger. It seems to indicate a great spirit. Maybe the secret of life is hidden somewhere in that design.

The next day we leave at daybreak. About a half-day's trip downstream we approach Ribbon Cliff, where the waters house the monsters of the whirlpools. I signal the clerk, who is steering, and he immediately moves the boat to the east side of the river, opposite the whirlpools. The other bateau continues on the west side, defiantly ignoring all warnings.

All of the men in our bateau watch with horror as the other bateau is caught up in the largest whirlpool and pulled under. The head man yells for our crew to stay their paddles and float as they watch the unfolding scene. For what seems to be an eternity we can see nothing but empty swirling waters. The boss signals for us to move back across the river below the rapids to watch for survivors. When we reach the other side, fur bales begin emerging below the rapids. Boxes and sacks of food and supplies also appear. Finally, Tanaka yells as he sees two boatmen struggling in the water near our boat. We quickly pull them in.

Then we notice the Indians from the nearby Entiat village have launched several canoes to help. They cannot save the large fur bales, because their small, two-man dugout canoes don't have enough room. But they do help rescue the rest of the crew. Luckily none have drowned, mostly because of the quick response of the Indians. If left to our crew, we couldn't have managed because our boat was already fully loaded.

We regroup at the Entiat village and take stock. Most of the furs are lost along with two barrels of rum and other supplies. The Indians report that some of their young men have the rum a few miles downstream and are busily testing the contents. The boatmen are too tired and shook up to care and don't pursue the matter. The other bateau eventually emerges and is towed ashore. Although the cargo is lost, the bateau appears to be functional. We rest at the village making minor repairs, redistribute the remaining load and leave the next day.

The remainder of the trip is uneventful. Tanaka and I talk about our adventures all winter at Fort Astoria and for many winters after. The story grows as details are added.

REFLECTIONS

My mom was very proud of her Iroquois ancestry. It was slight, just one person, who lived in the late 1700s and early 1800s. But Tawaka epitomized the more refined traits of the Indian Way. Most tribes have had difficulty maintaining their culture because they didn't have a written language that would give them the means to institutionalize it. A few recorded their history and culture in different ways and at least the essence of it has been kept. The Iroquois tribe is one of these and we have found much commonality among tribes. Tawaka married a woman from the Molalla tribe in Oregon; she was my mother's great-great-grandmother. That line of my mother's ancestors also included marriage into the Okanogan Tribe. This ancestral tie was reason enough for me to do research on the Iroquois, and when I was asked to work with the National Indian Policy Review Commission it came with the assignment. I was fortunate to work with Ernie Stevens Sr. of the Oneida tribe [one of the five Iroquois tribes], who was a leader in the commission.

When the five Iroquois nations, consisting of the Mohawks, Oneidas, Cayuga, Seneca, and the Onondagas [later six with the addition of the Tuscarora], became a confederacy about 1570 they were a true democracy. They put high value on individual rights but agreed to work together for their own protection from outside forces and to help their economy. Their agreement contained democratic principles of initiative, recall, referendum and women's suffrage. It also defined the responsibilities of governmental officials to the electorate and the principles of conservation. In decision making, they considered every issue to determine its effect on the succeeding seventh generation before proceeding. Of course to be able to do this, they had reached a certain level of economic stability. Day-to-day survival was not as critical as it had been. They established agriculture, such as growing corn, and could process food to keep over the winter.

The Iroquois were not the only tribes to create a confederacy; the Shawnee joined with a number of tribes to try to stop the western movement of the Shemanese [Europeans], and the Columbia Confederacy in the Northwest was formed to hunt buffalo and fight the Plains tribes. The Suyapenex [Europeans] were not a problem to them at the time.

Ben Franklin became aware of the Iroquois Confederacy early on because of his dealings with the Indians in the 1740s. He observed the so-called "savage" natives handle complicated issues with decorum and respect for each other. That was a lot more than he experienced with the "civilized" politicians of the thirteen colonies.[3]

One of his meetings with the Iroquois was on June 28, 1742, when one hundred and eighty-eight Indians gathered first in Stanton, Pennsylvania, and later on June 30 at Philadelphia, to discuss the validity of the 1736 Walking Purchase Treaty.

If my dad were telling this story, it might go something like this:

One of the Iroquois chiefs, Conasatego from the Onondaga tribe opened the discussion.

"We have come to complain about the White Man taking all of our land."

"How can that be? You have an agreement that sets boundaries," Franklin responded.

"Yes, we have an agreement that says, 'As far as a man can walk in one day.' This is how we normally describe it."

"Let me guess," said an amused Franklin, always fond of a good joke. "They found a runner who could cover more ground than you anticipated."

"Yes, you are right," Conasatego affirmed. "The runner covered more land than we occupy. Some of it we haven't even seen before. Now the other tribes are angry with us for giving away land they occupy. And we have no place to live now."

"Well, you have a point," said Franklin. "In a court of law it could be established that you didn't have a 'meeting of the minds.' That would make the agreement invalid."

"Your court of law is only for white men," Conasatego protested.

"I agree that it favors us. But that would be natural because it is based on our culture. You come from a different culture. In your culture, you occupy land but you don't own it. In our culture, we have introduced the notion of land ownership. If we own the land, we buy or sell it like a commodity. This came from Europe where land is scarce, so they had to develop rules to keep the multitudes from killing each other."

Franklin and Conasatego had many discussions while he picked the chief's brain. Another meeting was held in August 1749 in Philadelphia.[4] The next morning Conasatego got up feeling strange. He knew he shouldn't have stayed with those white men. They have an endless supply of the liquid that burns your throat on the way down but makes you feel happy later. You forget all your troubles and become the smartest man in the world, at least in your own mind. The last thing he remembered was all of them yelling "Yo-hee!"[5] He complained so much that his wife gave him a concoction from willow bark [a forerunner of today's aspirin].

Something said the previous night was still on his mind. The discussion was about the Iroquois Constitution. The Suyapenex couldn't understand why Indians gave women such an important role in the affairs of the tribe. Conasatego, or "Connie" as the men began calling him before the night was over, had difficulty explaining to them that this was the way it had always been in his tribe. His was a matriarchal society. Women always were predominant in tribal affairs. The women trained the boys to be leaders. They were tough on them, teaching discipline but also love. They eventually chose the leaders from the group of trained boys. But it didn't end there; women still advised the men leaders on serious tribal problems. This was so inherent in their tribe that there was no way they could separate tribal politics from family life.

The colonial men, including Ben Franklin, couldn't see how women could help with the serious affairs of the government. In their world, women stayed in the background, supportive but not really involved in complex affairs. Their culture had never allowed women to be in the forefront. Their women were trained in domestic affairs but had no knowledge or interest in politics. That was men's work.

The differences between the two cultures didn't end there. Individual tribal members had several rights within their government that colonial people didn't. The rights of initiative and referendum could override a dictatorial leader's unilateral decisions. Under the right of referendum, the leaders asked tribal members for their

---

3 William N. Fenton, *The Great Law and the Longhouse*, [Oklahoma   Press, 1998], 440.

[4] Ibid, 456.

[5] Ibid, 418, 456.

consensus; under the right of initiative, tribal members gave their decision even if not requested by the leaders. The members also had the right of direct recall of a leader, if it were the consensus of the tribe.

One of the more subtle differences was the qualification for leadership. As a community effort Indians trained their leaders from the time they were born. In the colonies anyone who had the time, energy, and resources could be a leader regardless of training.

After much urging by Franklin, the Virginia colonial government finally met with the Five Nations at Lancaster, Pennsylvania, on the ironic date of July 4, 1744.

Conasatego advised, "Our wise forefathers established union and amity between the Five Nations. This has made us formidable. This has given us great weight and authority with our neighboring Nations ... We are a powerful Confederacy and by your observing the same methods our wise forefathers have taken, you will acquire strength and power."[6]

Both Conasatego and Franklin were tired of the constant bickering among the Virginia, Pennsylvania, and Maryland colonial representatives. They said, "We heartily recommend a Union defining a good agreement between you and our English brethren."[7]

Franklin proposed it at the Albany Conference.[8] He explained that "Indians operate under a democratic, federal system with local clans, communities and bands coming together for Grand Councils as needs require."

The delegates did accept the concept in 1754, and in 1789 it was incorporated in the U.S. Constitution, although in a somewhat distorted form. The transition was completed in the series of amendments beginning with the Bill of Rights.

In my work with the National Indian Policy Review Commission, I had trouble convincing others of the concept that the Iroquois provided a basis for the U.S. Constitution. As more information became available, it became a common understanding. Kirke Kickingbird, one of the commission's Indian attorneys, even wrote a dissertation which compared the similarities of the U.S. Constitution to the Iroquois.[9]

Central to Tawaka's story are his journeys on the Columbia River. Indian people had traveled up and down the big river for eons. They hunted, fished and picked berries or roots as the seasons changed. The river was their economy. It was a natural one. All they had to do to maintain it was to conserve for future generations. This was easy for them to do because of their small population and their low-volume fishing technology. Their main export to the coast Indians, pemmican[10], was so labor-intensive the market was small.

Water was so integral to the Indian's life, it was spiritual. As the source of their food, recreation, and transportation, it was an everyday reminder of their Creator. Father Pat Twohy, a Jesuit priest who served on the Colville reservation, after talking with many tribal elders, including my dad, was inspired to write a passage in his book, *Finding a Way Home,* about the Indians on the Colville Indian Reservation.

> All bands shared the water
> Of the big rivers
> And the streams that ran into them.
> Each band camped together
> By the waters of certain rivers and lakes.
> These waters meant Life for the People:
>
> Water for salmon to come home in,
> Water for drinking and cooking,
> Water for the joy of bathing, swimming,

---

[6] Ibid, 432.
[7] Ibid, 592.
[8] Ibid, 720.
[9] http://www.kickingbirdassociates.com/articles/foundations-of-american-democracy/
[10] Lean dried meat pounded fine and mixed with melted fat

Water providing protection and distance from enemies,
Water for travel in dugout canoes to relatives and friends,
Water in which to feel close to the Creator of all,
Water in which to see one's self as one truly was.[11]

It was in this sacred arena that the collision between my ancestors and the Suyapenex would begin. As the availability of fur animals for trading was being exhausted in the East, new sources were in constant demand. A push up the Missouri River was sufficient for a while but soon peaked out.

In 1804, in an effort to open up a trade route to the Northwest, President Thomas Jefferson sent Meriwether Lewis and William Clark from St. Louis up the Missouri and points west. They reached the mouth of the Columbia, but the route was not commercially viable because it required a portage of 340 miles. Since the fur market was opening up in India and China, a Northwest route was needed.

The British, through the Northwest Fur Company, explored the Northwest between 1793 and 1811. In 1793, Alexander Mackenzie went from the Peace River, which emptied into the Arctic, to the Pacific, following streams he met at the Continental Divide. He followed the Fraser River over perilous and treacherous routes for six weeks and finally reached the Pacific Ocean. He mistook the Fraser to be the Columbia River. It was thought to be too dangerous to be a suitable trade route.

The Northwest Fur Company then shifted its efforts to the south and from 1807 to 1811, David Thompson searched through the labyrinth of ranges and trenches of the upper Columbia for a Pacific outlet. When he reached Blaeberry Creek in north Canada, he saw that it flowed to the Northwest and didn't realize that it was the headwaters of the Columbia. The fur traders eventually settled on a route that included Fort Okanogan, where the Okanogan and Columbia rivers met.

John Jacob Astor, an American working out of New York, established the Pacific Fur Company. Until he was forced to sell out to the Northwest Fur Company because of the War of 1812, he did a lot to establish the fur trade routes. He sent ships from New York to the mouth of the Columbia, a six-month journey, and established a fort, which he named Astoria. He had a lot of recruits to join the enterprise.

The Northwest Fur Company shipped furs out of the Columbia River region from 1813 to 1821, when it merged with the Hudson Bay Company. The surviving organization became the largest fur trading company in the world, involving hundreds of establishments and thousands of men covering millions of square miles from the Atlantic to the Pacific and up to the Arctic. Fur trading was at its peak from 1835 to 1840 and eventually was terminated in the area in 1850.

The owners and clerks of the fur-trading companies were either British or Americans, but the rest were French-Canadian or Indian, mostly Iroquois. Many of the fur traders who lived very long in the area married native women and raised families.

The boatmen were called voyageurs – a hardy and unique bunch. They liked to sing to pass the time and take their mind off the drudgery. The singing was very animated on the water and in the open air, but not necessarily harmonious. They all sang in unison, raising their voices and marking the time with their paddles. One always led, but there was a diversity of taste and skill. Ordinarily the steersman chose the song and gave the pitch. Sometimes he sang the stanza and the others joined in the chorus. Voyageurs were chosen partly by their singing abilities, and the effect of six to fourteen of them in full song was quite impressive.

They sang in French, of course, with songs about their canoes, their country, their life, their loves, their church – sentimental romances, old ballads, humorous jingles, lofty poems, and obscene verses. A portion of one of those songs, as quoted by Grace Lee Nute in her book *The Voyageur*, reflects the voyageur's abiding love for his vessel:

---

11 Patrick J. Twohy, *Finding A Way Home: Indian & Catholic Spiritual Paths of the Plateau Tribes*, [Gonzaga University Press, 1983], 56. Quoted by permission of the author.

You are my voyageur companion!
I'll gladly die within my canoe.
And on the grave beside the canyon
You'll overturn my canoe.

Indians, too, would go up and down the river but not as far as the fur traders. They had dugout canoes that were mostly used to cross the river. The Indians of the Pacific Northwest were quietly minding their own business until people of a different culture came and began trading for furs. Trading on a large scale was a notion foreign to Indians. Most of what they trapped was for their own use or maybe minor trading with friends or relatives. About the same time, horses began to show up from California and Mexico along with some Southwest and Mexican culture.

The Columbia River tribes were nomads – hunters and gatherers – as their ancestors were before them. They changed methods and location but their purpose was always the same, simply to provide for their family. For centuries they walked, following the salmon, deer, and seasons for roots and berries, living almost from day to day. The introduction of the horse in the 1700s dramatically changed their lifestyle. The increase in speed and carrying capacity made it easier.

This mode of life continued from aboriginal times until the late 1800s. The creation of the Colville Indian Reservation in 1872 destroyed their nomadic way of life. The boundaries were too small to maintain a viable nomadic economy. This was a major change to the Indian way of life and almost fatal to Indians themselves, both as tribes and as individuals.

My dad, the consummate storyteller, related to Tawaka as he took soundings along the same stretch of the river. He was working for the Army Corps of Engineers, doing preliminary survey work for Chief Joseph Dam. The surveyors were in two big power launches and were relatively safe. But the whirlpools were just as threatening and Dad could imagine the excitement Tawaka experienced.

My dad's ancestors crossed paths with my mothers' many years before they met. Tawaka married a woman from the Molalla tribe in Oregon and settled near what is now Salem, Oregon. His daughter, Susanne, was in the fur business through her husband, Amble Petit, a French-Canadian fur trader. They were married in the Catholic Church on December 27, 1838, and had a daughter, Marie, who was baptized on January 9, 1840.

In another branch of my ancestors, Marie Okanogan, who was from the Okanogan tribe, also married a fur trader, Andre Picard. The offspring of Marie Okanogan, Regis Picard, and Susanne and Marie Pettit, married and formed the basis of the Picard family. Tawaka's life flowed much like the rivers he so fondly traveled. He saw many changing scenes while at the same time, many things stayed the same. He surely became aware that the various tribes he encountered had much in common, even though they never or rarely had contact with each other. They believed in a Creator God who worked very close to their own Spirit. Much of their culture and beliefs were connected with the Spirit. Tawaka may have understood that the spiral pictographs he saw along the Big River were ancient explanations of how Creator God communicates with us. The Indians who drew the pictographs were in deep meditation, in touch with the Supreme Spirit. It was their legacy to pass on this information and revelation to future generations. Dad said that young Indians found their Spirit, or Sumax, by going to these sites, where they prayed, fasted, and stayed awake for several days. They meditated by watching the moving water and listened for enlightenment. They added to the images already there with images of their own visions. The radiating light coming from their heads is explained by the Hopi song [F. Waters Book of the Hopi 1959]:

The song resounds back from our Creator with joy,
And we of the earth repeat it to our Creator.
At the appearing of the yellow light,
Repeats and repeats again the joyful echo,
Sound and resounds for times to come.

Chapter Four
CHILCOSAHASKT

Aboriginal Times

A bullet twangs off a rock by his left foot, and Chilcosahaskt instinctively ducks. Guns are rare, and Indians can't get them easily. A few came from the East through early traders. He falls behind a rock ledge and waits for a few minutes before peeking over it. He sees his people in a brutal fight with the Xeman in the southerly wash below him. Both sides are in breechcloth, and he cannot distinguish his own people from the Xeman.

Dust clouds rise from horses galloping back and forth with their riders trying to take aim on their enemy. All he has is a single-shot musket that shoots barely further than he can throw a rock. He is on foot because his horse had stepped into a groundhog hole and broken its leg. He is scratched and bruised from the fall and can't move very fast. So he eases toward what he thinks may be friendly territory.

As he walks, he thinks about the fighting. It seems senseless. What do they gain? There are plenty of buffalo for both tribes. They will lose some of the best men from both sides. Their families will suffer for generations to come.

He walks up a small hill and runs down the other side. He anxiously looks back and sees one of the enemy following him. A sudden fear grips at the pit of his stomach and quickly spreads throughout his body. His thought process stops. He is in survival mode. He runs harder.

The enemy has only a knife, so Chilcosahaskt is safe if he can keep some distance between them. Just when he thinks he cannot go any farther, he breaks through some brush and stumbles into his camp. His people surround him and begin yelling at his pursuer, who stays at a safe distance. It is an impasse.

That night, after the fighting stops and everyone returns to camp, he thinks some more about the situation. He wants to help his people, but he doesn't know how. Finally he sleeps and dreams.

In the dream, his lodge is burning down. He can see through the flames that all his loved ones – mother father, sister and brother – are threatened. All will be consumed in the fire. But wait. Is it a fire? The flames rage, but nothing seems to burn. What is happening?

He notices a group of people in the background, strangers to him, who are fanning the fire, trying to make it burn more. But why?

He yells at them to stop, but they ignore him. He throws rocks at them, but he misses. He has no other options. Or does he? He remembers being taught that if his desire is intense enough, he can do anything. But how to increase this intensity? He also remembers that it must become the most important thing to him. He can't desire everything with equal intensity. He must choose and concentrate single-mindedly on what he wants most. He does, and his loved ones are saved.

When he wakes up, he vividly remembers his dream and ponders what it may mean. He thinks of the story told at campfires where Coyote brings fire to the people. He can't imagine life without campfires. Salmon don't taste very good raw. He somehow senses that the Sun also is part of the story, because it brings heat to people. Does the campfire somehow store energy from the Sun? If so, then Coyote must be very smart to figure out how to do that.

The first Chilcosahaskt was a good warrior because he was trained for it. Every two or three years they would make the trip to what is now Montana and bring back buffalo and sometimes women from other tribes. This was one way to keep up the hybrid vigor in the tribe. They were geneticists before their time.

Chilcosahaskt II was probably chief when the tribe started using tepees. They picked up the idea from eastern tribes, the Salish, Blackfeet, and Shoshone who in turn got it from the Sioux and Cheyenne of the Great Plains. The unique cone shape is ideal for letting smoke out at the top. A spiral also moves up and down in a cone shape.

Chilcosahaskt II was a good hunter but preferred to stay in his own territory. He explored the mountains of the upper Entiat Valley and over to Lake Chelan. He knew the patterns of the deer whether winter or summer. His family was never short of deer meat. His diligence was what eventually did him in.

It is early spring, 1790. Chilcosahaskt can't resist making one more hunting trip up in the mountains. He knows the dangers of avalanches but decides to chance it anyway. It isn't that his family is starving. They still have an ample supply of dried deer meat. He has spring fever and just wants to get out into the mountains and appreciate the cold, crisp snowy peaks in the early morning.

He is walking at a slow pace, studying the tracks in front of him. They are easy to follow in the snow, but he can see that the buck is stumbling occasionally for no apparent reason. This is unusual for a healthy animal. The buck is probably starving, as there is no sign of blood and it has been a hard winter. Maybe he has been chased by a cougar or a pack of coyotes but there are no signs of them now. They probably caught Chilcosahaskt's scent and are keeping out of sight. He can almost feel their eyes on him. He knows he will catch up to the buck within the hour.

But he has ventured too far. He has followed the trail leading down towards Lake Chelan. The buck is seeking water. Higher up in the shaded northern slopes the streams are frozen. The snow is deep but Chilcosahaskt has fashioned snowshoes and is making good time. He becomes intense in his search and neglects to watch for warning signs of snow slides. As the morning grows warmer, the sunny part of the slopes starts melting. The snow is already soft from several days of warm weather. Chilcosahaskt's trail leads under an overhang, which has tons of snow on the upper slopes behind it.

He hears a rumble, soft at first but quickly growing louder. He doesn't have to guess at what it is. Avalanche! He is still under the overhang when the snow breaks loose and instantly buries him before he has time to even think about what's happening.

Since no one knew where he was, Chilcosahaskt's body was never recovered. It was somewhere on the northern slopes of Lake Chelan. He left his widow and his two-year-old son, Chilcosahaskt III. At the farewell dinner the following words were spoken,

"I have known Chilcosahaskt for many years. He and I hunted together all over these hills and valleys. Several times we searched the general area where he was lost, because it is a good place to hunt. It had a trail where the deer go down to the lake for water.

We had good times and hard times together. I never once heard him complain, because he loved life. Every day was a new experience for him and he looked forward to it. He did everything with zest and was full of energy. But he was not without humor.

I remember one time he played a trick on his nephew. His nephew wanted to learn how to hunt, so Chilcosahaskt took him out one day. He knew where a mama bear and her cub were, so he brought his nephew close to the area and told him to go around the hill on one side while he went around the other. Then he hurried to reach the bears first and roused them so they would run - towards his nephew. Can you imagine his nephew's eyes when he saw two bears running directly at him? Well, lucky for the nephew, he was fast enough to jump out of the way, unharmed. Chilcosahaskt was watching from on top of the hill, laughing as hard as he could.

He understood his place in life. He was a role model for his nephew and trained him well. He was confident his nephew could handle the situation. But things didn't always go his way and he accepted whatever happened.

His main hope was that he would make someone happy. Every day he would get up in the morning, face East as the sun rose, and say:

'Creator God, [Hawiyencuten], I give you thanks [Lam Lampt] for giving me the strength and energy to see another day of this wonderful life. Please help me increase my faith so I will have the resolve to help my family and tribe adjust to the many challenges they face.

Until another day [aykast] Lam Lampt, Chilcosahaskt.'

I reach out to his family and friends who suffer from his not seeing another day. We do not even have his body to bury but we will keep him in our minds and know that he is better off in the Spirit World and is wishing us well.

We have lost a good member of our tribe, but his memory lives on. He has left a legacy to his two-year old son with the same name. Others will have to tell this young boy about his father so he can learn the ways of our tribe. He will carry on the tradition of our tribe and we will survive. We will actually profit from this unfortunate event because many of us will step up and take more responsibility for the tribe's welfare. In this way Chilcosahaskt's abilities will be multiplied. When the time comes, young Chilcosahaskt will become chief of our tribe. This is all I have to say. Lam Lampt."

The group of family and friends at the dinner answered with the customary "aaah" signifying agreement.

It is not known who was Chief after Chilcosahaskt II died. Chilcosahaskt III, who lived his very long life in the Entiat Valley, became Chief sometime after 1837. Chilcosahaskt III grew up with his extended family, which was very common then as it is now. Whenever there is a need, someone in the family takes over. In this case it probably was several people, like an aunt or uncle or both. Although Chilcosahaskt probably wondered about his father and would on occasion ask about him, he was not deprived of parental care. His mother, Kenemtiq't, was still with him and she received a lot of help. She probably moved in with a brother-in-law, most likely as a second wife. She adjusted to her new duties and life went on.

One of Dad's stories was about Chilcosahaskt III, in his 20s, observing the fur traders as they were travelling the Big River.

Chilcosahaskt would watch the fur traders as they passed his home in Entiat with their large double bow boats [bateaux] loaded with fur from Upper Canada. The fur was going to Fort Vancouver to be shipped eventually to the Far East. Other than logs and brush floating down the river in the spring that was the most traffic they had.

Chilcosahaskt looked with wonder at the stout, short boatmen rowing the bateaux. There were eight of them, four on a side, rowing in a well-synchronized cadence. They had a man ready to steer at each end. He'd heard a lot of stories about the French-Canadian and Iroquois boatmen. They looked like a carefree bunch, dressed in leather leggings and a fur cap. He didn't envy their work, though, as he had enough rowing just getting across the river and back. He couldn't imagine taking a round trip to this distant place called Fort Vancouver.

His half-brother, Wapato John, who lived at Chelan Falls, told many stories about voyageurs. They occasionally stopped at Chelan Falls for supplies or to re-caulk their bateaux with pine pitch. The Indians warned them of the monsters who lived in the whirlpools near Ribbon Cliff. But the boatmen were too worldly. They had seen everything there was to see and heard everything there was to hear.

So eventually one of the boats ignored the Indians' advice to stay on the other side of the river at Ribbon Cliff. They were caught up in the whirlpool and capsized, dumping the entire load into the water. Some of the children at Entiat, a couple of miles downstream, saw the fur bales floating down the river and told the adults. Chilcosahaskt and some other young bucks tried to retrieve the fur bales but they were too heavy for their small, two-man canoes but they did save the boaters.

Some of them found two barrels of rum [actually grog which is rum mixed with water] and brought those ashore. The adventurous ones tasted the contents and wound up happy for two days. Chilcosahaskt wasn't one of them as he had heard of the after-effects. Sure enough, those that imbibed were sick for several days afterwards and swore they would never do that again.

On the other bateau, a young Iroquois paddled with interest as his boat carefully went to the other side of the river and safely missed the whirlpools. They were able to retrieve some of the furs although the bales had broken apart by the time they reached them. It wasn't a total loss but it was a lesson well learned because the boatmen never again ventured on the wrong side of the river.

The Iroquois rower was the one who had warned the men steering the boat, so they knew how to handle the situation. That rower had already experienced a river whirlpool upriver in different rapids and had a healthy respect for them. His name was Tawaka. His descendants eventually married descendants of Chilcosahaskt.

Chilcosahaskt saw the entire transition from an Indian to a European world. Unfortunately, most of his thoughts and observations went unrecorded. His son, who made him proud, was Lahompt, later named Koxit George, my grandfather.

We always seemed to be stoking the fire at my folks' place in Wenatchee because they had a big corner fireplace that became the centerpiece when the fire was burning good. Such was the case on a cold and wintry morning when Dad stoked the fire while I stood behind him, in a pensive mood. Then suddenly, as I looked into the brightly burning fire, I had a feeling of déjà vu.

"That looks like the fires some of our ancestors had while they were holding Council."

Dad knew I was giving him an opening, so he took advantage of it and launched into one of his favorite stories.

"My dad, or your grandfather, who was called Koxit George by the Suyapenex and Lahompt by the Indians, told me about their conversations. I was just an teenager and not paying as much attention as I should have, but as I tell the story a lot of it comes back to me."

Mom joined in then.

"Tell him about preparing for the buffalo hunt. You remember more each time you tell it. I always learn something."

Mom didn't have to encourage Dad, but she did anyway.

"OK, since you insist. They were camped not too far from where we live right now. Down closer to the Columbia River so they could easily get water. It was a big encampment, the first one after the snow left. Everyone was excited to be there to see their old friends and to meet new people. They had horse races, wrestling, stick games, wye lukes[13] and dancing. The young people participated in the physical activities while the older ones just sat around and told stories. The little kids sat with their parents and grandparents and absorbed tribal history. The chiefs were eager to get down to business right away because they had a lot of work to do.

"I can see them exchanging greetings with each other and then sitting down in a rough circle. The circle is a practical arrangement because it allows everyone to face each other and no one can consider himself greater than the others. But everyone knew his place.

---

13 An Indian card game with the dealer betting against the other players. Similar to roulette but using the first turned up card as the one to be matched by a later one.

The elders spoke first, if for no other reason than to set the tone of the discussions. Through self-control, the youngest would rarely speak. As they grew older, they became more confident of themselves and had more to say. The chief acted only with the consent of the others. He never presumed authority.

"But getting back to the scene we are now envisioning …

The fire leaps towards the dawn sky as the young fire-tenders throw pitch on it; lighting up the faces of those huddled around in the chilly, April morning. Shooktalkoosun [Broken Sun] studies the faces of his friends whom he has called to this Council. They represent all the tribes who roam this area, primarily the Wenatchi, Chelan, Entiat, and Sinkuise [Moses-Columbia].

Shooktalkoosun begins: "It is that time again. We have depleted our caches of buffalo and need to return to buffalo country to replenish them. I have called this Council to prepare for a hunting party to leave within thirty days. Does anyone have anything to say before we get into the details of the trip?"

He nods towards Chilcosahaskt, who had raised his eyebrows.

"My brother, Wapato John, told me the other day that he is not sure he wants to go to Xeman [enemy - pronounced "haman"] country to hunt buffalo this year," Chilcosahaskt announces. "He says the Chelan tribe lost too many people during the last excursion and came back with less dried buffalo meat than ever before. Also, two years away from their families and homeland left them virtually impoverished, because most of the hunters went on the trip. The mobile hunting party of older men who were left behind to help the women, children, and invalids at home didn't work out very well. I agree with him. My Entiat tribe had the same problem. He can elaborate."

Wapato John nods in agreement: "He has described my thoughts very well."

Tecolekun, the Wenatchi Chief, raises his hand and, after getting the nod from Shooktalkoosun, states: "While I don't want to disagree with my fellow tribesmen, I would like to point out this will probably be the best trip that anyone can remember. The weather is starting off much better than before, our horses have wintered well and everyone is healthy. We can make the trip faster and, as everyone knows, it will greatly improve the welfare of our tribe. We need buffalo to provide not only food but for necessary tools and cooking utensils."

It is a good speech, but his position is somewhat tainted since he is the father-in-law-to-be of Kwiltninuk, and naturally is expected to support him. Kwiltninuk, sitting next to his father, Shooktalkoosun, is second in line to succeed him as leader of the four-tribe confederation.

Kwiltninuk is the most enthusiastic supporter of the hunting trip. He is a superb fighter in skirmishes with the Xeman, who jealously guard their buffalo, and he is an excellent hunter. Above all, he feels most alive when he is hunting or fighting. That is his entire life. Every day for him is preparation for action. But he is not a convincing orator and leaves that to others.

His father is the main spokesman for their tribe, the Sinkuise [Columbia], because he is chief of the Sinkuise and leader of the Confederation. Even the impetuous Kwiltninuk knows his place in councils such as this. It is customary for anyone to speak at Council if he feels the need. The others are obliged to listen but not necessarily to act. The words of the second eldest son of the Chief do not carry a lot of weight. Patsksteeweeya is the eldest, and Kwitalahn [Moses] the youngest. Moses does speak out occasionally when he thinks the conversation is heading the wrong way, while Patsksteeweeya is very quiet and somewhat unsure of himself, even though he is the next in line to be Chief if he proves himself. Moses, on the other hand, has a lot of confidence for his age but doesn't consider his opinion worthwhile amongst his elders because of his youth and inexperience. Moses notices that Kwiltninuk is having trouble containing himself even though he hasn't yet spoken.

Their father replies, "We understand your problems because we also have had difficult times since the last hunting expedition."

Shooktalkoosun has the ear of everyone because he speaks from the heart, has an excellent analytic mind, and presents well-thought-out suggestions for solving problems.

"I have been thinking how we can do better. I will leave my youngest son, Kwitalahn, at home this time to serve as hunter and provider for the home camp. I do this reluctantly because he is old enough to learn a lot on this trip and would be very helpful to us. But the times have been so bad, we can't afford to risk our families any more than necessary. Some of you have sons or nephews who could also help those at home. They would miss the excitement but would grow with the weight of responsibility of being the sole provider at home. What do you think of the idea?"

"It's a good idea," answers Wapato John. "But what about my brother, Chilcosahaskt, who does not have a son old enough to help.?"

"Aaah," agree the majority of listeners.

Tecolekun picks up on the point and suggests, "We could arrange to have a group of young and able helpers make regular rounds to each encampment to see what they can do to help. It will work better than the older men we relied on last time, because the boys won't mind riding their horses."

Chilcosahaskt nods in agreement and adds, "But they will have to be rotated, because it is a day's ride each way to my encampment and it could easily turn into too much work for one young man."

Shooktalkoosun interjects, "It looks like we are in general agreement that some sort of plan can be worked out." They all agreed.

"One more thing before we break up," concludes Wapato John. "Why don't we ask everyone to consult Karneetsa if they have a problem that requires a level head?"

"Aaah" everyone consents. They respect her judgment and experience as the wife of Shooktalkoosun.

Some leave the warmth of the fire to check their horses, and this marks the end of the discussions for the day. They will get together later that evening after dinner to discuss some more arrangements for the hunting trip. These discussions will carry on for days and weeks, if necessary, until every last person is satisfied with the plan.

I asked "When did this meeting take place?"

"This Council occurred in 1840, which resulted in one of the last buffalo hunting trips into what was later to be Montana. The trips were long and arduous because it required going through two mountain passes and probably meeting the Xeman"

The Columbia Indian Confederacy, which was the first of its kind in what is now north central Washington, was created by the four Salish-speaking tribes because they needed more people for the buffalo hunting trip to the Plains. They occupied a contiguous block of territory on both sides of the Columbia River and culturally were close – especially the Wenatchi, Entiat, and Chelan. The Sinkuise had a stronger tribal organization, more tendencies to warring activities, and more frequent and prolonged ventures into the Great Plains for buffalo hunting.

The Confederacy also provided the mechanism for the summer ceremonies. Individuals enhanced their political advantage by strategically marrying daughters of chiefs. This also applied, to a certain extent, to other members of the tribes.

The Columbia Indian Confederacy remained undiscovered for a long time and they were the last to feel the impact of white settlement. It was not until the 1890s that significant numbers of whites started settling the area. The city of Wenatchee, site of one of the main Indian meeting places, was not laid out for development until 1892. In 1910 all the land in Manson, on Lake Chelan, was still occupied by Indian families.

According to Dr. Verne Ray, who studied the tribes, said it was during the Pacific Railroad Survey and in the negotiation of cession treaties with Governor Isaac I. Stevens, that George Gibbs made brief ethnographic inquiries among the Chelan, Entiat, and Wenatchi, and learned of the existence of the Columbia Confederacy and of its pre-white origin.[14]

---

14 Verne F. Ray, PhD. The Columbia Indian Confederacy, University of Washington. 1960.

Ray also said that it was not surprising that a great confederacy developed among central Plateau tribes. Political organization was highly evolved among all of the Plateau tribes.

The offices, departments, and functions of government were laid out with precision, even though the overall structures were of modest proportions because of the small populations. The emphasis placed by such tribes as the Wenatchi, Entiat, and Chelan upon village autonomy in all local affairs made a larger organization either desirable or necessary for such purposes as the organization of buffalo hunting ventures into Blackfoot country. Tribal organization might have served these purposes, but a league of all the tribes which traveled together was a more logical mechanism. Intertribal affairs of other sorts, for example the summer ceremonies, found the same group of tribes in cooperative association.

Among the tribes of the confederacy and to the south [but not to the north] there was another powerful incentive to intertribal cooperation and organization: chiefly intermarriage. This pattern was so strong, it developed into a rule for the choice of mates and it applied not only to the tribal officials but also, to a considerable extent, to other members of chiefly families. The numerous chiefly genealogies, extending back five to seven generations, clearly show the extent to which this pattern of marriage linked the tribes of the confederacy and even those beyond.

The Columbia Confederacy was not the only such league on the Plateau. A comparable organization existed among the tribes immediately to the south. This was the Yakima Confederacy, comprised of the following tribes and perhaps some others: Kittitas, Yakama, Wanapam, Klikitat, and Palus. Its greatest leader was Kamiakin, a Palus-Yakama man whose name was most prominent in the treaty negotiations of 1855 at Walla Walla and in the so-called "Yakima War" which followed.

Shooktalkoosun [Broken Sun], the first head of the Columbia Confederacy, may have been responsible for its formation. His first remarkable feat was the acquisition of chiefly leadership over the Columbia Indians, despite the fact that his own ancestry was from outside the tribe. His father was an Okanogan Indian from what is now the Tonasket area; his mother, Cnaxo-mx, belonged to the Chelan tribe. Since this is seven generations back from the present, memory does not provide details of his parents' lives. It is certain that Shooktalkoosun went to live with the Columbia Indians at an early age, but again the circumstances are obscure. Such a change of tribal residence was not unusual, but only the most remarkable man would have been able, under these circumstances, to place himself in the chieftainship. The Columbia tribal rules for succession to chieftainship were extremely rigid, providing that a deceased chief should be followed by his eldest brother, or, in the absence of brothers, by his eldest son. Normally there was no deviation from such a line of succession – save in the case of incompetency of the normal successor due to extreme dullness, insanity, or some such affliction. Among the Northwest tribes whose rules of succession were the same, only two exceptions are known. One is that of Shooktalkoosun, the other that of Kamiakin of the Yakama Confederacy. The cases are parallel in that both men achieved their positions as a consequence of their abilities and martial leadership. However, Shooktalkoosun's exploits occurred previous to contact with the whites and were principally concerned with warfare against the Blackfoot and other Plains Indians, while Kamiakin's prominence developed as a consequence of his leadership in the wars with the whites following the Treaty of 1855.

It seems probable that the Columbia tribe either lacked a proper successor to the chieftainship at the time when Shooktalkoosun took over, or that such a successor was a very weak man. We know, at least, that Shooktalkoosun was a very strong man. There are more accounts of his remarkable exploits in war and his bravery in all critical situations than for any other chief within memory. Shooktalkoosun led large parties of Columbia, Wenatchi, Entiat, and Chelan Indians to the country of the Blackfoot each summer where the activities were twofold: hunting buffalo and fighting with the enemy.

Shooktalkoosun probably had a broader perspective of tribal affairs than any ordinary chief because of his ties to more than one tribe. There were also many cultural ties among them. Despite the vigor with which warfare was carried out against the Blackfoot, there is no record or memory of any conflicts between or among the four tribes which formed the confederacy. All four spoke a common language in contrast to some of their neighbors, particularly the Sahaptin to the south as represented by the Kittitas, Yakama and others. On the west, linguistically-similar Sanpoil and Colville tribes were not in the habit of making warring ventures against the Plains Indians. The Okanogan tribe, while always friendly with the four tribes of the confederacy, took pride in acting independently. The Methow, to the north, participated in some activities of the Confederacy, but at other times they were under the influence of their northern neighbors, the Okanogan.

It was inevitable that the unity among the four tribes involved in warfare with the Plains Indians – single ventures which sometimes were prolonged for two or three years – should be carried over into the less dramatic concerns of domestic and economic life in their home territories.

"Dad did my great-grandpa join the Columbia Confederacy?"

"During the time of the Confederacy," Dad answered, "Chilcosahaskt was the Entiat Chief and participated in it.

"Did great-grandpa Chilcosahaskt go on many of the buffalo hunting trips?"

"Chilcosahaskt had been on several hunting trips into Blackfeet Country. Their hunting parties didn't always meet local war parties. But they were prepared in case they did.

"During the two years before each trip they would work on real-life situations. This included how to meet direct attacks by the Xeman. They would set sentries to watch for a sneak attack, practicing both observation and stealth techniques. And, of course, they continually practiced shooting their bows and what guns they had. Hand-to-hand fighting was always an entertainment, maybe using wooden knives or just wrestling, which was a very popular sport.

"They didn't neglect their spiritual preparation either. They used the sweathouses regularly with groups of ten to fourteen men. The winter before the trip they dedicated a dance to the hunting trip with many petitions for their success and safety. And finally, shortly before leaving they would participate in a three-day ceremonial dance.

"Even though it was primarily a hunting trip, there was always the chance of encountering the Xeman. It was their country they were invading. The Xeman, always ready for a fight, welcomed the opportunity to challenge them. They were probably preparing for such an event, too. The only thing that prevented it was that the Xeman also had to hunt. They had limited time to get enough food to last the winter. Their country had long and hard winters so successful hunting was necessary. Sometimes it took all their time and energy.

"Ironically, there were times when the two enemies were hunting almost side-by-side, too busy to stop and fight."

I wanted to keep Dad talking.

"I understand that Broken Sun was not only a good hunter but a fierce fighter in battle, too," I said.

"Broken Sun, or Shooktalkoosun, was a legend. He obtained a guardian Spirit aid that helped him win all battles. He never was defeated in battle. His Spirit was superior to everyone else's. His tribe knew he had supernatural help that always helped in battle. His enemy was not only respectful of his spiritual power but also overawed by it. His reputation grew with each battle. The Blackfoot shamans worked diligently at trying to counteract his Spirit. But his will prevailed. His desire was greater. His focus was complete. He was one with the Universal Mind.

"Broken Sun's hunting and war parties grew larger because of his reputation. Everyone wanted to see him in action, first hand. His young warriors became aggressive, feeding on Broken Sun's power, so they too became confident. They would taunt the Blackfeet warriors, daring them to come forward and fight. At first the Blackfeet were more than willing but, after a series of defeats, they became cautious.

"Broken Sun would put on a certain red blanket when he saw the Blackfeet were ready to attack. This was his sign of invulnerability. The Blackfeet were amazed at how bullets would usually miss him and if they did seem to hit him he wasn't hurt.

"It was in 1840 that Broken Sun was finally shot in the arm and fell off his horse onto the ground. His sons attempted to carry him from the battlefield while others fought off the enemy. But Broken Sun would have none of that. He ordered his sons to leave him and to return to safety. He felt he had lost his honor and would fight no more. His guardian Spirit had failed him. His desire and will were gone.

"And then, as Chilcosahaskt watched from a distance, a bloody scene occurred. A Blackfoot warrior killed the fallen Chief, cut off his head, and dismembered his body. Chilcosahaskt could not forget that scene for the rest of his life. For either tribe, this was not typical treatment of their enemy, especially a respected Chief with such a reputation in battle. They honored brave battle exploits in ceremonial dance and other occasions.

"The Xeman were convinced that Broken Sun had such extraordinary powers that he would come to life again to fight. They felt extra precautions were needed to prevent that from happening.

"Shooktalkoosun's death was the beginning of the end of the Great Plains buffalo hunting trips. Although the Columbia Confederated Tribes took more hunting trips to Blackfeet country, Chilcosahaskt never went again."

Patsksteeweeya, eldest son of Shooktalkoosun, succeeded his father as Chief, and the next year he returned to Blackfoot country, engaging in several battles and fighting valiantly. But it soon became apparent he did not have his father's "medicine." It ended with his death in a battle that was the last fight with the Blackfeet, because there was no more buffalo hunting in the Great Plains.

The next eldest son was Kwiltninuk, who became Chief in 1841. Kwiltninuk spent most of his effort in matters of war with the Suyapenex. He was Chief during some turbulent times and sometimes the people asked his younger brother, Kwitalahan [Moses] to help them with their peacetime negotiations. Kwiltninuk didn't mind because he was more the war chief. Moses, who was fifteen years old when his father was killed, worked closely with Chilcosahaskt, trying to keep peace with the Suyapenex. Kwiltninuk remained Chief until his death in a battle with some miners in the Wenatchee area on July 11, 1858.

Moses became Chief officially after his brother's death. Moses was more of a pacifist and tried to negotiate instead of going to battle. He was thirty-three at the time of his brothers' death and ready to assume command. When he was a boy, his father had sent him to a mission school at Lapwai where he learned English and Nez Perce, a Sahaptin language. He received religious training and became familiar with the ways of the Suyapenex, their modes of thinking and culture. This was very useful later during his negotiations in Washington, D.C., because the officials there didn't know he understood and could speak English. They used a Yakama interpreter, and Moses would speak through the interpreter, even though he knew English.

REFLECTIONS

When the boys grew older they became interested in our family lineage. I helped Rick make a family tree as a seventh grade project. I had to do some research to fill in the blanks. Chilcosahaskt was a mystery to our children, because all they knew was that he was their great-great-grandfather. Dad discovered from the Jesuits that there were actually three Chilcosahaskt's. The first one was probably the son of Wapiti. He lived in the early 1700s. The second died in 1790 in an avalanche near Lake Chelan. His son was only two years old at the time. The third Chilcosahaskt, the one we know most about, was born in 1788, lived through the 1800s and died in 1904. He is buried at Manson. This basic information was used to build the family tree, but it didn't enlighten us on how they lived. So I added to it by putting together the bits and pieces that were handed down from my dad and grandfather, Lahompt.

Wapiti was one of the founders of the Entiat tribe in the late 1600s. He named his first son Chilcosahaskt [Standing Cloud] because of the standing cloud that led him to the Entiat Valley, where the child was born. The Entiat tribe was started from remnants of the Kawachin tribe, which had been decimated by the Xeman [generic word for enemy]. A few Wenatchi and, later, Chelan tribal members joined them. They all spoke the same language, had the same customs and lived in the same area. They mixed frequently while hunting, fishing, and root/berry picking.

The Entiat Valley proved to be very comfortable for the small tribe. In the winter they would live at the mouth of the Entiat River, where it entered the larger Columbia River. The weather was warmer and there was less snow. In the spring they would gradually move up the valley until, during the heat of the summer, they were situated in the cool forest of the Cascade Mountain range

At first they built below-grade pit houses on the east side of the Columbia. They could catch the winter sun longer during the winter months. These well-insulated houses were very warm as they were about three to five feet below the surface. Poles covered with brush and mudpacks on the roof kept out the elements.

These gradually went out of favor as conditions changed. When someone died they would relocate. This took a lot of time and effort. They found more mobility in a similarly built pole house, but above grade. These they used at their fishing sites along the Columbia. They moved the house as they searched for food.

Chapter Five
CHILCOSAHASKT –

Modern Times

Later in life, a major event would significantly change Chilcosahaskt's life and that of his descendants. Dad told the story in his grandfathers' voice, beginning on the morning of December 14, 1872:

"Why don't you put some more wood on the fire?"

I hear my wife, Suzanne, but I'm not sure it is cold enough to deplete my precious woodpile. If I use it all tonight I will have to make a trip up the Entiat River to get some more. I have seen 84 winters and it is getting harder each year. I growl and say, "Put on another blanket. It is not that cold." Before she can answer we hear a loud, low rumble and the log cabin begins to shake.

Our twenty-year-old son, Poker Joe, who is sleeping on the floor, jumps up and says, "What's that?"

We all stagger toward the door, grabbing to hold on to whatever we can. Outside it is clear with the early morning stars brightly shining in the December sky.

Poker Joe is the first to see a large dust cloud upriver north of us. He points and says, "Look!" The ground is still shaking. The big cliff by our home is falling across the river, stopping up the river.

We are all frightened and don't know what to do. Our cabin is close to the Entiat River, just a little up from where it meets the Big River that white men call Columbia. From there it is a gentle rise to maybe 100 or 150 feet above the river. Going towards Ribbon Cliff, the ground is flat for two or three miles. Because of the layout I figure the mountain can't reach us if it all falls. I try to reassure my family, but it doesn't do much good.

I worry about my oldest son, Lahompt, who has moved up near the land of the new Reservation. His mother, Yow-yowt, was my first wife, an Okanogan Indian from that area. Lahompt married Skumk'nalks from the Chelan tribe. They have one child, Chilaeetsa, who is about ten now.

A few of our neighbors come out of their dwellings to see what is happening. Others stay inside, afraid to move. Nobody notices the cold. After the ground quits shaking, everyone stands there for a few minutes, just looking at each other. Not in all our oral history has anyone heard of anything like this. We don't know what to make of it.

I finally break from my trance and tell a couple of the young men to make a fire outside where we sometimes gather to talk. While the fire is being coaxed along on the cold, damp ground I am trying to put my thoughts together. Before long the flames are leaping skyward, and everyone huddles around the blaze.

I have only recently heard that the Suyapenex have given us land up north called a Reservation. We have all been asked to move there and make new homes. Moses had told me it would happen sooner or later. Moses is trying to make the best of it.

I cannot imagine living anywhere but the Entiat Valley. Over the years, I have traveled over a ten-day ride in each direction and never found any place like it. Toward the west there is too much rain and not enough sunshine. Toward the east and south there is too much sunshine and not enough trees. Yes, if I have to choose a second best site, north would be it. It has places very similar to my home site; plenty of trees and just enough sunshine.

But here I can catch salmon on the Big River in the fall, dry it and have enough to last most of the winter. I spend the winter at the mouth of the Entiat River, where it is relatively warm with less snow. Then as spring comes, I gradually move upstream on the Entiat until I am high in the mountains when the long, hot days come during the summer. The trail through the thick forest was built by my ancestors over many generations. There are plenty of trout and deer to feed us. Some of these are dried for the winter months, too. And the huckleberries! There is no better treat than a mouthful of huckleberries. Just last summer is when the Reservation was offered. And now the earth shakes. Is there some relation? Is the Great Spirit telling us to wake up? What is the message?

I tell the others standing around the fire of my thoughts and get an immediate reaction. Some think the message is to refuse to go to the Reservation. Others think just the opposite. I summarized:

"It is an omen, no question about that. Whether it is a good omen or a bad omen, we seem to differ. A good omen would be optimistic about the future and tell us to move ahead with confidence that we will survive. A bad omen would be pessimistic about the future and tell us to be cautious about what we do for we may find a situation where we can't survive.

"So what is it? Good or bad? Let's take stock. We are here and nobody is hurt. We have yet to find out if everyone survived to the north and south. We can see the river's edge receding here. Does this mean we will not have salmon in the future? If not, how will we survive? Maybe we need to change our ways. We must adjust to the new conditions. We cannot live using the old ways anymore. To survive we must learn what is in store for us and adapt. Is this possible? We have only to look at our ancestors who adjusted to many changing conditions. We have the ability; we only have to use it.

"So the omen is both good and bad. Bad in that it warns us of changing conditions. Good in that we know we can adjust to the change. To do this, though, we have to study the changing conditions and learn from them. We cannot let events rule our lives; we must take control and run our own lives. That is all I have to say for now."

In unison, everyone agrees by saying, "Aaah." By this time it is getting to be daylight and we can see the river bottom with just a trickle of water moving through it. It is indeed an omen.

We are at the end of an era. We will not be able to live as we have been for generations and generations. I feel sad. I remember many good times. The hunting trip to the east for buffalo was probably the high point of my life. Nothing was more exciting or more difficult.

Change. Was that what was needed in my life? I have seen so much change that I am distrustful of it. Yet change seems to call out to me, seems to be the cure for the restlessness I sometimes feel. More and more of my tribe are beginning to build houses like the Suyapenex, falling trees, hewing logs, using the plentiful timber of our forests to build permanent homes. But is permanency good for us?

From the beginning of time our ancestors have lived well in the wilderness, hunting and fishing. Now more and more Suyapenex are moving into our traditional hunting grounds. Game is not as plentiful.

Several weeks later I need to calm down, so with the sun high in the sky I sit watching the Entiat River merge into the much larger Columbia. It is so natural and peaceful that I soon slip into a dream state. A fuzzy vision appears showing my tribe merging with the Suyapenex. At first it looks like we would be overcome by the massive numbers. But I can see most of us adapting and moving with the current. To do this we learn how to live amongst them without *being them.*

Since that historical time railroads, highways, dams, and cities have overrun the quiet and peaceful countryside. The towns which grew up along the Columbia River are named Chelan, Entiat, and Wenatchee in commemoration of the tribes that once lived there. The earthquake itself is remembered only by a small monument placed at Ribbon Cliff alongside Alternate Highway 97.

Every time I drive by Ribbon Cliff I can imagine how my great-grandfather felt when the earthquake loosened the massive rocks and caused them to roll into the Columbia River to dam it up.

He, of course, never witnessed the fourteen dams that now control the flow of the river. If he did I am sure he would wonder why. If he were told that it was for flood control he would wonder why the Suyapenex didn't just build their homes above the flood plain. He would also wonder why firelight wasn't sufficient for lighting and heating. He would say nature takes care of itself. Trees die and dry out so we can easily burn the wood. They give up their life so we can live. That is nature's way.

As for dams providing jobs so people can earn their living, he would ask why then do they take such great pleasure getting away from their jobs to hunt and fish. The Indian's job is to hunt and fish.

He wondered about his Suyapenex neighbors. They liked children; he liked children; they liked horses; he liked horses, they liked to socialize; he liked to socialize. So how were they different?

One major difference was that they believed they must own land. This alone causes major problems. He knew Indians didn't need to own land as long as they could can stay where they wanted.

He would wonder why the Suyapenex were so determined to dam up the river that they forgot about the salmon. They didn't seem to realize they were threatening the salmon life cycle until after the fact. Then they spent a lot of time and effort building fish ladders so the salmon could go upstream and regulating the water flow downstream to prevent excess nitrogen which was fatal to the salmon. They seemed to create problems so they could be heroes when they solved them.

The Suyapenex didn't seem to care that the salmon was a primary source of the Indian diet that couldn't easily be replaced. Many generations would suffer. But the Suyapenex sports fisherman liked salmon too so they became the catalyst to replace the salmon runs.

If Chilcosahaskt meditated and tuned into the future he would see that eventually there would be too many people to be able to live by hunting and fishing so they created jobs for them to earn a living. The dams flooded all the good farmland along the river so farming was not an option. They created many industries that he didn't understand. Wires hung from the dams across what was once beautiful, empty land. The Suyapenex houses and towns would have heat and lights from the electricity produced by the dams. It would be a weird world.

His conclusion was that the omen not only threatens our lifestyle but suggests that we will be overrun by the Suyapenex. There are just too many of them. To survive we will have to adjust to their ways. But we will still be Indian; that will never change.

My great grandfather chose to remain at Entiat. My grandfather, Lahompt, was his oldest son who eventually moved Kartar Valley on the Colville Indian Reservation to start a cattle ranch.

While Lahompt was struggling to keep his cattle ranch going, his father passed away at Entiat. He hadn't seen him for some time. The hundred mile trip just wasn't possible during these trying times. Chilcosahaskt was buried at Manson, where the grave would be protected by the Chelan Indians. Lahompt heard about it too late to attend the funeral but did visit the grave later.

Lahompt wasn't aware of the problems his father had. He still operated essentially as his ancestors had by ranging his cattle all over the unfenced Colville Indian Reservation. One of the reasons he eventually decided to leave the Entiat Valley was the encroachment of the Suyapenex. He knew his tribe couldn't co-exist for very long because their interests were different and conflicts would soon arise.

And he was proven right, because things didn't develop around Chilcosahaskt but right through him. This was because his long-term home was at the intersection of the Columbia and Entiat Rivers, a good and logical location. South of the Entiat River stood a large rocky, steep hill unsuitable for a home, so he chose the north side next to the Columbia. It was part of a flat area that continued north for a couple of miles sloping upward to the beginning of Ribbon Cliff, the site of the 1872 earthquake. It was a natural spot for travelers to stop before continuing their journey to Wenatchee, fifteen miles south along the steep, winding, and dangerous horse trail. Later, when steamboats came, the best landing location was next to Chilcosahaskt's home. His corrals extended across what was eventually to be Entiat's original townsite. His old log house was on the right side of the boat landing. In 1896 steamboats were the only transportation between Wenatchee and Entiat except for the pony-trail on the west side of the Columbia River.

Emma Mead's vivid description of Chilcosahaskt in her 1908 story [an unpublished letter] was very enlightening:

"The sun was setting on this beautiful May evening of 1889 and my husband, the doctor, went out to see about the horses, which were tethered for the night and feeding on the bunch grass. We were on the east side of the Columbia River about two miles up from Orondo.

I strolled down the river bank to get a close view of the great surging stream, half a mile wide at this point and rushing by in a fierce and roaring current. The big watch dog was with me, and feeling secure with him about, I became quite absorbed in the world grandeur of my surroundings, when suddenly my eye fell upon a red Indian, robed in a bright red blanket, standing bolt upright in a log canoe, and paddling or polling himself along the near shore. Whether he saw me or not I do not know, and whether his intentions were friendly or unfriendly I did not stop to find out. The whole scene in that golden light was startling in its weird picturesqueness, as if a specter came before me in a vision of unearthly scene and then became reality.

An idiotic alarm took possession of me, and I retreated with hurried steps in the direction of our camp, too much concerned for my own safety to make further observation, though I did manage to see across the Columbia, in the region where we were to land the next day, the huts of an Indian settlement. I thought this then was my fate: to live alone among blanket savages; to be hauled out of bed at midnight and scalped with fiendish ceremony or lack of ceremony; most likely to "suffer a fate worse than death", as in the books of my childhood.

I had some things to learn about the Indians of the Entiat Valley, and my story will not be a tale of Indian outrages on inoffensive white settlers, though later I may have a word to say about white outrages on inoffensive Indians. I reached camp unharmed, my ferocious watch dog following tamely, and the Indian left behind.

The next day, after the steamboat left us on the west shore of the Columbia, we were met by an Indian reception committee. Sitting in the sand were eight or more Indian men and women. The oldest rose from the sand and approached with an extended hand and said, "Hullow" which was about the extent of his English. He shook hands with each of us smiling as he did so, an evidence of welcome that we understood and appreciated. I then recognized him as the lone boatman at whom I had taken fright the day before.

We became good friends in our eleven years at Entiat Valley."

Chilcosahaskt loved talking to new people so he would always meet the steamboats despite their irregular schedule. The only road to that landing wound between his house and his big cattle pens. The Indian presence was noticeable by the sweat houses dotting the banks along both rivers. Indians often visited at his place as did white traders and horse racers. They would swap things or tell stories, and Chilcosahaskt was always in the middle of the action.

Impromptu rodeos were held by Indians sitting on the rail fence which formed his corral. They would bet and then leap from the fence onto the back of a horse running by. They usually landed safely on the horse barebacked with no ropes or bridle. It was exciting with everybody yelling and whooping.

But this serene existence was not to last. Chilcosahaskt suffered from the intrusion of the white man. He had cattle and horses that ranged all over the Entiat Valley before they came. His reputation for raising fine horses was far and wide as told by A.J. Splawn, who met him in December 1865 near the Rock Island rapids. He traded twenty horses with him and stayed at his lodge. In 1858 Chilcosahaskt gave Qualchen, a Kittitas Indian warrior, a fine bay horse that was proudly displayed at Qualchen's memorial with all the trappings it carried on the day Qualchen voluntarily rode into General Wright's camp, where he was immediately hung.

Chilcosahaskt's livelihood and whole purpose in life was threatened. The quiet, peaceful ranch life with his tribe would be no more unless he resisted change. He watched as the first settlers announced their claims by laying down timber in a square where they planned on building their house. That move was obvious to

Chilcosahaskt but he didn't agree that they could move in at will. Tribal custom was to consider the impact on others before making such a move. Civility was the rule. The concept of anyone owning land was new to Chilcosahaskt and his tribe. Land was for the use of everyone. The Indian Way was to share, but not to the extent of being forced out. He knew that the incoming permanent ranchers would eventually usurp all the grazing areas of his and his tribes' stock.

J.D. Bonar was one of the early settlers [No. 3 by some counts] who caused Chilcosahaskt trouble. Chilcosahaskt would remove the house squares, tear down fences and steal fish out of their traps.

It was all to no avail so Chilcosahaskt eventually built a fence of his own around his highly prized little peach orchard [neighbors said he grew the finest tree-ripened peaches you ever tasted]. This forced the white men to go far out of their way to get around the fence. Even so the white settlers regarded Chilcosahaskt as a good Indian, but in those days the whites hardly looked upon Indians as being human, only a phenomenon of the country.

Then on February 10, 1903, [tribal enrollment records show 1904] the likable Indian Chief of the Entiat tribe passed away quietly. He was well-known in the Entiat community because he had lived there all his life, spanning three centuries from 1788 to 1903. But people there only knew him in his later declining years from 1872, when he was 84, to 1903 when he was 115. In his old age the locals said he was "wrinkled like a dried prune" and totally toothless. But he loved to tell jokes and thrived on company both Indian and white.

Upon Chilcosahaskt's death, Bonar immediately induced E.F. Morris to petition the Chelan County Court for letters of administration of the estate of Chilcosahaskt, which were issued on April 7, 1903. Morris, as administrator, then petitioned the court to sell the property. It was purchased by Bonar on July 20, 1903.

Court records the estate as duly probated [See Appendix Chapter Five *Chilcosahaskt – Modern Times 1*] in the Superior Court of Chelan County on May 4, 1903. And the land belonging to Chilcosahaskt and his heirs had subsequently been sold to Bonar. It was presumably sold for $2,600 but no heirs received anything.

Bonar needed the sworn word of Indians that they had sold the land, "fair and square." So Bonar went to the Colville Indian Reservation to hunt up Chilcosahaskt's heirs and other witnesses. At first they shook their heads. Then a vagrant Indian who Bonar had once fed was discovered and vouched for him. He and his wife urged others to sign for sake of "Skookum Bonar who gave heap big handout to hungry Indians." He even claimed to be Chilcosahaskt's kin.

Several years later it was discovered that the property had a cloudy title. This was mostly the concern of J.D. Bonar who was with the Entiat Delta Orchards Company which was located on the property. He filed suit on December 15, 1913, to quiet title to the land in question. Chilcosahaskt's trust patent covered the whole townsite as well as the Great Northern Railway running through it.

The patent that Chilcosahaskt received on October 22, 1896, for the land in question from the United States was still in effect. It contained a clause which provided that the U.S. would hold said trust lands in trust for the sole use and benefit of Chilcosahaskt and his heirs for twenty-five years, which would end on October 22, 1921.

These patents were issued to Wenatchee, Chelan and Entiat tribal members who choose to stay at their ancestral homes instead of moving to the Colville Indian Reservation. There are still Indian trust land around Cashmere and Manson.

Just before Chilcosahaskt died, J. D. Bonar tried to solve the trust patent issue by influencing him to apply for the cancellation of the twenty-five year patent and to issue "in lieu of" a patent in fee simple on September 6, 1902. This was against the desires and wishes of Chilcosahaskt, who at the time was 114 years old and, most likely, not capable of understanding the complicated legal issues of the white man.

Land in question: Lots three and four of Section Sixteen and lots 1 & 2 of the NE quarter of Section 17 of T25R21EWM totaling 146.25 acres.

In 1955 after Eva Anderson wrote six Wenatchee World articles about Silico Saska [Chilcosahaskt], Sam Sumner, an attorney from Wenatchee, reminisced about a case he had in 1914. He said: "A young Indian woman, Lucy Freer Snider, who was a descendant of Chilcosahaskt, and her Aunt Minnie Freer came to see me at my office in Wenatchee. She had contacted a young attorney from Brewster, Jack O'Conner, and he suggested they meet with him. Lucy said a summons and complaint addressed to the 'unknown heirs of Silico Saska' had been served on her Aunt Minnie Freer Smith and her to quiet the title to the Town of Entiat."

Sam was young, short of money and always challenged by a good fight. He agreed to join Jack in the battle on behalf of the Saska heirs. They immediately identified the legal question of the 1896 trust patent the U.S. government had issued to Saska containing a clause providing that at the end of twenty-five years a "fee patent" would be issued to his heirs. They rightfully concluded this was for the protection of Indians so they could hold the property until they learned the ins and outs of the white man's system for owning property.

"In view of this clause," Sam said, "Jack and I wondered how that land could legally be sold in 1901." They thought the trust patent should have been effective until October 22, 1921.

The argument of the opposition was that Saska had become a citizen and thus separated himself from the Indian tribe and for that reason the trust patent feature was negated. They claimed that Silico was an Indian born within the territorial limits of the U.S. and that in 1879 and again in 1889 he renounced, in writing, his tribal relations; that he took up his residence separate and apart from any tribe of Indians, and adopted the habits of the whites; that he became a citizen of the U.S.; that by virtue of his residence on and cultivation of the land in question, and of his citizenship he became entitled to a patent under Section 2289 of the Revised Statutes of the U.S. without any restrictions upon his right of alienation; that erroneously a patent was issued to him containing the twenty-five year trust or non-alienation clause in the Cross Complaint referred to; that said patent was thereafter duly cancelled, and a patent issued to said Silico Saska in fee simple, and containing no restrictions on alienation; that plaintiff and its predecessors in interest have been in the open, actual and notorious possession said land for more than ten years prior to the commencement of this action; and that plaintiff's claim of title is deducible of record from the United States of America.

The Superior Court disagreed and ruled in favor of the plaintiff. Several years later the State Supreme Court overturned that decision. [See Appendix Chapter Five *Chilcosahaskt – Modern Times 2*]

REFLECTIONS

Sam Sumner, who was so successful in Superior Court, did not get to present his case to the State Supreme Court. He was in Washington D.C. working with Senator Curtis to get an amendment to an act that would quiet all Indian titles. While he was away, Supreme Court Judge Chadwick wrote the decision reversing the Superior Court decision.

This questionable action was in addition to the totally inadequate effort by Bonar and the probate to identify Silico's heirs. Heirs alive but not listed on May 4, 1903, when the probate was issued were:

Achmeen [Margaret]	1840-1922
Mary	died 5/8/1917
Squen-hn-malx [Suzanne]	1840-6/23/1925
Cecile Antoine	30 or 40 years old in 1903
Heirs of Qui-hn-meetsa [Mary]	died 1890

Before Qui-hn-meetsa [Mary] died she married Franklin Freer of the Miller-Freer trading post in Wenatchee. They had daughters Mattie, who died in 1941, and Minnie Freer Smith, who lived from April 29, 1887, to July 20, 1917. Mary also had a son by Franklin's brother, David, named Johnny who lived from April 2, 1879, to June 28, 1956. Daughters Lucy Freer Snider lived from Nov. 15, 1885, to Sept. 26, 1936, and Hattie Freer lived from 1889 to Jan. 26, 1918. Minnie Freer married John Smith and had the following offspring:

Son Ben Smith, 1898 – 1978

Daughter Leona Smith, 1900-1957

Son Sam Smith, 11/25/1902 – 1/22/1978
Son Johnny Smith, 7/9/1905 -5/31/1972
Daughter Eva Mattie Smith, 1908 – 195_

The spelling of Alma for Almira and Nesplin for Nespelem indicates an oral research as the correct spelling was commonly in written form and filed.

George Saska from Alma must be Koxit George [Lahompt], who lived in Kartar Valley on the Colville Indian Reservation about twenty miles southeast of Okanogan. He did not live in Alma [or Almira]. He shipped cattle to the railway there occasionally. Koxit was well known in Okanogan as he traded there and even had a bank account. However, he and most of the heirs did not speak English and therefore did not read newspapers or posted bulletins so were totally unaware of the legal proceedings. The spelling was so bad that even those that read about George Saska would have a hard time associating the notice with Koxit George.

If this situation were to arise today it would be met with a barrage of legal actions. Native American Rights Fund [NARF], American Civil Liberties Union [ACLU], and a bevy of well-versed Indian attorneys would attack the problem with a vengeance. Their arguments would center on:

1. The 25-year Indian Trust Patent.
2. The comparative competency of the participants: Chilcosahaskt never had any legal advice nor could he read.
3. The fairness of the court notices at a time of minimum communications and travel accommodations.
4. The accuracy and completeness of the probate. It should have been done by the U.S. government who had jurisdiction and better records.
5. Counter-argument to opposition:

At the times Chilcosahaskt was claimed to have renounced his tribal relations in writing [he couldn't write so someone did it for him] he was 91 years old in 1879 and 101 in 1889. His relationship with the tribes was good so it had to be an external reason to make him do this. It was common practice in those days for outsiders to pressure Indians to do things so they could take their property.

He was always with his Entiat tribe as Entiat was their ancestral home. He was the recognized Chief of the tribe.

He could not have become a citizen of the U.S. because Indians were not given citizenship until 1924. On June 2, 1924, the Indian Citizenship Act of 1924 was signed by President Calvin Coolidge. Many people thought the Fourteenth Amendment to the U.S. Constitution guaranteed citizenship to all persons born in the U.S., but that was "subject to the jurisdiction thereof," which excluded the indigenous Native American. Even after passing the act many states didn't allow Indians to vote until 1948, when New Mexico and Arizona finally relented.

He was born in 1788 and the U.S. did not ratify its constitution until 1789 so he could not have been born within the territorial limits of the U.S. In addition Washington did not become a state until 1889.

The last chapter of this contested property began when Rocky Reach Dam started construction in 1956 and ended when the whole area was flooded by the dam backwaters in 1960. The new townsite is located above the flood plain on the land previously ceded by the Colville Confederated Tribes.

Although too late for Chilcosahaskt's heirs the Cobell case against the United States resulted in a $3.4 billion settlement approved in 2010 by Congress. This was for mismanagement of individual tribal member land sales, timber sales, oil leases and grazing permits by the federal government.

Entiat Chief Chilcosahskt,
My Great Grandfather

For many years I traveled the Big River alone in my dugout canoe. I knew where all the rapids and whirlpools were. Every year we would catch and dry Salmon to feed us through the winter. Then I saw my first Suyapenex. He was a sign of what would come. First, the fur traders, then the miners, the soldiers and farmers. One day the earth shook, the big cliff by my home fell across the River, and it ceased to flow. This was another sign. Soon we Indians were told to move north. We could no longer follow the game along the river's shores. My son went but I could not. After me the people saw the River become a Lake. It too was told to remain in one spot, just like the Indian.

—Wendell George

At Entiat Rapids

Unknown photographer, ca. 1950   *The Spokesman-Review*

483 miles from ocean[1]

Lincoln Rock, shown at the beginning of this chapter, is halfway between Wenatchee & Entiat. It was discovered in 1889, the same year Washington became a state. Lincoln was born February 12, 1809 and my dad the same day in 1906.

1 Page 66 used by permission of the University of Washington Press. William D. Layman's 2006 book "*River of Memory, The Everlasting Columbia*".

Entiat Valley

Kwitalahn [Moses] looked at Chilcosahaskt and sighed, "We need someone to go to the Council at Walla Walla called by the Chief Suyapenex."

Before responding the old Chief threw another log on the fire. The pitch caught and the flames jumped higher with a loud crackle. The tepee grew warmer and took the chill off of the cool spring temperature.

"Any ideas?"

"Te-cole-kun will be one. I went to his camp at Wenatchee and talked to him. He agreed but I cautioned him to just go and listen. No decisions. Kamiakan sent a message to me that only tribes from the south were invited. We will essentially be intruders so we probably will not be asked for any input."

"That is our way anyway. Even as Chief I must consult my people before we make any decisions. If I did it any other way I would not be Chief very long. A Chief can only do what his people ask him to do. Very seldom do they approve anything before they talk it out at length".

"That is why I came to you. You are my elder and have the wisdom of the years. I'm only twenty-nine and still learning. Actually my older brother, Kwiltninuk, is Chief of the Sinkiuse tribe and the Confederation. People only consult me because I am not as quick to battle as he is. But he knows this so he brings me to every Council and asks my advice.

"But from my experience, the Suyapenex do things different from us. The head person at the meeting has the authority to make a lot of decisions. It works for them because they seem to all think alike. They usually approve it. The negotiator loses face if they don't approve his actions."

"I suppose that'll work if the negotiator man knows his limits and the desires of the people involved."

"They have so many people involved that I don't know how that would be possible."

"Such an involved process also gives them a built-in excuse to say no if it suits them."

"That's what we call being two-faced or speaking with two hearts."

"So who else should go?"

"We know that Kwiltninuk is too volatile and I will not go because I am not Chief. I know they think Kamiakan can speak for all Yakama tribes but we are a separate tribe. What we need is someone to be the eyes and ears for our tribe"

"Wapato John and I are too old and decrepit to go. I'll be sixty-seven soon."

"What about Lahompt? He is young and energetic. He and Te-cole-kun are good friends and would work well together."

"He is pretty young, only fifteen."

"I was fifteen when my dad was killed. I did a lot of growing up fast. He'll do all right. Our young men become warriors when they are teenagers. He has had some experience and a level head.

"I'm glad you think so. He's smart but I don't want to push my own son on you."

"You're too modest. I know you have been training him since he was born. He could ride a horse almost before he could walk."

"You're right. I am very proud of my son. He will be a good leader some day."

When his dad told him about the trip Lahompt became very excited. His anticipation was so great that he missed the last few words of his Dad's instructions. Something about bringing a horse that was a good swimmer. He didn't have to worry; his favorite horse was also the best swimmer. He wasn't real big, about fourteen-and-a-half hands, but had a good gait, was extremely alert, and tuned into everything. They were a team.

But his dad was talking again,

"Son, your mother and I worry about you. Not because you're not capable, because you are. But on every trip there are things that happen that can upset you. Unexpected things. People don't do what they are expected to do. Weather changes. Horses acting up. It could be anything."

"Dad, I have been to Lake Wenatchee on our annual huckleberry camping trip and all the way to Kettle Falls during the salmon season. I can handle this trip easily."

"Son, you are only fifteen years old. You think because your grandpa and great-grandpa were that age when they went to battle that it is easy. It is not. There are many things you haven't seen yet. I would go on this trip but I do not look forward to two weeks on a horse no matter how thick and comfortable the blanket I'm sitting on. I am sixty-seven years old now and have been thrown from a horse more times than I want to remember. You on the other hand have all this to look forward to."

"You're right, Dad. This is the most exciting trip I can imagine making. All the tribes from a hundred miles around will be there. I will see people I have only heard stories about. I will be able to tell many stories to my grandchildren that I don't have yet."

"Lahompt, let me tell you again how you are to represent our Entiat tribe. As you know, I have been close to Moses for many years. I had many good times with his father and older brothers going to the Blackfeet and Salish country to hunt buffalo. We have a mutual trust that only time and many experiences together can develop.

Moses is concerned about the purpose of this meeting you are going to. He doesn't trust the head man, Governor Stevens. He tells me he is an ambitious man that has little time for details or for doing what is right. What's worse is, he doesn't understand Indians at all and doesn't want to.

Moses says the Suyapenex have many soldiers, good horses, and rifles. We have no way to stand up against them. They can demand anything and get it, by force if necessary.

Moses says they also have to get approval from their headman back east. This means they can agree to something and then change their minds later.

Moses says Stevens has only invited the tribes from the south; the many bands of the Yakamas. But he is sure that Stevens intends for those tribes to speak for ours.

So Moses wants representatives from our tribes in the north to go to the meeting. He wants them to be there as observers only. He wants them to learn everything so they can and come back and report. Then we can discuss it and decide what to do together. This is the same approach that the Suyapenex use which works for them and it should work for us. Do you understand?"

"Dad, what's to understand? I go down to the meeting, enjoy the ceremonial dancing which they are sure to have, maybe meet some girls and then just listen to what is said. I am to do nothing but come back and report what was said. Right?"

"The thought strikes me that you should try to explain to them what you are doing. Explain to them that you do not have the authority to make decisions but that you are only a messenger. Explain that even as Chief I cannot make such decisions. I can only enforce decisions that have already been made by the people. On new issues everyone gets a chance to speak, and it may be weeks before a consensus is developed. Do you think you can do that?"

"I can try but didn't you tell me that the Suyapenex cannot speak our language? I remember you saying that they use interpreters. If our tribes were not invited then there may not be anyone who can speak our language. The Yakama tribes all speak the Sahaptin language, which is much different than our Salish. Some of us can speak it but not everyone. The Chinook language that everyone tries to use is not that useful to discuss such an involved subject. I don't think it will work."

"Do what you can. We don't have a choice at this time. The meeting is in two weeks and no time to get a message to anyone who can fix the problem. It will take you almost two weeks to get there."

Lahompt took that to be the end of the conversation. He had to get ready. He was to start out the day after tomorrow. After he packed he had to get in the right frame of mind. He went around the village asking his sweathouse buddies to join him in a sweat. A couple of cousins were due in from Lake Chelan in the afternoon and he wanted to be ready to start then.

Their sweathouse was on the Entiat River beside a quiet pool and set near some brush that shielded them from outside observance. This was a private affair. Only the participants were to know what went on. There was a tacit understanding that they wouldn't discuss anything outside the sweathouse unless it was with other participants. It was a cleansing process and you had to be in the right frame of mind to accept what was said in the sweathouse. To get in this frame of mind you would go from the very hot temperatures in the sweathouse to the very cold after diving into the river. It was an initiation no matter how many times you went through it.

Some tribes do it a little different than those in the Northwest, but most use the sweathouse in some way. It is important to have the right kind of rocks for heating. Some will explode when heated. Luckily in the Northwest we have a lot of cooled lava rock. They are the best. A fire is started in a pit outside the sweathouse just big enough to hold the number of rocks you intend to use. They have to be small enough to handle when they are hot but big enough to hold the heat as long as possible.

Before starting the fire a petition is made to the creator-God [How-we-en-chuten] to allow the sweathouse to be used in the manner it was intended. Usually this is done in the four directions East, South, West, and North. A statement is made for each direction recognizing what it brings to our life. East is the source of our energy, South brings comfort, West ideas, and North the power and strength to do things.

The fire is started and rocks heated with as many as 10 or 20 for a two-round sweat. The participants gather around the fire outside the sweathouse. They talk and tell jokes on each other and get in the mood for the sweat.

When the time comes, the leader -- usually the one who calls for the sweat -- brings them into the sweathouse. Most sweathouses are small, maybe big enough for four to six people. Others may hold twelve to fourteen. They are made of bent willow sticks covered with hides, blankets, heavy canvas or anything to hold in the heat. The small door is closed after every one is in sitting in a circle around the pit, which will hold the hot rocks.

A bucketful of red-hot rocks is then brought in and the rocks dropped in the pit. The first speaker, maybe the leader, maybe not, will sprinkle some rose water on the rocks creating steam. The temperature immediately increases.

During Lahompt's sweat he said,

"Thank you [Lam lampt] Creator-God [How-we-en-chuten] for allowing me to serve you. I have spent many hours preparing for this trip which is so important to my people. I hope I am deserving of this responsibility. I know I am young and inexperienced but my father and the other elders have faith in me and I'll try to live up to their trust.

"Thank all those who are here today and those who couldn't make it but are thinking of us.

"This is all I have to say for now. Lam lampt".

The others said "aaah" in recognition and support of his statement. He then passed the rose-water bucket to the next person who sprinkled the rocks three times and made his statement:

"I also give thanks for this good life. But I want to make a special petition for my friend, Lahompt, who is going on a very important mission for our people. Please guide him and give him strength to do his job. Give him the wisdom to understand the situation and be able to deal with the Suyapenex. We will all be with him in spirit. Lam lampt".

These petitions were presented until everyone had an opportunity to speak. Several brought their drums and sang a song dedicated to their petition. There were other petitions asking for help for loved ones and for the sick. They went through two rounds before everyone was satisfied. After every round they left the sweathouse and jumped into the icy-cold water of the Entiat River yelling as they went.

The next day Lahompt got up at sunrise and made his usual acknowledgment to the sun, thanking the Creator-God for allowing him another day. He then said his good-byes to his mother, Dad and friends. Everyone in the village turned out to see him go. They knew that whatever happened at the meeting it would mean a major change to their lives. Chilcosahaskt III had been telling them to expect this and to prepare themselves. Exactly how they were to do that they didn't know. Maybe Lahompt would find out at the meeting and come back and tell them.

Lahompt figured he would be gone about a month so he brought a second horse to carry supplies and to use as a backup in case his riding horse became lame. He was first going to Wenatchee, about fifteen miles south, to join up with the group from there. They left the next day.

As he rode through the rocky cliffs along the big Columbia River he thought about his dad, grandfather, and great-grandfather all making a similar trip to join up with local tribes to go all the way into the Blackfeet and Flathead country to hunt buffalo.

Sometimes these trips took two years, depending how successful they were and how well they were able to travel after they battled with those tribes. They weren't too receptive to us hunting in their territory. And, when our party captured any of their women that was a cause for a determined chase. They didn't give up easily.

Chilcosahaskt III had told him about Moses' Dad and two brothers getting killed in these battles. The game was serious and they played for keeps.

The story of how Moses became Chief was especially interesting to him. He was the first son and natural heir to become Chief after Chilcosahaskt III so the progression didn't apply to him but it gave him a good insight on what it took to be a good Chief and leader of your people. It was a big responsibility and he wanted to do well when the time came. With the changing conditions he knew he would have to adjust his approach so he analyzed all the situations he encountered.

Upon arriving at the Wenatchee encampment at the meeting of the two rivers, Lahompt was greeted by Te-cole-kun, Chief of the Wenatchee tribe. Te-cole-kun wasn't much older than Lahompt so they were good friends. They had a lot in common. They spent a lot of time together on hunting trips and other tribal gatherings. They would enjoy the trip together.

The trip to the Walla Walla country took about ten days. They were in no hurry and they didn't want to get their horses footsore. The trail wasn't that friendly. They followed the Columbia River as much as possible but they had to take detours when the cliffs became too steep. They also crossed it a few times. They arrived towards the end of May. Some of the tribes were there but most hadn't arrived yet.

Walla Walla is beautiful in the spring with green grass and rolling hills all around and plenty of trees and water for their campsite. The Blue Mountains are about ten miles south. They form the southeast boundary of the Great Plains along the Columbia River.

Since their party was small, only about ten in number, they didn't have a problem finding a campsite.

The next day the Nez Perce arrived in big numbers, about 2,500 total. They made a show of it. They approached Governor Stevens and General Palmer on horseback in a single, winding line. The men were mostly naked, painted and decorated with furs and plumes. Their horses were painted in bright crimson and white. Some of the horses didn't need to be painted as they were already blanketed with white, contrasting their darker color [Appaloosa]. The bridles were fringed with bead of bright colors and plumes of eagle feathers interwoven in the mane and tail. They presented quite a show. Lahompt and Te-cole-kun were impressed. The entourage stopped about a mile from the governor and his party, who were standing at a flagstaff out on the plain. About a half a dozen chiefs rode forward and were rattling their shields, singing and beating their drums as they rode past.

The rest formed a circle and rode around the governor's party. They would gallop up as if to make a charge and then wheel around and around yelling war whoops in intense excitement. About a dozen or two dismounted and danced in a circle for twenty minutes while the rest kept time with their drums.

After the performance, maybe twenty chiefs, including Lahompt and Te-cole-kun, went into the governor's tent, where they sat for a while, smoking the peace pipe and then all returned to their camp.

The Nez Perce had the largest numbers present, with the Walla Walla and Cayuse next. Of course, this was their home ground but they, like all the other tribes, had their numbers greatly diminished, mostly from influenza and smallpox diseases they got from the Suyapenex.

They were in early contact with the traders of Hudson Bay Fur Company who had a trading post at the old Fort Walla Walla on the left bank of the Columbia River near where the Walla Walla River empties into it.

Lahompt visited the Nez Perce on Sunday. It was raining hard enough to want to stay under cover. They were holding services in one of their larger lodges with two chiefs leading. One of them was quoting the Ten Commandments and at the end of each sentence the other chief would repeat it in a louder voice. They then all would sing. They had prayers in their lodges every morning and evening and several sessions on Sunday with no trading allowed on that day.

This was all due to the influence of the early Roman Catholic missionaries who melded the church beliefs with the Indian beliefs.

By Monday, most of the tribes invited had arrived. Their encampment and lodges were scattered over about a mile along the valley. The Council was to begin on Tuesday, May 29, 1855. Although scheduled to start at noon it finally came together about two p.m.. Only about eight tribes were represented at the meeting. But interpreters hadn't been assigned and there was no set agenda for the meeting.

Governor Stevens did make an address to the group but it started raining again and the meeting was adjourned to ten a.m. the next day, weather permitting. It didn't matter anyway because most of the Indians at the meeting couldn't understand what was said.

There were about five thousand Indians, including women and children, on the grounds by that time. Lahompt and Te-cole-kun had never seen so many Indians in one place. They visited as many camps as they could, talking to old friends and making new ones.

The Cayuse had some dancing in the evening, which they were able to join. During the day there were many horse races with betting on who would win. Lahompt wished he had brought his racehorse that was undefeated. He was long-legged but sure-footed and stood seventeen hands high. As it was, he had to bet on horses he didn't know and, of course, he lost.

The next meeting was on Wednesday at one p.m.

A small arbor had been erected directly in front of Governor Stevens' tent and several in his party were ready to take notes of everything said, although in English. In front of the arbor sat Governor Stevens and

General Palmer on a bench. Before them, in the open air and in concentric semi-circles sat the Indians, chiefs in the front rows and women and children in the back. Lahompt and Te-cole-kun were in the middle of the chiefs, but as guests because their tribes hadn't been invited.

There were about a thousand in attendance. After the traditional smoking ceremony, the Council was opened by a short address by General Palmer. Governor Stevens then rose and made a long speech outlining the objective of the Council and what was desired of them. As he finished each sentence, the interpreter, who was a Delaware Indian from back east, repeated it to two of the Indians who announced it in a loud voice to the rest – one in the Nez Perce language and the other in Walla Walla. Of course, Lahompt and Te-cole-kun were not fluent in either language or in the English spoken by the Suyapenex. The Delaware Indian was experienced in treaties because his tribe made the first treaty in 1787 with the Colonial government.

Through their friend Moses they had learned some Nez Perce and English words and phrases, because Moses had spent three years at a mission school in Lapwai, the home of the Nez Perce. This process caused the business to move slowly. Lahompt and Te-cole-kun didn't understand much of what was going on. Some neighboring Indians tried to help but it was sketchy.

On Thursday, the discussion was resumed. Governor Stevens and General Palmer made long speeches to them explaining the benefits they would receive from signing the treaty, and the advantages that would result if they moved to the new lands offered in exchange for their present hunting grounds. Lahompt could tell from the reactions of the Indians that it wasn't received very well.

On Friday, June 1, there was no meeting as the Indians were discussing the proposals among themselves. All of the Indians Lahompt and Te-cole-kun talked to said they did not favor signing.

On Saturday at noon the chiefs began their reply to the proposal. They did not commit one way or another but were unfavorable to signing the treaty. Sunday was a day of rest.

On Monday they met again at one-thirty p.m.. Chief Lawyer of the Nez Perce spoke for the first time. Several other Chiefs spoke and finally they adjourned at 5 PM without any significant progress. The Indians sang and danced every evening until late at night during all these proceedings.

The negotiations continued like this for several days from Tuesday through Sunday. Many memorial speeches were made by Indian chiefs. Chief Lawyer described how this country was discovered by the Spaniards who left the Indians the legacy of the horse. The horse greatly improved the mobility of his tribe and improved their economy. If Governor Stevens did half as good, the change would be welcome. He expressed his approval of the treaty but urged the Suyapenex to act in good faith, as he seemed to have some premonition.

Young Chief of the Cayuse was opposed to signing the treaty because they had no right to sell the ground, which Creator-God had given them for their support. He asked if the ground, water, and grass could answer him and tell him if the reason to sell was the right one. He also said the money was not in his hand. What was he to receive? The promises were vague and didn't mean anything. Five Crows of the Walla Walla tribe agreed with him. Pe-pe-mox-mox also agreed and said tomorrow evening he was going home regardless.

General Palmer asked Kamiakan to say something: "You are the Yakama Chief so you must speak for your people," but Kamiakan responded with "I have nothing to say. I am Palouse and cannot speak for the other tribes."

Owhi, Chief of the Kittitas, said his people were far away and did not know anything about this proposal. He could not do anything unless they agreed.

Governor Stevens again asked Kamiakin to speak and he again refused.

General Palmer said the chiefs who did not understand the proposal wanted to bring the gristmill, blacksmith shops, wagons, and tents to show their people. He said he couldn't build schoolhouses or other dwellings in a day. He said to bring all the money that those things would cost was impossible. It would take more than all their horses could carry. But he said whatever we promise you will get.

Lahompt and Te-cole-kun were able to learn later that Governor Stevens carried it even further by admonishing the chiefs to speak for their people so he wouldn't be ashamed of them. They agreed that the governor didn't understand Indian people. In their culture, it didn't work that way. They also tried to communicate to the others that even the Suyapenex didn't work that way. They had to get approval from a bunch of people in Washington D.C. before the treaty would be final. Those people were elected similar to Indian chiefs but they had power to approve treaties. The people they were negotiating with did not have the authority so the actual agreement could be changed drastically without consulting the tribes. They knew this to be true because Moses had told them.

On Friday, June 8, General Palmer made a concession. He told them if they did not wish to go to the Nez Perce reservation he would offer them another reservation, which would include some of the lands on which they now lived. After this offer had been clearly explained to them and considered, all agreed except the Yakamas.

Te-cole-kun and Lahompt decided, after some consideration, that the treaty was going to be signed regardless of what they did. They would not have time to bring the proposal back to their people for consideration. Their choice was to ask for forgiveness or permission with no opportunity to get permission. So they decided to take advantage of this offer. They cornered the Delaware interpreter and through sign language and mixed dialects were able to convey to him their desire. He helped them draft what was later to become Article 10 of the Treaty, the Wenatchapam reservation quoted exactly as follows:

ARTICLE 10. And provided, That there is also reserved and set apart from the lands ceded by this treaty, for the use and benefit of the aforesaid confederated tribes and bands, a tract of land not exceeding in quantity one township of six miles square, situated at the forks of the Pisquouse or Wenatchapam River, and known as the "Wenatchapam Fishery," which said reservation shall be surveyed and marked out whenever the President may direct, and be subject to the same provisions and restrictions as other Indian reservations.

General Palmer was quick to include it so he could convince the other tribes to also agree. This turned out to be the final agreement although Looking Glass of the Nez Perce then arrived and caused turmoil throughout the weekend.

On Monday, June 11, 1855, at ten a.m., Governor Stevens opened the meeting with a short speech and asked the chiefs to come forward and sign the papers. Lahompt stood near the table and became the fifth mark indicating his signature on the Treaty right after his friend Te-cole-kun, who was the fourth.

On the way home they discussed their reception by their tribal members when they learned of what they had done. They knew they violated a time tested process by signing without consulting the members but their tribe had never been faced with such a crisis before. They hoped their friends and relatives would understand.

This bothered Lahompt considerably. He was missing something. He didn't know what it was but he longed for it. He had a dream where he was searching for balance in his life, so he got up early one morning and walked directly **East.** He soon saw a shadow coming towards him. He couldn't tell what it was. Then, as it came out of the bright sunlight, he could see it had a limp. When it got closer he could see it was a coyote with a bad leg. When the coyote saw Lahompt he quickly ducked into the brush and disappeared, demonstrating his strong will to live.

The next time he saw coyote he was walking **South.** His leg was healed and his eyes shone brightly. They showed compassion, not only for Lahompt, but also for the whole world.

Later, as he was heading **West,** Lahompt began to understand what was happening. Coyote was showing him The Way.

Finally, he turned **North** and moved with confidence towards his ultimate goal.

The message then came to Lahompt that he, as a Native American, has maintained his oneness with nature, just like Coyote. This oneness holds the key to understanding.

Te-cole-cun and Quitenenock died in the Clockum battle with miners in 1858. Lahompt started working with cattle and eventually moved to the Colville Indian Reservation in Kartar Valley.

The change to a reservation environment was not easy for any of the tribal members. Lahompt, like the other Entiat boys, led a carefree life style in the Entiat Valley. He hunted and fished up both the Entiat and Wenatchee rivers. He and the other boys would swim in Lake Wenatchee while their families were camped in the area during huckleberry harvest. He spent many hours lying on his back in the shade listening to the cool mountain breezes rustling through the branches of the tall fir and pine trees and dream of climbing the snow-capped peaks on the steep ridges of the Cascade Range.

Lahompt rode horses before he learned to walk. Riding a horse was much preferred over walking. He became an excellent horseman. None of the Indians of that time wanted to move to the Reservation which was an unfamiliar area to them.

But their leaders had a lot of foresight. They could see the changes coming. Beginning around 1826, Half-Sun and other chiefs, including Chilcosahaskt, would go on trading trips down the Columbia River to the Hudson Bay Company trading post at Fort Vancouver. They brought back to the Sinkiuse, Wenatchee and Entiat tribes cattle, hogs, and chickens. The Indians were amused by the tame grouse. The women of the tribes prized the cooking pots, knives and spoons. The chiefs also brought back how to plant and grow potatoes, corn and squash. This was the beginning of the transition to farm and ranch life. Tending cattle herds was a natural because it involved riding horses.

Lahompt saw the advantages of it and become a farmer and cattleman. He married in his early twenties and settled on some good land on the Entiat River. His wife, [skumk'nalks], tended the garden and chickens while he raised hogs and cattle. The young couple didn't mind the hard work because it gave them plenty of food, warm clothing and blankets to get through the bitter cold and deep snows of winter. They were happy with their peaceful and bountiful life in the Entiat Valley. But not for long because it was soon shattered with the threat of war with the Suyapenex.

In July 1878 a small group of Umatilla Indians, mostly women and children, were fired upon while crossing the Columbia River near the Dalles by a group of Oregon Volunteers. Several women and children were killed. The survivors scattered into the hills. This resulted in a counterattack by friends and relatives of those killed. Five Indians attacked and killed Mr. and Mrs. Perkins in reprisal.

The settlers in Yakima City requested soldiers to protect them and that the army capture Chief Moses and hang him. A typical case of misplaced anger. They knew he was capable of organizing all the tribes in the area.

The rumors spread all over Indian Country. Up the Entiat, Lahompt and his tribe gathered their women and children into one encampment for protection. Gardens went untended, berries and roots ungathered. The women and children were afraid to leave the safety of the camp. The stories circulating described young Indian girls being raped and their throats slashed. Babies were said to be impaled on the bayonets of the Oregon Volunteers. The rumors ran rampant on both sides. Someone was needed to save a confrontation.

Chief Moses sent messengers to all Indians on the Columbia River and asked them to meet at his camp on Crab Creek. Lahompt and several others from the Entiat and Wenatchee tribes attended the meeting. Moses opened the meeting,

"We have a serious situation to solve. Both Suyapenex and tribal people have been killed. These were innocent men, women and children. It is unfortunate but it is causing hatred and fear on both sides."

A young aspiring warrior said, "They started it but we are going to finish it!"

Moses raised his hand before he lost control of the situation and said quietly but firmly,

"We may be able to fight for a while but they eventually would overpower us with their greater numbers and firepower. Their soldiers are professional, full time, and trained to kill."

Another young hot blood said, "It would be better to die in war with pride than be pushed around by the Suyapenex forever!"

"I agree but we could negotiate some limits to their heavy handedness. Since childhood I have watched the Suyapenex creep westward with increasing numbers. They are now like a *kinkint* [dangerous] river at flood stage. They occupy our green valleys and the best lowlands all along the Columbia River. We have been pushed back into the highlands and dry deserts."

"I hear they want us to move to the Yakama reservation, where we will be corralled like a bunch of wild horses."

"That's right and even though we have many relatives down there we speak a different language and have a different culture. There would soon be rivalries and bad blood between us."

The young hot-blooded warriors shouted for war.

"We have always lived here, as our people before us. We will not be forced from our homeland. We will fight until death."

The older tribal leaders quieted down the others by reminding them that all major tribal decisions were made after full consideration of all options.

Chief Moses took the cue and rose to his full height of over six feet and said, "I do not believe we should go to war with the Suyapenex. Many people will be killed and in the end we will still lose. Then we will have nothing left and probably be sent to Oklahoma like Chief Joseph and the Nez Perce. General Howard has promised to give us a reservation of our own. I trust him to do this for us. He is in Washington, D.C. right now pleading with the U.S. President Hayes.

I have been asked to help the Yakima citizens' posse capture the killers of the Perkins family. This will prove our innocence in the matter, and show our good faith. I need nine volunteers to ride with me to help capture the killers.

The young warriors still weren't satisfied. They protested,

"Chief Moses, you are an old woman, afraid to fight!"

Lahompt stood up and interrupted,

"Hear me now, everyone. I will go with Chief Moses to hunt the killers. Our chief is right; we should try to keep peace. Our way of life is changing and we have to adjust or we will not survive. Who else among you wants to go with us?"

So nine volunteers, including Lahompt, went to meet the posse. When they neared Yakima Valley they camped and built a huge fire to announce their presence. It wasn't long before the posse discovered them and moved to capture them. Moses cautioned his warriors to lie down and rest to look peaceful. They were not to grab their weapons when the posse arrived. In the early morning hours the posse surrounded their camp and they surrendered peacefully.

Lahompt liked to tell the humorous story about Chief Moses. During the excitement of their capture in the Yakima Valley, a posse pack mule got away and dashed through the center of their camp directly for Moses. Moses was sitting down and didn't want to be trampled so the big man raised both knees up to his chest and kicked the mule so hard it fell into the campfire. Only a man as big and powerful as Moses could have done that.

Moses was then taken to Yakima City and put in jail with chains on. While in jail Moses was able to contact General Howard and they agreed that Moses should go see the President in Washington D.C. This is where his three-year schooling at Lapwai began to pay off. He was able to create an edge on the negotiations because he didn't tell them he could understand some English. They would speak in front of him like he wasn't there. That knowledge came in handy later.

Moses asked all tribal members to keep the peace and await further developments. So Lahompt and the others all returned home. At his family home on the Entiat he passed the time caring for his cattle and horses. But his heart was heavy worrying about the safety of his family and what the future held for them. Days became weeks and the waiting became unbearable. Their gardens were planted, berries picked and roots dug. They were just waiting for the crops to grow so they could harvest them. This extra time was an opportunity to start more rumors.

Fellow tribal member Yah-Mount said, "How can we be sure that the soldiers haven't already taken Moses to the Oklahoma Territory where they took Chief Joseph? Only yesterday I met five men coming back from the Yakima Valley. They said the settlers there are telling the Washington Territorial Governor Ferry that Chief Moses is a troublemaker and they are asking the governor to send Moses and all his people to Oklahoma. They threatened that if the governor didn't do it, they would chase the Moses tribe all the way to Canada. The settlers want to clear out all Indians from the Yakima, Wenatchee, and Okanogan valleys."

At last, Moses came home and called for a tribal meeting on May 29, 1879, near Sam Millers' store in the Wenatchee Valley.

Nearly all of Lahompts' family and friends went to the meeting. Just a few stayed behind to watch over the garden and animals. The Sinkiuse [Moses-Columbia], Wenatchee, and Chelan tribes did the same. The many tepees surrounding Millers' store was a once-in-a-lifetime scene and very impressive. The future of all was at stake and they all wanted to hear about it.

General Howard opened the meeting, "We ask God to please help us create peace and goodwill between the Indians and their new neighbors, the settlers."

Using an interpreter he continued, "Chief Moses had a very successful trip and brought back a written agreement signed by President Hayes, which includes a map showing the new Moses reservation, called the Columbia Reservation. The President promised that all Indians who want to make their homes there could do so."

Then Chief Moses rose to his full impressive height and with a deep, melodious voice he said,

"Be peaceful and friendly with the Suyapenex and the U.S. government. It is useless to resist the infiltration of the Suyapenex settlers. My eyes were opened when I traveled east to Washington, D.C. The Suyapenex are as numerous as the grains of sand, too many to count. They would easily overpower us in numbers alone.

"But the U.S. President wants us to have our own reservation. He thinks that will prevent a war with the Suyapenex. It is located north of us starting at the Columbia outlet of Lake Chelan; all land north and west of the Okanogan River to the Canadian border, then west to forty-four degrees longitude which follows the summit of the Cascade Mountains, then south back to Lake Chelan, the point of beginning. It is big and covers much of the land we already use, especially the Chelan tribe. We will be happy with it."

"What do we have to give up?"

"We have to promise to give up all our homelands down here and our usual habitats, and promise to live on this reservation in peace. To help us they have promised protection from any further intrusion up there. We should prepare to move right away."

Lahompt went back to his Entiat home with mixed feelings. It was natural to be sad about leaving his familiar Entiat country for an unfamiliar place. He felt he should be glad because all their troubles seemed to be solved. But he had a deep inner feeling of foreboding.

This became reality as he was gathering his few cattle and horse for the move. Moses and a small group toured their new reservation and found that some miners and a few cattlemen were already there and refused to move.

This made it easy for Lahompt to stay at home on the Entiat until the U.S. cleared the new reservation of intruders. It looked like the same story they had encountered before; no matter where they went they were pushed out again. Lahompt knew that their old way of life was finished and it was going to be hard to adjust to a new way.

An Army detachment and a special Indian agent did travel through the Columbia Reservation, giving written notice to the miners and cattlemen that they had to move out immediately. They also offered payment for any improvements they had made which, of course, was very little. None of the Suyapenex moved out. And even worse, the lives of the few Columbia tribal members who dared to move onto the reservation were threatened. The Indians found their fences cut and gardens and crops destroyed by cattle run through their ranches.

Then a personal disaster hit Lahompt when the dreaded small pox spread amongst his tribe. Many of them died, including his wife, leaving him with two children. If that wasn't enough misfortune disaster struck again.

While chasing horses down from the steep canyons of the upper Entiat River, Lahompt fell from his horse into a rocky ravine. When his friends found him it looked to them that he couldn't survive more than a few hours because his left hip and foot were broken. All the muscles and ligaments in the leg were cruelly torn. Of course, there were no doctors to set his broken bones so they did the best they could.

For weeks his family and friends watched him suffer horrible pain and each night they expected him to die. He was naturally tough as were most of the Indian cowboys, because accidents always happened. That's when he met the Black Robe missionary from Cashmere who stopped daily to visit and pray with him. Finally, Lahompt did start to heal, but it would be months before he would ride his beloved horses again.

Lahompt did finally learn to walk again despite his left hip, leg and ankle being shriveled and deformed. He used a cane the rest of his life when he wasn't on a horse, which wasn't often. He exercised his upper torso to compensate for his disability and developed into the muscular build of a wrestler.

Lahompt started attending the services of the Black Robe who helped him recover. His life seemed hopeless with all the problems he faced and he found some hope at the mission. It helped that the missionary spoke the Salish language fluently. Since the priest was left-handed they called him "Lefty." Lahompt accepted the teachings of the Catholic Church and Father Lefty baptized him with the Christian name of "George".

After George Lahompt started riding horses again he would travel to Sam Miller's Trading Post at the confluence of the Wenatchee and Columbia Rivers. It was the only local place to trade and buy provisions. One day another trader lounging in the store observed him hobbling on his cane and called him "Kokshut lepee" which means "broken legged" in the Chinook jargon. This was later shortened to "Koxit". The nickname stuck, so the rest of his life he was known as Koxit George by the Suyapenex.

The months dragged into years and still trouble brewed with the miners on the Columbia Reservation. Lahompt was glad he hadn't moved there. He decided to stay at Entiat until things settled down. His dad, Chilcosahaskt, never intended to move and resolved to spend his remaining years at Entiat.

Not only were the Indians hassled but the miners began lobbying to restore a fifteen-mile strip of land on the northern border to public domain. The reason soon became clear; gold was discovered there!

On February 14, 1883, the new Secretary of Interior, Henry M. Teller, drafted an executive order to restore to public domain a ribbon of land, fifteen miles wide, across the northern end of the Columbia Reservation, including all mineral rights. Secretary Teller's home was in Colorado, so he understood the miners' desire and was sympathetic to them. The Indians were never officially involved in the negotiations and weren't even notified until the Suyapenex settler told them.

Rumors started again with some element of truth. The story going around was that the reservation would be cut up into small pieces until nothing would be left for the Indian.

Moses was again invited back to Washington, D.C., but this time along with Sarsarpkin and Tonasket of the Okanogan and Chief Lot of the Spokane tribe.

Meanwhile gold was discovered at Ruby on the Columbia Reservation. This sealed any hope of keeping the reservation. After five years of harassment by the locals and being ignored by the U.S. government, the Indians lost again. The chiefs had no other choice but to agree to move to the Colville Reservation and relinquish all claims to lands elsewhere. Of course, the Indians already on the Colville Reservation were not consulted about this decision. This created bad feelings among the tribes.

The executive order cancelled the Columbia Reservation and returned it to public domain. Congress didn't get around to ratifying this action until one year later on July 4, 1884. In today's world, the tribes would have lobbied against this action and maybe would have won.

"Dad, didn't my Sxxapa [Grandfather] Lahompt sign the Treaty of 1855? I would like to hear how that all happened."

"He told me that story [see Appendix *Lahompt-Entiat Valley* 1.] many times but at first I was too young to remember much about it. It would be while we were eating. Nobody was allowed to talk unless he called on them. He repeated his stories many times. Repetition is one of the techniques teachers use even today. We had no radio or TV so story telling was our only form of entertainment. Young as I was, I still listened as best as I could."

Dad said these stories were always told in the kitchen of their log house. I remember the old log house because I ate there many times. I usually sat on the bench next to the wood stove. I could turn around and look out through the small window facing north. The house faced east. I would say just like the old days but it was built in the old days, the late 1800's.

My grandfather was the first in our family to successfully make the transition from a nomadic lifestyle to a land-based commercial enterprise. Instead of a hunter-fisherman he became a cattle rancher. To him his horse was an extension of himself. The famous Japanese photographer Frank Matsura took many pictures of him in the early 1900's, most of them on a horse. One, probably the best, is shown at the beginning of this chapter and the cover of the book.

He got his name "Koxit" from his broken leg which never properly healed. Koxit is a word from the Chinook language meaning "broken." Of course, he broke his leg while riding his horse. The horse fell on him in the rugged, hilly country of Entiat Valley.

Dad continued, "The last time I remember him telling the story was in 1920 just before I went to Chemawa after the St. Mary's Mission school burnt down. Dad said my Sxxapa Chilcosahaskt was very worried about sending him on such an important trip.

Kwa-ni [Christine]

Therefore, the last of the holdouts were forced to move to the Colville Reservation. Their only other choice would have been Oklahoma, and the Nez Perce didn't fare well there. They were called "The Driven People" because no matter where they went, they were driven out. They had no chance because all their fishing and hunting grounds, berry and root gathering spots were now over-ridden by the Suyapenex.

So Lahompt gathered up his family with their few cattle, horses, meager belongings, and moved to the southwest corner of the Colville Reservation at a place called the Tumwater Basin. It suited him because it was as far away as possible from populated areas. It was on a high plateau which contained many small pot-hole lakes with plenty of water for his stock and bunch and rye grass as high as a man's waist.

During this time Lahompt married Kwa-ni [Christine Pe'el] in 1894 who he had met during a huckleberry picking trip to Lake Wenatchee or possibly at the Icicle River while salmon fishing. Kwa-ni was from the Kittitas tribe, one of the Yakama bands. Her mother Hannah Weneches was the granddaughter of Chief Seattle from the Suquamish tribe. Hanna's father was Aleck Patwankt, who is the source of my Indian name.

Although it was new and exciting, life wasn't easy on the Tumwater. A small log cabin was built by Lahompt and Sam, his son by his first wife by hauling logs from miles away at the east rim rocks, which held a sparse stand of pine trees. Firewood was also hauled. They raised pigs and chickens to supplement their beef and venison diet. Achmin and Mary, Lahompt's two daughters by his first wife, helped with the garden, which grew very well in the virgin soil. The cattle grew fat and sleek in the summer, feeding on the north slope grass. However, the calves didn't fare well in the late spring blizzards. And the winters were harsh and long so the Georges didn't say long in the Tumwater Basin.

Lahompt found a small basin he called Achmin Basin after his daughter. It was on the edge of the plateau in the Duley Lake area. It had several fresh, cold springs, level acreage for farming and high rimrocks on the western side which provided excellent protection from blizzard winds from the Cascades.

The miners on the reservation were also busy. They infiltrated the north half of the Colville Reservation and found it to be rich in minerals. But now instead of a fifteen-mile strip the miners were pushing for returning the north half of the reservation to public domain and opening it for mining.

After that the U.S. government intended to allot eighty acres to each Indian man, woman and child to be held in trust by the federal government. The purpose of this was to open the residual of the South Half of the Reservation to homesteading and mining.

On hearing of this, Lahompt scouted the entire southwest part of the reservation for the best place to claim as an allotment. He settled on Kartar Valley at the southeast end of Omak Lake. The valley was called "Kartar" because it was where a creek entered the valley and a row of tall trees formed in a random formation approximating rows. It was low altitude with mountains on three sides and the large lake on the northwest side.

My grandfather, Lahompt, later to be called Koxit George, migrated from Entiat Valley because our tribe was forced to the Colville Indian Reservation. His was the transition from a nomadic life to farming. He successfully established a cattle ranch on the Rez in the late 1880's. Kartar Valley became his base. They ranged their cows all over the southwest part of the Rez. There were no fences so he moved the cows to the best pasture as the seasons progressed. They did dryland farming for winter feed.

Some may say that it was halfway to nowhere, but once you get into Kartar Valley you know it was worth the time and effort. I tell everybody who'll listen that nobody goes there accidentally. You have to want to go there because it is out of the way.

It is not large as valleys go, but it is unique. It may only be unique to me because my grandfolks first settled there. The valley was formed about 12,000 years ago during the Ice Age. Glaciers slowly pushed top soil unto the floor of the valley until it had a bed of about 200 feet average. In the middle of the valley, where my alfalfa field is now, you can't find a rock of any size. It is a mix of volcanic ash and topsoil.

When the glaciers melted it established streambeds which run into the valley to an underground lake about 140 feet from the surface. The lake eventually provided water for my dad's alfalfa and house. It seeps down to the lower part of the valley and ends up in Omak Lake that is about two miles northwest and at a 300-foot lower elevation.

The valley is ringed with a pine forest. Lahompt was a genius for picking the valley for his Indian allotment. But deep wells weren't known to him. They tried to hand dig a well but couldn't go more than ten or twelve feet. They used Kartar Creek for their water, which was minimally sufficient for their needs. That was back in the days when mountain water wasn't contaminated. But it wasn't a green valley in those days, in fact very dry. They had to work hard to survive.

He decided to locate his ranch headquarters there but he first had to convince his neighbor and friend, Saii, to trade with him. After some discussion it was agreed that Saii would give up all claims to the valley for a certain amount of gold and several good horses.

Lahompt gave the Tumwater Basin to his son, Sam, who wanted to start his own cattle ranch. To his daughter, Achmin, who had recently married, he gave Achmin Basin. These would be their choice of allotments if that happened.

Lahompt and Christine made their final move when they located at Kartar Valley, where they developed a successful cattle and horse ranch. Victor Jangraw, a Frenchman from Oregon, built a log house for them so carefully that it still stands today. People are amazed at the way he squared the big logs and mortised the corners perfectly. The house faces east as is the Indian custom, and the back has no windows or doors because of the prevailing winds.

They planted a grove of poplar trees for shade and a windbreak. Their orchard consisted of apples, peaches, pears, apricots, and cherries. In the garden, potatoes, corn, beans, peas, squash, onions etc. all

75

flourished. Also raspberries, strawberries, and watermelons grew well. The long hot seasons were conducive to growing as long as Kartar Creek was diverted by irrigation canals. Christine filled their cellar with canned fruits and vegetable every year.

Kartar Creek went underground just below the house. Lahompt had his crew build a dam on the creek form a pond. Ditches were dug to irrigate the garden, orchard, and even a few acres of alfalfa below the forty-tree orchard.

The Georges became devout Catholics because Lahompt remembered what the Black Robe Father, "Lefty," did for him. They helped St. Mary's Mission with donations including beef, fruit and vegetables. They also helped buy the statues of Mary and Joseph for the church.

It was about thirty-five miles by team and buggy around Goose Lake Flats, Cold Springs, and down corkscrew grade and up Omak Creek to the mission. This prevented them from attending mass every Sunday because of work schedule or weather. So they, and others, built a cabin on Omak Creek near the mission. On all feast days the Georges, and others, spent up to a week attending the service and visiting with friends.

Besides religious services, the St Mary's students gave band concerts and plays. Of course, there were always those ready to give speeches. Father DeRouge took advantage of this and asked the Indian leaders to talk about how to live the good life with church, family, community and tribe.

In this way, Lahompt became known as a good speaker and eloquent philosopher. He, Alex Smitkin and Alex Nicholson were respected by all the Indians because of their honesty, logic, and excellent reputations. They acted as consultants, advisers and as a liaison between the priest and Indians and even between the mission and government. Lahompt received a medal from Father DeRouge for his good works, of which he was very proud.

Another innovation by the priest was to give these community leaders permission to hold prayer meetings at their homes on Sunday because of the long distances. When Fr. DeRouge couldn't attend funerals or baptisms, the leaders conducted a simple service in his place. As a result, the Georges' ranch became the prayer meeting center in Kartar Valley. Friends and neighbors would come faithfully each Sunday. After the meetings Christine would serve a big dinner with the help of the women and girls attending. This was a time for renewing old friendships and visiting among neighbors. Even during the week the welcome sign was always out.

Eventually Lahompt became an unofficial "deacon." Unofficial because he didn't go through the long Suyapenex "schooling" required for an official church deacon. He would hold what we call today a communion service at his home in Kartar Valley.

Christine worked hard all her life and became a remarkable cook, especially in baking bread. This was highlighted when she went to Yakima to visit her sister and, while there, helped out by baking a batch of bread. Her brother-in-law thought it was so good he entered some loaves of bread in the state fair. She was surprised and delighted when she won the blue ribbon first prize.

Contrary to today's practice, Lahompt shipped his range-fed steers when they were three years old. Even then they had a long ways to go to ship his cattle to market. He and his cowboys would round up his cattle, cut out the steers, and herd them to Wild Goose Bill Condon's ferry on the Columbia River. After crossing them on the ferry they would wander over to the rail head at Almira. He would then sell his steers and pay off his help, usually in gold coins. He carried large amounts of cash in his saddle bags so he wore a Colt .45 on his hip. His reputation preceded him as a fearless and self-reliant man so no one took advantage of him. He deposited most of his cattle sale proceeds in the Okanogan First National Bank.

Lahompt bought purebred Hereford bulls to improve his cattle and his cow ponies were bred up to be bigger and stronger horses with more stamina by two full-blooded Morgan stallions.

After the railroad reached the Okanogan Valley he shipped his cattle from there, a much easier task. He set up a line camp at Duley Lake and cut out four or five hundred head of prime steers. They were then driven over the breaks to the railhead at Okanogan.

By then, the ranch was so well organized that Lahompt found time to enjoy his favorite pastime, horse racing. He bred and trained horses until he became well known in racing circles throughout eastern Washington. His horse named Bob Wade, a miler, and Captain Billy, a quarter-miler, were his favorites because they were outstanding and became consistent winners.

For training, a one-half mile track was laid out in the valley. When Lahompt's son, Moses, became old enough to ride race horses, it was his job to race them on the track while his father timed the horse. When the horses were entered in a race, a professional jockey was hired to ride them.

In December 1885, Chief Joseph and the remnants of his Nez Perce band arrived in Nespelem at the invitation of Chief Moses. They just returned from Oklahoma, poverty-stricken and hungry and in ragged clothes. Chief Moses asked for help and many people responded. Lahompt sent beef cattle to help with that first winter; others sent clothing and blankets.

If Lahompt happened to be in Okanogan at noontime he always invited friends or acquaintances, both Suyapenex and Skint [Indian], for lunch at the restaurant. He also let it be known when butchering time came. He never lacked for help with the work because they would go home with a generous portion of beef hanging from their saddle or tucked in the rear of their wagon.

About every five years Lahompt would have a bad year. On dry years the spring rains would arrive too late to germinate the oats which resulted in a shortage of hay the next winter. In 1887 the winter was a real disaster. The range grass disappeared by October first and November brought blizzard winds and a massive snowfall. By December the snow was deep and the temperature stayed at ten degrees below zero. Snow kept coming until mid-March and Lahompt ran short of hay. He was desperate, so he had his crew cut birch limbs along the creek and haul them in sleds to feed the cattle, which were in the lee of Boot Mountain to protect them from the wind. He lost at least a quarter of his herd, numbering about a thousand head.

Lahompt then hired Saii to skin the dead cattle for a dollar a head. Saii made $800 for his work as about two hundred hides were rendered useless by coyote damage. Then a Jewish man came with large wagons and four-horse teams, bought the hides and hauled them away, a small return for such a large loss.

But he was to sustain a larger loss a few years later by cattle thieves. He didn't mind someone who needed food to take one or two head. But he hated professional cattle thieves who stole for profit. One day his range riders came rushing back at full speed. They said they couldn't find most of the 1,200 prize Herefords who were summer grazing just north of Kartar. Lahompt strapped on his Colt .45 and took ten cowboys with him to search for the missing cattle. After two days of fruitless hunting they found a trail of several hundred head of cattle. They were being pushed north and had already passed west of Omak Mountain.

Lahompt sent a cowboy to Conconully on his fastest horse to get the sheriff while he and the others stayed on the trail of the cattle thieves. The sheriff and posse caught up with them just east of what is now Tonasket. They followed the thieves to the Canadian border where the trail disappeared. When he returned to Kartar he estimated about a 900 to 1,000 head loss.

There seemed no end to the bad luck for Lahompt and the tribes. The U.S. President finally opened the south half of the reservation to homesteading. On opening day September 5, 1916, hundreds of land-hungry settlers flocked to the land offices. The Colville Reservation was located on land the Suyapenex thought had little value. Who would want to live on arid, sagebrush and rattlesnake infested land? But they did and found out the dry land farming was difficult at best. Most of the homesteaders abandoned their claims within a few years leaving crumbling cabins and sagging sheds leaning bravely against the winter blizzards as proof of their failure.

When the north half had been opened for homesteading all tribal members were issued allotments. But sometime between 1913 and 1916 the reservation was closed to any more Indian allotments to save land for homesteading.

Therefore all Indian children born after the closure did not receive allotments. After the south half was opened for homesteading, tribal members could not even apply for homesteads because they were not citizens of the United States but wards of the federal government. So tribal members born after that date can only inherit or buy allotted land. As a result, only Mattie and Moses were allotted because Edward and Peter were born too late.

After 1916, as more and more homesteaders moved on the Reservation, the grazing range disappeared under the plow and behind fences. Lahompt and the other Indian cattlemen lost their range. When they rounded up their herds they found their numbers depleted due to cattle thieves and hungry settlers. The horseshoe lightning brand was brought down from the range for the last time. A diminished herd of 500 was all that was left of a once proud cattle operation.

Lahompt was weary and tired of the struggle to keep ahead of the challenges he had to face. His oldest son, Sam, had died the year before from injuries received when his horse fell on him. His next oldest, Moses, was only twelve. So one day Lahompt asked Moses,

"Son, I want you to saddle your horse and ride with me today."

Moses thought that was great because his dad seldom asked him along. He followed Lahompt up the trail north of the valley. They tied their horses in the shade and slowly walked to the top of a sheer rock point overlooking the valley. Lahompt used his cane but Moses didn't dare try to help his proud father. They sat down and quietly enjoyed the warm sunshine.

Lahompt was feeling his age as he stared out over the isolated valley and became lost in his own reflections. Moses sat quietly, waiting and listening. He sensed that this was an important step in his growing up. The happy song of the meadow lark in the willow trees below them and the sweet aroma of the purple Johnny-jump-ups blooming in the spring sunshine highlighted his appreciation of the valley.

He felt like jumping up and climbing the rocky cliffs because it was spring and time for doing things. But he sat still and waited as he was taught to control his excess energy in respect for his elder. At last his father turned to him and said,

"Son, I brought you up here to tell you about life. I come up here often to look down at our ranch with the green oats growing in our fields."

Of course he was speaking Indian because that is how they always conversed. Moses didn't learn English until he went to the Mission.

"This valley is our home and this earth is our mother. The sun is our father. Treat it well and you will live well. Do not allow greed or selfish pleasures to control you and not mistreat your mother."

Moses could only say,

"Yes, father."

"Our cattle herds have vanished. Our herd has been reduced to a level that will make it difficult to make a living. When I am gone they will disappear entirely. You are now a boy but you will soon be a man and have responsibilities. Do not be in a hurry to quit school. You must learn the Suyapenex way in order to survive in his world. But don't follow all the Suyapenex as many of them are cruel and live by a different set of rules. They are greedy and selfish. Live by the laws of the Church. It is very similar to our culture and if you combine the two you have the best of both worlds. Always be willing to help others.

"When I was a young man I did things I am not proud of. I wasn't prepared to handle the adult situations. My father and mother advised me but I did not listen and became arrogant. I am pointing this out so you won't make the same mistake."

"What did you do?"

"One day while visiting my aunt in Entiat she asked my cousin and me to ride down to Miller's store in Wenatchee Valley and buy some flour and sugar for her. We decided it would be easier to just row across the Columbia and buy what she wanted from the Chinese miners camped there. We climbed into an old dugout canoe and rowed over to the opposite shore. We didn't realize how savage we looked with our revolvers strapped to our hips. Those poor Chinese must have thought we were going to scalp them. They all ran away and hid in the bushes except the cook in the back cook tent. We went over to the tent and asked in our language to buy the supplies.

"Of course, he didn't understand us so he started shaking and chattering with fear. I walked over to the table to show him what we wanted and he suddenly grabbed a shotgun and pointed it at us. I grabbed a pan of hot water off his stove and threw it at him. He ran screaming out the back tent flap.

"Determined not to go home empty handed we snatched a sack of flour and sugar and ran down to our dugout canoe and started rowing back across the river as fast as we could. About halfway our canoe sank and we started swimming for our lives. The current carried us about a mile downstream and we were exhausted by the time we managed to crawl up the river bank. We lost our canoe, flour, sugar, and nearly our lives.

"So I finally understood what my father meant when he said, "You get out of life what you put into it'".

Lahompt then stood up and smiled at him. "Come! Your mother is waiting dinner on us."

My grandfather, Lahompt, was one of my role models although I never knew him. He passed on twelve years before I was born. I knew him through my dad, who told me many stories about him. Even my dad knew him only as a youngster because he was 15 when Lahompt had the stroke that ended his life. My grandmother, Kwa-ni, was Lahompt's third wife. His first two died of either the flu or small pox, which swept through our tribe. Kwa-ni outlived Lahompt by thirty-eight years, because she was much younger than he was. Coincidentally though, they were both 82 years old when they died.

We visited her many times in Kartar Valley. I remember sitting on a bench in the kitchen while eating. I could turn around and look out the window on the north side of the log house. Grandma was still a good cook. I can almost taste those fluffy, large brown biscuits and bread covered with real homegrown butter.

She was remarried to Sam George, Yakama Indian with the same last name but no relation. I would listen to my dad and his mother and stepfather tell stories well into the night. The kerosene lamp on the table gave a steady hiss that eventually put me to sleep. I could follow the stories somewhat because they would throw in a few English words once in a while. Some of these were Wenatchee, Okanogan, Methow, and Yakama that were Indian words used by the Suyapenex. They were talking mostly in Yakama and sometimes in Wenatchee. Their stories were very animated and resulted in a lot of laughter. They liked to tell jokes on each other or someone they knew well.

One time my mother grew tired of listening to them because she couldn't follow their stories. So she decided to go out and read in our car, parked just outside the log house. She became totally absorbed in her book, squinting because of the dim dome light she turned on by opening the car door. Subconsciously, she could hear the crickets and night birds in the trees around the house. She suddenly became aware of total quietness in the dark night. She put her book down and listened, nothing. Then she heard a low whistle behind the car and turned to look but, of course, she couldn't see anything in the total darkness. The whistle sounded again but on her left. She could feel the hair on the back on her head stiffen and stand up. It came again from the front. She decided her best move was to hurry into the house just to her right before she was surrounded. She quickly but quietly stepped into the house. Kwa-ni looked at her and smiled. She told Dad in Indian that his wife just confronted the "Stick-Indians". Dad translated for Mom who thought she returned with dignity but then realized her looks gave her away. My grandparents had many encounters with the Stick-Indians and said they were harmless but liked to pay tricks on humans.

Lahompt died of a stroke in June 1922 while he was driving a wagon to Okanogan for supplies. He is buried at the Kartar cemetery overlooking his land with all the other Georges. He was indeed the Last Chief Standing as the chief system was destroyed by the Suyapenex.

Lahompt was the last chief because our tribe was forced into a different kind of organization. But our leaders maintained, to the extent possible under the circumstances, much of the same way of operating. In the old days they listened to the tribal members before they made any decisions. A consensus to them meant everyone was in agreement, some to a lesser extent than others, but still in agreement. There was no counting of votes to see which side had the majority. Even one dissenting vote could hold up the process until that person was satisfied enough to change his mind.

I remember reading James Michener's book on Poland. The people of Poland called it a "liberum veto" when they had a meeting of this type and one dissenting vote would prevent any action."

Dad said, "Indians do not call it anything special, because it is a way of life. Individual rights are foremost. Every group tries to accommodate individual wants and desires. This is very frustrating at times for those who want immediate action, like Kwiltninuk. Patience was not natural for him, but he learned it in order to fit in with his people. Like the Poles, Indians seem to be a very lumbering, slow-moving society. Indians do not respond to situations that call for immediate decision and action because they feel there is always another day to take action".

Time is forever and, in fact, it does not exist, except for convenience. It is not the dictator of events, but only a method to identify when events occurred. Indians dictate events and later measure, by time, when they happened. Today, we call this 'Indian Time.' Indian Time dramatically demonstrates the difference in philosophy between the white society work ethic and the Indian society. Indians with this background will often be late to meetings and have difficulty keeping any schedule. But they spend as much time as necessary to accomplish each mission. In contrast, the schedule-driven people of today are forever trying to achieve 'quality time' with their kids, spouse, friends, or relatives.

However, it must be recognized they had more manageable numbers in that the tribe was small. Everyone knew everyone else. This was, in different situations, either an advantage or a disadvantage. In any event people would realize when someone was being selfish and putting himself above the tribe. If that happened several people would take that person aside and try to convince him to do what is best for the tribe. Usually they were successful. This helped to prevent small disagreements become large ones. It also helped people get to know each other.

I sold my ranch in Kartar Valley to the tribe with the agreement I could move my grandfather's log house 1 ½ miles NW. The site I chose is adjacent to the old property and towards Omak Lake. I am renovating it so it can be used as a memento of my family's history. In this way we hope to preserve some of our Indian culture.

Before move

After move

Moyese George, son of Chief Kwan George

Kwa-ni and Lahompt had four children who survived birth, Mattie, Moyese, Eddie, and Pete.

My dad was born in a tepee in Kartar Valley. He may have been the last one from our tribe to do so. It was on a cold winter day February 12, 1906, the same day as President Lincoln's birthday. Some would say that was prophetic because both had compassion for people. Lincoln wanted to heal a divided nation. Dad wanted to stop world wars. My grandparents' log house stood next to Dad's birth tepee. They were practicing only one of many of their Indian traditions.

Eddie died at about seventeen of leukemia. Dad remembered a bright light shining above the Kartar cemetery the night Eddie was buried. Dad said he was a good person, better than most. Dad also said we are all put on earth to become good persons. He said the Indian word for it is "Sqoo-lel" meaning "going into goodness". Eddie arrived at an early age. To do this we must believe in oneself and feel good about ourselves. It is self-esteem at its peak. Indians would call it "sees-use," meaning able.

How can we go into goodness? We must first realize that the keys to the miracle of life lie in our own consciousness. What society thinks of as reality today is the hypnosis of social conditioning caused by induced fiction in which we are all collectively participating. It seems our only fate is to be born, grow old and die.

Life will bestow miracles on us when we begin to see it as an expression of the miraculous. When we desire to become co-creators with God we will be "Sqoo-lel." Then we will realize that the Circle of Peace is a world we can dream into actuality from the purity of our hearts. If enough of us do that our collective consciousness will bring about a transition in our civilization.

Lahompt and Kwa-ni wanted their children to get a good education so they sent them to the St. Mary's Mission school. This was really their only choice for a dormitory school and the distance prohibited them from daily commuting.

Dad remembers Lahompt telling him when he was about twelve years old, "Do not be in a hurry to quit school. You need to go until you learn all that the Suyapenex's school can teach you. You cannot survive now or in the future unless you know what they know."

Dad went to the Mission school when he was eight years old in 1914. He was ready to start the sixth grade when the Mission school burned down in 1919, so in 1920 his folks sent him to Chemawa, an Indian school near Salem, Oregon, where he graduated from high school in 1928, specializing in carpentry.

Two descendants of my Aunt Mattie, her daughter Anita Cheer and granddaughter Karen Sam, went on to college and became teachers at the St. Mary's/ Paschal Sherman Indian School. At one time or another they both taught fourth grade in the Koxit George building named after our grandfather. Since then the school moved into a new building in 2005. There has been some talk by the PSIS administration to name a wing in the new school after Koxit George. Our family would certainly appreciate that.

My dad was a very quiet and reserved person in his younger days. I know this indirectly, of course, but one example is the exchange of letters written after he graduated from Chemawa High School.

August 17, 1928, letter to O.C. Upchurch, superintendent of Lapwai Indian School from O.H. Lipps, superintendent of Chemawa Indian School:

….Moses George, a full blood Wenatchee Indian….He is 21 years of age, well developed physically and has had an excellent record as a student here. He has remained at Chemawa all summer working at his trade of carpenter on our new dormitory. He is a rather quiet fellow but he is anxious to have a position [as disciplinarian at Lapwai boys' dormitory] and says he will do his best to make good……He is a very good carpenter and especially good on cabinetwork. I have a table in my office that he made of various colored woods, the top being inlaid in a Navajo design. It is a rather remarkable piece of cabinetwork…

On August 23, 1928 from and to the same people:…and [Moses] is somewhat reserved and quiet….

One of the stories that Dad would tell me while he was reminiscing was about his experience as a wrestler at Chemawa Indian School. He was in good physical shape from working on his folks' ranch in the summertime but he worked hard to get in condition for wrestling. He did neck exercises until he had a "bull" neck. That was his strength and advantage over other wrestlers. The story took place in Salem, Oregon, in 1924:

I stepped into my opponent with the classic stance; my head and back upright, arms and elbows in, bent at the hip and perfectly balanced on the balls of my feet. Just like my coach had taught me. I did a back arch throw, which landed us on the mat. I quickly slipped my arm around my opponent's head and pinned both of his shoulders to the mat. The move was so fast that the referee had to move into position to count and was a little late starting. In desperation my opponent pushed off and barely escaped the count of three which would indicate a pin. He looked at me with surprise not expecting to be challenged by the high school student from the small Indian school near Salem, Oregon. After all, he was a senior at Oregon State University and had never been defeated in a wrestling match.

We continued, evenly matched, for several more minutes. The OSU wrestler was fast, very fast. And he seemed awfully strong for a 134-pounder. But I was in the best shape of my life. My 18 years had been spent on a cattle ranch at home and doing sports of all kinds at the Chemawa High School. Physical conditioning was a way of life for me. My strength was my neck muscles, which had helped me throw more than one opponent.

This time it would take more than strength. It would also take agility, technique, and speed. Twice my opponent went on offense.

First, he did a lifting duck-under move by exploding his hips through me. As we fell to the mat, I managed to roll out of the hold by a brute-force slip of the headlock. I stood up and circled my opponent looking for an opening. I then realized this was the most challenging match of my life. I had never met such a graceful opponent.

Finally, my opponent took a back step and threw me to the mat from a hip lock position. I fell so hard I lost my breath, jarred my teeth, and had an instant headache. For a while it looked like I might be in trouble as my opponent tried a body jam with a sweeping motion that pulled my body out of position. We were locked at an impasse for several moments before I was able to break the hold again solely with the superior strength of my neck.

The match continued for several more minutes and time was beginning to run out. We each became anxious to make a pin as we felt the match was about even so far. But I suddenly felt tired. The initial adrenaline surge I experienced at the beginning of the match had peaked out and I was fast losing my strength. And strength was what I needed at that point.

I kept in motion as I was trained to do and made one more valiant attempt to pin my opponent. I by-passed my opponent's arm and reached for a high double lift move.

I managed to get my hips under my opponent but in doing so I reached too far and couldn't keep my head and back straight up which was necessary to get leverage. This was a fatal error quickly detected by my more experienced opponent who countered with a quick back step move and threw me from a hip-lock position.

This time I couldn't escape the inevitable pinning. The match was over. My opponent would move on to the next qualifying match for the Olympics.

I lost but with dignity to Robin Reed, who went on to win the Olympic Gold Medal for the 134-pound weight class in Paris in 1924. Robin was never defeated in any wrestling match at any weight limit. In the Pacific Northwest tryouts for the Olympics, Reed entered four weight classes, from 145 pounds to 191, and won all four. On the boat to Paris he defeated every American wrestler at every weight classification except 167 pounds. This included Russell Vis, the eventual Gold Medal winner at 145 pounds.

I was proud of my accomplishment. I would have liked to share it with my dad, but he had passed away two years before. My mother was an avid supporter and it was her idea to send me to Chemawa in the first place. The St. Mary's Mission school on the Colville Indian Reservation I was attending had run into some hard times in 1920 so she sent me to Chemawa to make sure I received a good education. It was at a great sacrifice for her as I was just reaching the age to be very helpful at their cattle ranch.

Chemawa had over 1,000 students in the late twenties. I attended during the peak growth period. Athletics always played an important part in student life at the school. An attempt was always made to furnish opposition to match the age and maturity of the boys. During the early years of the school, young men actually of college age were enrolled at Chemawa so competition was necessarily arranged with state universities, local colleges and athletic clubs. The first high school graduating class was in 1927 so my class was the second. the 1927 squad is shown in their annual picture.

I am the second from the right in the last row.

84

The school was started in 1880 with fourteen boys and four girls. Students came from tribes in all western states, Rocky Mountains and Alaska.

After my defeat by Robin Reed I never wrestled competitively again. Instead I wrestled wild calves during branding time back home at my folks' cattle ranch.

After graduation from Chemawa I returned home. When I got back my brother-in-law, Felix Grunlose, a rugged Lake Indian from the upper Columbia, met me at the railroad station in Okanogan. It was a two-day combined bus and train ride from Salem to Portland to home. Felix was the first to speak: "Good to see you, Kemosape." We kidded each other about who was the Indian and who was the Lone Ranger. Tonto, the Lone Ranger's Indian companion, called him Kemosape meaning friend.

I gave him a tired smile. I had a big letdown after my wrestling match. I spent a lot of time thinking about it on the way home. I came to realize I couldn't have gone to the Olympics if I had won the match. I was broke and too proud to ask anyone for help. My Dad, Koxit, had passed away with a stroke in 1922 and the Kartar ranch was in shambles. The cows were gone and the horses were disappearing fast. There was nobody to look after them. Felix worked in the woods. He was not a rancher. He had to work out because he had just married my sister, Mattie, and would be starting a family soon.

We had a lot of catching up to do as we rode the buckboard back to the ranch. We spoke in Salish. From Wenatchee to Colville on the Columbia River all the tribes spoke Salish. The language changed somewhat as you moved up the river but most Indians had no trouble making the adjustment. Felix was a Lake so he spoke the upriver Salish and I spoke Wenatchee, the down river Salish.

As we came over a hill seven miles east of Okanogan we could see the Omak Lake. I always enjoyed seeing the brilliant blue-green water several hundred feet below the wagon trail. The lake, about a mile wide in places, was carved out of rock formations and wandered for almost ten miles to the entrance to Kartar Valley and the George cattle ranch.

Lake water came from snow meltdown in the mountains and stayed in the lake basin as there was no outlet. This caused the water to be somewhat alkaline and no fish existed in the lake until the tribe planted Lahontan trout from Pyramid Lake in Nevada about 1969. It was discovered to be 350 feet deep in places at the west end. Maybe this caused the rumor to be circulated that the Okeefanokee monster fish occasionally visited the lake through an underground stream from Lake Okanogan in Canada.

My father, Lahompt or Koxit, and mother, Christine or Kwa-ni, filed for allotments shortly after 1916 when the Reservation was allotted. When my sister, Mattie and I, were born our parents also filed for allotments for us.

Felix sensed that I didn't want to talk about wrestling. "Are you still going to Haskell next year?"

I thought about it before answering and finally said: "Yes. It's the only place I can afford. It's sorta like Chemawa; everything is paid for but incidentals. I hope to save enough this summer to carry me through the year. Do you think that is possible?"

"Sure, I'll help you do it. If you don't do it now you'll never do it. Your dad would have wanted you to get as much education as possible. Your mom knows you'll do well and will encourage you. Your dad never went to school but in his own way he was always learning. There was never a smarter Indian on our Reservation than him. He learned how to raise cattle where nobody ever raised cattle before up at Achmeen Basin. Your grandfather taught your dad about horses but not cattle. You know horses and have worked your dad's cattle. But things are changing. We can't run cattle the way your dad did. It isn't only the homesteading Suyapenex moving in but other things, like fences. When Suyapenex came to the Reservation they fenced everything. Your dad ranged hundreds of cows all over the southwest part of the Reservation. We can't do that anymore. He could pasture his cows according to the season and keep them on good grass almost year around. Now, you watch, cattlemen who wish to stay in business will have to put up lotsa hay. Not just some hay like we do for our horses but tons of hay for the cattle too. This will limit how many cows you can keep. Koxit chose the best farmland in the country but the creek can only furnish so much irrigation. It is not enough to grow much hay. And you know every couple of years the valley has a drought. There were years when we didn't have any crop!"

I agreed with Felix's analysis but a thought struck me: "What about the 200 head that we are missing from the range? Can't we go look for them?"

Felix said: "I wondered when you would think about that. Let's do it!"

REFLECTIONS

I can truthfully say this was all started by my grandmothers' attitude and desire to have her family educated. She was a good linguist in her own Yakama and Wenatchee dialects but limited in English. Her passion was reflected in her statement to Sister Maria, author of the "Black Robes" book, on May 3, 1960, just two months before she passed away. She said, "No school – no good!"

Because of his folks' encouragement to become educated he went on to Haskell in Kansas, a two-year Indian Community College. He wanted to go on to the University of Kansas and become an architect but he didn't have the money. His father had passed away and the ranch was in shambles.

Here is the original letter Dad wrote telling of his desire to go on to college.

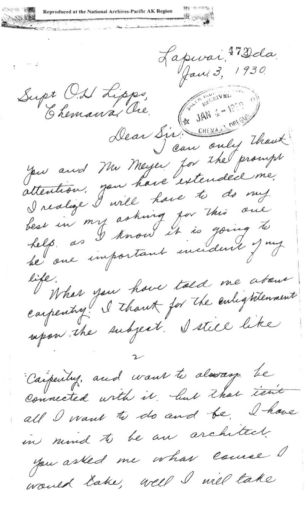

architecture and plenty of it. of
course I'll take other required subjects
but that is what I want to be.

It interests me very much and
I take to it the same to better that
I want to be one.

I understand about transportation
tuition, and other expence. as long

3

As I have room and board. I
can see to my expenses for such.

After I complete my course I will
go out and find employment in
some architect's office and work
there to get it thoroughly from
the ground up.

I realize that a College
education is almost the most
important thing in asking for
employment nowdays and whats
more I can't become an architect
so easily by just going out and
trying to do the work without having
some advanced schooling of it.

At Chemawa when we had

4

Mechanical drawing I was so
interested that I did my work the
best I knew how.

Mr Lipps I am earnest about
this, and feel that I will not fail
if I get my chance. so I very much
hope you can arrange this. and
have your trust and confidence.
If so how can I fail my
friends?

Everything is fine here, and
I wish you and family the very
best this new year can give you—
Very sincerely
Moses George

87

Click, click, click…..

Moyese, now called Moses, listened to the hypnotizing sound of the rocks caught in his tires as he drove back to Wenatchee from the Colville Indian Reservation. It always happened when he drove up to the reservation. It was especially disturbing to him because he was a roads engineer and critically analyzed every road he encountered. He now worked for the State Highway Department in Wenatchee but he had worked on the Colville Reservation during the Civilian Conservation Corps [CCC] days and surveyed roads that are still in use. He especially remembered talking his boss into letting him lay out a one-mile straightaway a couple miles north of Nespelem. He had to work hard to assure the balance of cuts and fills to make it cost-effective because that was the prime measure of a good road for any road engineer.

But since then very little improvement had been made on reservation roads. He'll have to lobby with his present bosses because state highways did run through the reservation.

That wasn't why he was here though. This was one of several trips he had taken to work with the Tribal Council. They had asked him to serve on a committee charged with the task of coming up with a plan in case the reservation was terminated. The others on the committee were all councilpersons: Shirley Palmer of Nespelem and Bud Stensgar of Inchelium were still on the Council. Lorraine Misziasek of Inchelium and Glen Whitelaw of Keller had been on the Council and worked on the committee. Moses more or less represented Omak because he was a former councilman and that was his home. In addition, his present job added experience the others didn't have.

To provide more expertise they hired Stanford Research Institute to review the reservation resources, appraise the value and make recommendations of what to do. Going in, it sounded pretty straightforward but they soon found that the BIA didn't have sufficient information to do a good study. They didn't have a handle on the forest, which was the main asset of the reservation. The minerals survey was nonexistent even though gold was discovered all over the north half and Republic had an operating mine for years. So the committee had to make do with what it had. There wasn't enough time to do anymore. The deadline was next year, 1965. Tribal members were undecided whether to terminate the Reservation or not.

Dad's thoughts turned to the day he won a seat on the first Council in 1938. He could see himself sitting in the old Council Hall watching them count the votes. He remembered that he would go from high anticipation to disappointment as the votes were counted. There were eleven candidates for the four Nespelem District positions of the Charter Council. The highest two vote-getters would be assigned the two-year term positions and the next two highest would be assigned the one-year term positions. He had spent the last several years going to meetings during which the proposed tribal constitution was formulated, so he was familiar with the process.

They had proposed several versions of a constitution and had been rejected because it gave the tribe too much power. He could still hear some of the conversations of that time.

Cleveland Kamiakin:

"How can they take power away from us that we already have? Our Chiefs have served us for generations and will continue to do so. They do not recognize them as our governing body because we have not written things down. Our language is oral, not written."

C.B Susan Timentwa:

"We already have the Chief system that works for us so we don't want to change."

Moses participated in the meetings leading up to this election from 1934 to 1938. He didn't side with either group because he understood both arguments. His dad, Lahompt, and grandfather, Chilcosahaskt, were traditional Chiefs and, as the oldest, he would have been in line if the Chief system prevailed.

But that system was decimated with the mass move to the Rez. Members of his Entiat tribe now lived all over the Rez. It would be difficult, if not impossible, to organize such a group into tribal affiliation. They developed the interests of their area, which included several other tribes. They began intermarrying and the lines became even dimmer.

The new system allowed for geographical representation, which solved one problem but increased the potential for tribal jealousies within and between districts. The Nez Perce and Moses Columbia bands formed a coalition, which was at odds with the San Poil and Nespelem that were the original tribes from that district.

He felt that the new organization would have one major advantage in that it would be recognized by the Bureau of Indian Affairs. They didn't know how to work with Chiefs and essentially ignored them. On June 8, 1938, D'Arcy McNickle of the Feds summarized the situation:

"By what right do we ignore an existing organization, however inefficient and undemocratic it may be? Of course, we have the power to do it, but is that enough?"

He also said it was a mistake for the tribe to adopt a constitution in which no provision was made for representation by the tribal chiefs. He suggested a Mr. Faris should go to the Reservation with a copy of the Pawnee Constitution and attempt to have the Colvilles adopt an amendment along the lines taken by the Pawnee, which allowed for Chiefs. There is no record that this ever happened. The Pawnee still have a traditional Council of Chiefs in addition to a tribal Council.

As he remembered it, Dad was trailing until about half the votes were counted. He kept a rough count of his votes as they were read off. He then started pulling away from everyone but Marcel Arcasa and Albert Orr, who stayed very close. Dad and Marcel Arcasa received the most votes with Albert Orr and Hiriam B. Runnels filling out the ticket. [Appendix Chapter Nine *Moses* 1.]

89

Dad felt lucky because there were some strong candidates running. Many of these were to serve on future Councils.

After he was sworn in, Dad asked the Council to support education of tribal members. His folks had repeatedly told him the only way our tribe could survive was to learn the ways of the Suyapenex. It wasn't easy because most of the Council hadn't finished school and didn't consider it necessary. In addition, some wanted to continue the old ways of tribes. But the seed was planted and eventually the tribe became big time supporters of education of their young.

While he was serving on the Council, Dad was able to find out more about how the Constitution actually came about. On September 3, 1936, a letter was sent from the Washington, D.C. office to Harvey K. Meyer the Colville Indian Agency Superintendent.

The letter said the BIA couldn't approve the tribal constitution passed by the tribal members because the powers were too broad. Those powers can only be given to a tribe which is under the Indian Reorganization Act [IRA] which the tribal members previously voted down. The letter did not say why, which makes it a Catch 22 [can't win] situation. [See Appendix Chapter Nine *Moses 2*].

This significantly reduced the sovereignty of the Colville Confederated Tribes because, as tribes, they had previously full control of tribal property.

I remember going with my folks to the Circle Grounds at Nespelem to watch the ceremonial dancing. We listened to the steady beat of the drummers and the high-pitched, lonely-sounding voices of the singers. This was the first powwow held in Nespelem after World War II. There wasn't a big turnout, as a lot of vets hadn't returned yet. Some would not return at all. But there was a feeling of renewal and that made everyone glad that things were returning to normal.

The beat seemed to get into your bloodstream and make you move with it. It was hypnotizing. The same kind of feeling must have driven the warriors of old to go to battle.

The distinct beat of the war drums were heard throughout the whole nation in 1941 and we went to war. It was especially loud on Indian reservations. History has shown that about thirty percent of the eligible tribal people join the armed services during wartime. This is a higher percentage than any other culture group. This was also true for World War I, which became an embarrassment for the federal government so Congress passed a bill in 1924 giving Indians U.S. citizenship. All other people who were born in the U.S. are automatically given citizenship.

There were 17,000 Indians who joined the service during World War I even though they were not citizens. Those veterans were given citizenship by Congress as they were discharged after the war. The reason was not to correct an oversight but to assimilate the Indians. Neither the Indians nor tribes solicited this action. They were not trying to prove a point. They were joining the service for two reasons.

First, the conditions were so bad on the reservations-- no jobs, no businesses, and no hope -- that they just wanted to find something better.

The other reason was the adventurous ones wanted to see the world, and this provided that opportunity.

WWI was beyond my immediate family's memory but when WWII cane along 27,000 Indians joined the services. All my family of the ages 17-30 joined the service. My dad was 35 years old when the war broke out so he wasn't eligible for the draft. In addition, he was exempt because he worked for the U.S. Army Corps of Engineers building gun emplacements and airports. He finally succumbed to the beat of the drum when he was 38 and joined the Navy Seabees.

1945 - Dad

"Dad, why did you join the Seabees? You didn't have to as your job was critical to the war effort and you were past the draft age."

"I joined because everyone else did. But I don't advise you to go to war. When I was in Japan I drew Shore Patrol [SP] duty to guard the perimeter of Nagasaki after it was hit with an atomic bomb. We were to keep people out because it was still contaminated with radiation. I never saw so much devastation in my life. The city was leveled. Nothing stood except for an occasional brick or concrete wall. I could imagine how the thousands of Japanese were demolished. I hope we never see that again."

After the war my folks moved to Wenatchee where Dad worked for the State Highway Department. For the first time they were able to settle in one spot. Dad made the most of it by building his dream house after I went on to college. [See 1963 pictures below]

NOV   63

He enjoyed his work designing highways all over north central Washington. One of his projects was the rest stop at Blue Lakes but his proudest accomplishment was convincing his bosses to build Interstate 90 between George and Vantage at two levels so oncoming traffic wouldn't be looking into headlights at night.

He also studied and worked hard to get his Land Surveyors license. He had the years' experience and knew the fundamentals of land surveying but had to study for the legal questions. He made several attempts before passing the test but that was an accomplishment because many couldn't pass it.

Every time we visited the folks we would swap stories about Indian history.

"I will fight no more forever. Those were the words spoken by Chief Joseph during his surrender speech at the Bear Paw Mountains in Montana. It was the end of an era."

Dad was describing the flight of the Joseph Band. He had just finished telling our kids a Coyote story and that led into the Chief Joseph battles.

"We have some relatives that were in that battle. Some of mom's Yakama kin married into the Nez Perce tribe. The Johnson family is one of them. Unfortunately, she was too young to know them. She was about 16 when she married Dad in 1894 and moved to the Colville Indian Reservation. Chief Joseph moved there about the same time at the invitation of Chief Moses. Moses and Joseph were good friends although they didn't always agree on things.

"Like school, for example. Moses wanted a boarding school at Nespelem. Joseph didn't want anything to do with a Suyapenex school. It is easy to see that their experiences greatly influenced their attitudes. Moses learned a lot during his three years at the mission school at Lapwai. He wanted his tribe to have the same advantage. Joseph, on the other hand, was still feeling the persecution and didn't want his tribe's kids brainwashed.

"Moses spent part of one winter at our ranch in Kartar. I don't know the exact year but it probably was in the late 1890s. They discussed many things. Moses wasn't too keen on the black robes [Jesuit priests] and their mission at St. Mary's but dad was an avid supporter of it -- so much so that he had services at Kartar when the weather was too bad to go to the Mission. He was a religious leader of local Indians. Many people came, mostly because mom was a good cook and they always had a big meal after the service."

This prompted a question I had to ask,

"Dad, the Carlisle Indian School in Pennsylvania is an example of Joseph's fears because their motto was 'Kill the Indian and save the child.' It opened in 1879; just two years after Joseph's surrender, and operated until 1918. I know you speak highly of Carlisle but maybe you didn't realize their purpose."

"I liked Carlisle mostly for the football program that Coach Pop Warner put together. Pop Warner was a great promoter of Indians. He later coached at Stanford and was instrumental in getting their name changed to Stanford "Indians". Unfortunately, they changed it again later because they thought it was insulting to Indians. I was proud that they would recognize us because usually we are ignored.

"Pop Warner had great teams at Carlisle and even beat Harvard 18-12 in 1912. Jim Thorpe was their star player. Later I had the pleasure of meeting Jim when he visited Haskell in 1930. But Thorpe wouldn't have done very well without our tribal member, Alec Arcasa, who was his blocking back. Do you know that there were at least forty of our tribal members who attended Carlisle?"

"No, I didn't. But did you know that Carlisle was Captain Pratt's idea, conceived in 1875 while he commanded the POW camp at Fort Marion, Florida? Before that he was a mercenary Indian fighter supporting white expansionism during the post-Civil War period. He commanded a regiment of Buffalo Soldiers [blacks] and Indian scouts. At Carlisle, his purpose was to civilize Indians. He cut off their hair, replaced their traditional clothing with military uniforms and taught them English. Carlisle was set up to break spirits; destroy the traditional extended families and cultures, to obliterate memories and languages, and especially to make the children deny their Indian-ness, inside and out."

"I know it didn't work very well. Most Indians eventually returned to the Reservation. Not because of the Reservation which had so many economic problems and no jobs to speak of, but because it is home to them."

"You're right, Dad. Ten thousand Indians attended Carlisle over the years and most of them returned to their reservations."

Dad retired in 1969 so my folks moved to Kartar Valley on the Rez. They had been planning that move for a long time. My dad was the first to drill a well at Kartar Valley in the early 1970's. That changed everything. Of course, they had to get the tribe to sponsor them to have the Rural Electrification Administration [REA] bring electrical power to the valley. Then they could pump the water. Before long the valley was green. Then I helped my folks get a Bureau of Indian Affairs [BIA] grant so they could start an alfalfa farm. Alfalfa hay was always in demand in this area, so it was a good enterprise.

As dad grew older he developed a deep, resonant speaking voice, probably from his love of singing. He eventually played in a dance band as a drummer and singer and that is where he met my mother, Marie Picard. They both went to Chemawa but never meet there. Later, he and his brother, Pete who was also a singer, played for many country-dances around Eastern Washington. With that voice he could hold an audience spellbound because he spoke fluently with a sprinkle of big English words that sounded good but most people couldn't interpret. His lifetime ambition was to learn as many English words as he could. He was also fluent in both Yakama and Wenatchee dialects. He loved to joke and you never knew when he might spring one on you. He did this one time that people still talk about today. It was when he spoke at the Salmon Festival one fall at the Leavenworth fish hatchery. He was asked to address the audience in his native Wenatchee tongue. He stood up and looked around the audience and quickly surmised that most of them were of European descent so he began his speech in a loud resonant voice. He spoke for several minutes before smiles started showing up, especially on the tribal members present. He was speaking deceptively fluent German complete with a guttural accent. Many of the words had the same guttural sound as the Wenatchee language. When he saw his ruse was discovered he quickly reverted to the Wenatchee language and mockingly apologized for his deception. He then spent a few minutes delivering a flowery speech in Indian and thanked [Lam Lampt] them for listening. He was given an enthusiastic applause.

Later in life he was always called upon to say a prayer or talk about Indian culture.

His passion, besides education or maybe because of it, was truthfulness. He said in the old days members could be expelled from the tribe for intentional lying. He said that today it is the norm. He thought you could only believe half of what anybody says and you don't know which half. He felt so strongly about it he wrote a short essay:

PUBLIC SPEAKING

As to composition and structure of the speech, the rules of that art maybe summarized thus:

1. Speak <u>only</u> when you have something to say.
2. Speak <u>only</u> what you believe to be true.
3. <u>Prepare thoroughly</u>.
4. Be <u>clear.</u>
5. <u>Stick</u> to your subject.
6. Be <u>fair.</u>
7. Be <u>brief.</u>

FAITH – Speak when you have something to say. Be sure that you have a message to deliver. Speak inspired. Sincerity. Never tell an audience what you do not believe or are indifferent about. It is immoral and worse. It makes you a public liar from lowest point of view. To speak against convictions or without convictions is fatal to speaker. Sooner or later, the public "gets on" to the situation. The speaker's influence is impaired. No matter how talented the speaker is, if he is not in earnest he can lose public influence.

Be not inconstant, and be felicitous. Use no trickery. It's obvious politicians are the worst offenders but the news media and anyone who has an axe to grind also falls prey to the temptation of lies.

It would be a better world if today's politicians took his advice.

In the fall of 1980 Dad was asked to go to Lake Wenatchee to look for areas that had previously grown huckleberries. He and T.B. Charley rode horses to Raging Creek on the Chiwawa Ridge. The picture shows Dad on Dusty, a Forest Service horse overlooking the valley. The picture was taken by Heather Murphy of the Forest Service.

Frank Matsura was a Japanese photographer who stayed in Okanogan taking pictures of Indians and early pioneers. My family appeared in many of them. JoAnn Roe published a book about Matsura in 1981 entitled *Frank Matsura – Frontier Photographer*. My grandfather Koxit George's picture is on page 48, taken in 1910 at St. Mary's Mission. Another probably more famous one, taken in Okanogan, is on page 128 in that book and Chapter Six Lahompt in this book. I had it enlarged and hung with the other tribal Chiefs in the Council chambers. On page 129 is another well-known picture of dad in a fur coat when he was about four years old [1910]. It is also in Chapter Eight Moyese of this book. Unfortunately Frank died about 1913 or he would have taken many more pictures.

The Japanese honored Frank with a film they came to Omak to make between February 11, 1982, and July 2, 1983. It was in Japanese with English captions. Dad was in it and became a star. The picture at the beginning of this chapter Nine was taken during the making of the film at Omak Lake. The filming ran into problems when it rained for several days continuously, very unusual for our area during July. But it gave the film crew the opportunity to get to know my folks.. They were all in the folks' small doublewide in Kartar Valley but were entertained with Dad's stories. He didn't speak Japanese as well as German but he managed.

It was sort of ironic because Dad first encountered the Japanese in 1946 while in Japan. It was just after we dropped the atomic bomb on Nagasaki that ended World War II. He was an SP [Shore Patrol] for the Navy and assigned to keep people out of the devastated city. He took that memory home with him and welcomed the chance to rectify some of damage we did to the Japanese. He felt his was a small but sincere gesture. It was confirmed by the signature of the film crew in his copy of Frank's book. Some of the Japanese members' comments: Jake Yamada said "Frank Matsura was the greatest photographer of Japan and I met many nice people in Omak and Okanogan" Tadao Hayakawa, the director said, "Thank you" and signed it on 7/2/83.

Hirshi Jamigata signed it in Japanese but said "To the great Chief [Moses George]" in English.

Nothing contrasts the Indian Way with the modern world more than the work of archeologists. We seem to be at the opposite ends of the spectrum. A case in point is the discovery of the Clovis point in East Wenatchee. That area is part of the land our tribe ceded under duress. We had used it for thousands of years. As recently as Chief Moses' time, the Columbia Confederacy had many camps there. After World War II my folks bought a house with five acres and moved to East Wenatchee in 1948. Their house was a mile or two from the Clovis dig. The story is best told by several Tribal Tribune and Wenatchee World articles I wrote at the time.

SOFTLY SPEAKING - May 17, 1988 - We are here to stay.

A few weeks ago a team of archeologists excavated some Clovis points in East Wenatchee. My dad, who is an elder of our Tribe, says these points should be named the Wenatchee points after our aboriginal ancestors who lived in the area at least 11,500 years ago.

Our ancestors were nomadic hunters and root gatherers who made a reasonably comfortable living traveling up and down the Columbia River with the seasons. They only took what they needed to survive and were very careful not to pollute the air and water which was so critical to their welfare.

They were the original environmentalists and conservationists. They didn't need technology and lengthy engineering reports to tell them when they were doing something wrong; they just used common sense. We, as their descendants, are living proof that their logic was valid.

Typical of their common sense technology was the below grade houses they built along the riverbanks. These houses were warm in the winter and cool in the summer. Modern architects are now promoting such houses to help conserve electricity and reduce heating costs. Yet in the 1950s and '60s power companies were promoting electric heat in homes to increase their sales. This is a vivid example of excessive economic development finally being moderated by conservation.

When the dams were built on the Columbia River they ruined our traditional fishing sites which were the heart of our economy. No thought was given to replacing our economy. The only goal was to produce as much electricity as possible. Now excess power has to be sent to California because we can't use it all in the Northwest. We don't have an economy so we can't afford to buy the electricity that is generated on our own reservation. We "sacrificed" our fish for this.

But some of us have become educated in the way of the New World. We have learned how to develop a new economy on the river such as our houseboat/marina activity and, although not as good as the old one, it is showing signs of improving. We have learned to be wary of any new development because of the environmental impact. We have learned how to hire expensive lawyers and engineers to do the proper analysis and write the proper reports to tell others what we know, as did our ancestors, from common sense.

Now descendants of the New World are telling us we have learned their way too well and are yelling foul because of our environmental concerns about the proposed resort at Crescent Bay near Grand Coulee Dam. They are saying we should not use their methods against them and that we should "cooperate." To our ancestors "cooperate" meant to give up their homes, land, water, fish, and their very existence for "progress." Many of our ancestors lived in Wenatchee but were forced to the Colville Indian Reservation because New World people wanted to live in Wenatchee. We are now at our last refuge and cannot retreat anymore. For our descendants to exist we cannot make any mistakes in judgment so we have to be very careful.

This is not to say that we aren't willing to cooperate with our neighbors. But who are our real neighbors and who are the carpetbaggers? Even the people who built the dams are gone now with an occupational force left behind to maintain the "conquered" river. Our neighboring towns, whether they like it or not, have to turn to us for a catalyst to boost the areas' economy. We are certainly willing to cooperate with them but not with the fast-talking outsiders who are looking for a quick profit at our expense.

So it boils down to who is the most sincere in saying "We are here to stay," us, or an out-of-state developer who is making grandiose plans and promises to financial backers that he can build a resort/marina at a cheap enough cost to make them a profit. Time will tell.

As always, your friend and Councilman from the Omak District.

Wendell George

World photo/Mike Bonnicksen
Colville Tribal Elder Moses George, center, prays for dig director Michael Gramly, right

CLOVIS POINT DISCOVERY
1987-1990

In the May 17, 1988, issue of my Speaking Softly article called "We are here to stay" I said "A few weeks ago a team of archeologists excavated some Clovis points in East Wenatchee. My dad, who is an elder of our Tribe, says these points should be named the Wenatchee points after our aboriginal ancestors who lived in the area at least 11,500 years ago."

The Clovis point discovery was a symbolic event for our tribe. It gave us a tie to our past that, up until that discovery, we only knew by stories handed down from generation to generation. You can imagine how much is lost when retold 575 times over 11,500 years [assuming 20 years per generation]. It is a wonder anything survived. But some things were written. We have hieroglyphics up and down the Columbia River. They are still subject to interpretation but they do tell a story that has been undistorted by time.

For example, the rayed arc of halo is a common feature in the Columbia River Basin and extends as far north as British Columbia. The most common interpretation is that it represents a person of high status and a special person called a shaman. The so-called "high" status was derived from the Western Culture. Native people could all achieve spiritual power if they wished.

Even today anyone can achieve it if they work at it. The symbol really depicts the Sun energy coming to man in the form of spirals. It is the connection of the Spirit World to the Physical World.

In 1987 some orchard workers were digging an irrigation ditch and discovered a cache of artifacts almost 12,000 years old. It was dated sometime after the Glacier Peak eruption 11,250 years ago. The artifacts included some rare Clovis points including a 9-inch fluted one, which is the largest ever discovered. These were thought to be a ritual site where First Americans performed rites of passage such as birth, death, manhood, and marriage. The cache included 30 stone pieces, including 14 finished spear points, the most ever found at one site.

The Colville Confederated Tribes asked Dr. Michael Gramly to stop the dig and said they would stage a sit-in if he didn't. Governor Booth Gardner requested a week delay to see if an agreement could be worked out. It wasn't and the sit-in was held on Monday October 22, 1990.

About 100 Indians showed up including most of the fourteen-member Tribal Council, some elders, women and children, and sympathizers.

Gramly, wearing a bulletproof vest, locked himself inside the seven-foot high chain-link fence surrounding the site.

"It's a sad day for American science isn't it when one has to wear a bulletproof vest?" Gramly asked no one in particular.

He said he locked the gate to protect the site from anyone who would molest it. A pit containing artifacts was covered with about five layers of orchard prop poles.

The day was cool, but not uncomfortable. Gramly was plenty warm in his light jacket over his bulletproof vest. He also felt secure behind a seven-foot chain link fence around the Richey Clovis archaeological dig site. He was comforted with the knowledge that the sheriff and five deputies were on site with a sixteen-member riot-squad nearby at the Pangborn Airport.

He instinctively moved back as the hundred-plus group of Indians started mingling around the site. But no hostilities erupted. The Indians stood with protest signs and bowed their heads as tribal elder Moses George gave an opening prayer [a tribal custom for any notable event]:

"We ask this day to give us your blessing. To erase a shame that has been put on our race. Some people believe we came over a land bridge, but we know if ever there was a falsehood that was one. We grew up here out of the ground.

"There are no arrows, lances or M-16's among us. We came in peace, dear Lord…How can someone come here from across the country and dig to put items on display. We never go into a non-Indian cemetery to dig up relics and put them on display. We came smiling yet our hearts are bleeding."

At one point, tribal leaders moved close and spoke to Gramly. Tribal Chairman Jude Stensgar shook Gramly's hand through the fence, asked a question or two and then asked if it would be all right for George to pray for him.

Gramly said it was.

"Those responsible for burying their lances, Great Spirit today we hope we are not desecrating this wonderful hallowed dirt," George began. He closed in his native language and then said to Gramly, "God bless you. May He keep your heart straight."

Gramly turned away misty-eyed when George finished. Gramly later took off his bulletproof vest. There was no need for it or the six sheriff's deputies present and the sixteen backups waiting at the nearby airport. The National Guard had even been put on alert for possible action.

Wenatchee Indians hadn't fought since our Chief Quitenenock was killed in a battle directly across the Columbia River with miners in 1858. We are a peaceful people.

REFLECTIONS

The issue polarized the local residents. Some wanted the scientists to proceed; others supported the Indians' concern over the possible desecrating of their ancestors. I finally wrote a letter to the editor of the Wenatchee World, published on December 3, 1990 titled: Science not needed at Clovis dig.

The aftermath of Dr. Gramly's visit leaves us with an image: contemporary Indians with no appreciation of scientific research trying to stop the Clovis Dig; of local people who, through Dr. Gramly's misrepresentation, are convinced that Indians should be pushed aside in the interest of science.

Before you grab your pen to make an angered response, let me clarify. We did not expect to stop the dig but did hope to include provisions for safekeeping of human remains and artifacts.

In the 1890s my great grandfather, Chilcosahaskt, had to move his family's gravesites from Orondo to Entiat to protect them. Many of our graves have been robbed by artifact hunters [see Aug. 12, 1954 Wenatchee World article on Indian skull collection]. Chief Moses' personal belongings that were buried with him were found in a New Zealand museum. The Smithsonian still has the remains of some of our people. Our own museum has had to purchase artifacts from private collections that came from burial sites.

Second, the dig site does not have to be a grave to be sacred. To us it is similar to pyramids, which have a spiritual value that cannot be measured in scientific terms. According to our legends these sites were carefully selected and revered to keep nature's balance. The throwaway society we live in has not given us confidence that this balance will be maintained.

And, finally, we question the motives of the hurry-up methods used by Dr. Gramly. This is not consistent with the slow, methodical approach used by other archeologists and actually endangers proper analysis. We, as much as anyone, want to learn from this dig if it can be done with dignity and respect for our ancestors.

Add to this the underlying profit motives of those involved and you have exploitation of a business opportunity rather than scientific research.

Science alone cannot prove the answer to the mysteries of creation because it ignores the spiritual. Native Americans, and others, can discern much from this site without analyzing physical evidence. Our spiritual beliefs are based on intuitive knowledge that needs no physical evidence.

<u>All science can do for us is to verify what we already know.</u>

I wrote this article for the Wenatchee World partly out of frustration because I was no longer on the Tribal Council and partly because of my deep feeling for our tribe. This was a classical conflict between science which dealt only with the physical and our collective tribal customs which are primarily spiritual.

My dad always disputed the archeologists' theory of the land bridge when he had an opportunity. Vine Deloria Jr. made the same argument in his 1995 book Red Earth, White Lies. He tied it in with tribal creation stories. Even the scientists are not in total agreement on the land bridge theory. Some are more prone to believe the Eastern people went island hopping when the glaciers receded. All their theories are oriented to physical happenings and do not include a psychic transfer of knowledge. The ability to "tune in" to the "Universal Consciousness" was predominant in both Eastern and American Indian cultures. The monks of Tibet travel all over with ESP and observe other cultures and happenings. This could work both ways.

There are many similarities to both cultures. Is this coincidence or intentional? We'll see as we move into the contemporary phases of our family history.

Exploratory Phase

My early years were a jumble of one move after another. Soon after my birth at my grandfolks' house at Owhi Lake we joined dad at the Coyote Creek survey camp. I remember:

*Cold showers in the community bath house.

*First phone call wondering how dad could fit in that small box.

Then my dad did survey work at Grand Coulee Dam and I remember:

*Beating a blue racer snake out of the hole next to our house.

*Mother shooting at cows in her garden with her .22 Special.

*Riding in a Model A convertible speeding at 30 mph.

*Seeing the turned-over outdoor toilets after Halloween.

My dad then worked for the BIA and we lived at the Agency where I:

*Missed the bus home after my first day at school.

*Lived in a two bedroom house with bathroom, water, and lights.

We then moved to the Fort Hall reservation for my second school year.

*I shot at and missed rabbits with a .22 rifle.

*My folks listening to reports of the Japanese bombing Pearl Harbor on Sunday December 7, 1941.

That changed our lives forever because my dad worked for the Corps of Engineers and joined the Seabees. I bounced around schools in Mount Vernon, Bellingham, Cutbank, Montana and back to Nespelem for the third grade.

Then I remember Mark Twain once said; "Every boy should have a slingshot that he made from scratch." If he didn't say it, he should have. I wanted a slingshot just like my cousin Calvin's.

He was good at making things. He could do everything better than I could or so it seemed. This could have been because he was thirteen and I was only seven. His slingshot would shoot straight and far. He could shoot big rocks and hit tin cans at twenty-five paces. I couldn't even pull the big rubber bands that he made from truck tires. So I decided I had to build one of my own.

As I was tagging around behind him I asked, "Will you help me make a slingshot like yours?"

"If it was like mine you couldn't even shoot it."

"I mean like yours but smaller so I could shoot it."

"Go away, Sonny, I'm busy."

"Busy doing what? You're just shooting at those tin cans."

"I'm practicing so I can hit a moving target."

"Please help me?"

"You can make your own just by copying mine."

He had a point. A slingshot only has three parts: the "Y" crotch, the two rubber bands and the leather pouch for holding the rock missile.

So I started looking around kkiya Grandma's [mothers' side] Grandma's house for the parts. We spent a lot of time at our Grandma's because our parents were working away from home. Calvin and his twin sister, Cleo, were there until they went away to boarding school at Chemawa. Although she lived on a farm Grandma didn't have very many chores for us to do so we had plenty of time on our hands.

The "Y" crotch was hard to find from our limited selection of willow trees with the right size limbs. To shoot straight, the "Y" had to be even on each side. I must have inspected dozens of willows before I found a balanced branch. To cut the willow I had to use an old rusty knife that I found. It wasn't very sharp so I had to saw the limb. My uncle sharpened his scythe with a wheel you turned by peddling it like a bicycle. I was too small to peddle it. Calvin wouldn't let me use his good sharp knife. I didn't realize it at the time, but it wasn't because of stinginess. He just didn't want to get in trouble with our grandma if I cut myself, which he was sure I would do.

I then notched, just like Calvin did, the two ends of the "Y" so they would hold the rubber bands from slipping.

Finally, I cut eyelets out of the leather pouch so I could loop the other end of the rubber bands through it and tie the loop. I did this by doubling up the leather and cutting it with scissors. The scissors I sneaked from Grandma's sewing basket.

After several tries I finally built a slingshot that worked. I practiced for hours trying to hit tin cans in the front yard. I never seemed to get any better.

Then one day Calvin took me with him to the pond near the barn. We laid in the brush and tulles waiting for the ducks to land as they did every day. Finally, they flew right over us and we each shot into the middle of the flock. At least I did, but I suspect Calvin actually aimed because he hit one and it fell into the pond.

Calvin whistled for his dog, who came running and enthusiastically jumped in the pond and splashed [his version of swimming] after it. But before he reached it, the duck recovered and flew away, quacking and scolding us for our intrusion.

But we didn't mind. We just leaned back and looked up into the clear, blue sky and enjoyed the rest of the summer, which always seemed too short.

After a while we grew tired of shooting slingshots so Calvin somehow got a .22 revolver for plinking. It had a short, four-and-a-half- inch barrel that made it difficult to shoot accurately. We would walk the mile or two to our Uncle Bill's ranch and shoot at mud hens in the ponds. They were never in any danger because we couldn't hit them. In fact we usually didn't hit close enough to scare them away.

My twin cousins Calvin & Cleo holding me, me riding horses.

I stayed with my Kkiya grandmother [mother's mother] in Nespelem during the fourth grade. My folks bought the three room house in Nespelem for $400, which is where Grandma and I stayed. It had an outhouse like all the others in Nespelem. By mutual consent, nobody noticed the blanket substituting for a door from the bedroom to the living room. I slept on the couch in the living room next to the wood stove. The other room was the kitchen with a table for two.

We moved to Seattle in 1945 after my dad joined the Navy Seabees. My mother went to work for Boeing as an electrician installing electrical wiring in B-17s, and B-29s. I went to three different schools during my fifth and sixth grade years.

After World War Two my dad had trouble finding a job when he got out of the Navy. So I spent the seventh grade at Nespelem with my grandma and my Uncle Pete and Aunt Laura after Grandma fell and broke her kneecap. Dad finally took a job in Wenatchee with the State Highway Department. Wenatchee is the aboriginal home of our tribe. I moved there in the fall of 1947.

Since my dad was an engineer my folks just assumed I would take all the math and science offered. They expected me to be an engineer, too.

In the ninth grade I discovered the library on Mission Street in Wenatchee. I would go in and browse. It was about six miles to the city center from where we lived, so I would have to either hitchhike or ride my bike. There wasn't much traffic in those days so it was mostly hiking. One day I started researching careers and learned that engineers were in demand and were one of the highest paid professions. Electrical engineers made up to $10,000 per year, which was a fortune in those days. So that's what I decided to be. Math and science were pre-requisites, and I took them all.

I had discovered girls at the same time and became distracted in my ninth grade algebra class. At midterm I came home with a D on my report card. My dad was extremely disappointed, but he didn't say anything. He just wouldn't talk to me. That hurt more than any physical punishment. It was a wakeup call. I improved my grade by the end of the semester. In high school I got all A's or B's in math and science.

My best sport was baseball. My batting average for three years was .333, but my junior year was the best. Coach Jack Barnes made me the leadoff hitter. I especially remember the game we had against Yakima at their home field. They were one of the best teams in the state so it was a big challenge for us.

I was facing one of the best pitchers in the state. Chuck Rabung had a hopping fastball and a wicked curve, both hard to see let alone hit. And if that wasn't enough, four major league scouts were in the stands to watch him.

Before the game started Coach Barnes called me over and put his arm around me and said a ball hit to the right of the light pole fifty feet in from the left field foul line was a home run and to the left only a double. I laughed at him and said, "Coach, don't worry about it I'm not going to hit it over the fence on either side!"

He replied, "As the lead-off hitter, you will set the pace!

My vision became crystal clear as he started his windup. Everything became silent and I saw only his arm. I was in the "ZONE." I calmly watched the ball as it left his hand. The ball seemed as big as a watermelon. I had already started my swing to meet the ball in front of the plate.

The ball was about shoulder level, but I had already decided to swing at the first pitch. I felt, not heard, the ball hit my bat. It seemed soft but I immediately knew I hit the "sweet spot." It sailed beautifully high in the air in a perfect arc right at the light pole. I couldn't tell at first which side it would go to, but I knew it was over the fence.

I started running to first base while I watched the ball sail over the fence just to the left of the light pole. I pretended I didn't see it and went past second towards third. The base umpire waved me back to second.

So I stood at second in total silence. My team was too surprised to yell and, of course, the fans were all from Yakima and were too shocked. But I didn't care, I had set the pace.

It was a good season all the way around. One day after baseball practice that spring my teammate, Pat Fogerty, offered to take me by the tennis courts. On a whim, he said "Let's go by the tennis courts. There's someone I would like you to meet."

I went along because it was on the way back to our baseball lockers anyway. We stood by the fence around the courts watching her volley with her partner. I didn't know that much about tennis but I could tell she had a strong, decisive stroke.

Barbara was everything Pat said she was. Tall, athletic and good-looking. Of course in high school we always said we were looking for someone with a "good personality." I didn't know about that because I hadn't met her yet. Looking back, I think this was an example of synchronicity. As Carl Jung said, there are no coincidences. Things just fall into place and make other things happen.

We just said hello through the fence after Pat introduced us. That was that for the moment.

While we were courting I brought Barbara up to the Rez. I was showing off just like any young buck courting his life mate. I told her we were going to live off the "fat of the land." First we went to Gold Creek up by Moses Mountain, which is north of Nespelem, isolated and no traffic at that time. The only problem was I couldn't catch any fish, so we were pretty hungry. I went to see my Uncle Bud [Emery Picard] at Owhi Flats where my grandma used to live. We bummed some food and I borrowed his .30-30, which is my favorite gun. While we were there we saw his beautiful stallion, very tall and kind of a blue-gray. Barbara wanted to go for a ride so Uncle Bud saddled up two horses. The one he picked for her was a nice, tame, small, nondescript mare. He suggested that I ride the stallion because he liked to run.

Of course, as soon as we got out of sight Barbara wanted to trade horses. I guess these were her alpha-male genes talking. I couldn't talk her out of it so we traded horses.

She got on big blue and he took off running. I got on the little mare and couldn't get her out of second gear. I yelled at Barbara to pull up on the reins and turn him. There was a barbed-wire fence just a few yards ahead. She had trouble stopping him because I think he clamped his teeth down on the bit. I kept kicking my horse to no avail and started imagining the worst case scenario. I could see in my mind's eye Barbara and the horse being tangled up in the fence and all cut up. She finally turned the horse just before reaching the fence. As I came up with my pony she started reading me the riot act for letting her get on such a wild horse. I didn't say anything and assumed that was the end of our short ride.

My uncle smiled when we came back so soon. He knew exactly what we did and the result. He admitted the horse was a racehorse and knew nothing else.

The next day we went up Central Peak hunting for deer. We were typical road hunters and didn't see anything. Finally, a pheasant started across the road about 150 feet ahead of us. I got out and said I was going to shoot it. She said,

"With a .30-30? There'll be nothing left of it."

"I'll aim for the head. That's only sporting."

She smiled and reminded me when she, Pat Fogerty and I were up Number Two Canyon near Wenatchee and I wanted to shoot a cigarette out of Pat's mouth with my .22 single shot.

"Yeah, I remember you yelling because you thought I was going to try it and fully expected me to hit Pat instead."

"Pat was so macho that he went along with it like he had full confidence in you."

"You made so much noise that I gave up and told Pat to stay back and I put the cigarette out 100 paces by itself. Remember what happened?"

"You big show off! You split the cigarette in two!"

"Yeah, with one bullet. I've always said you only need a single-shot rifle unless you wanted to get more than one deer."

"So go ahead, smarty pants. Let's see you do it again."

Luckily the pheasant waited while we were having that conversation. I leaned on the car, took careful aim and noticed my front sight covered the entire head of the pheasant. I shot anyway. The pheasant fell over and we went up the road to retrieve it. I missed the head but creased his neck just enough to get him. We ate well that day.

We then went to Owhi Lake to catch some good Eastern Brook trout. Unfortunately it was midsummer and the fish weren't biting. My friend, Dorland Palmer, came over to visit. His folks were staying at the only cabin on the lake, just about a mile away. We started telling Stick Indian stories and then went down to see if his mother would cook us dinner. For some reason, Barbara stayed at our camp. At that time of the year nobody was on the lake. I guess I stayed too long because when I came back Barbara was hopping mad. She said,

"You told me all those scary stories on purpose, didn't you?"

"No, not really."

"Then you waited until almost dark to come back. The trees were talking to me and I could hear all kinds of noises in the brush. I was scared to death!"

"Sorry, but come on down to the house. Adeline [Dorland's mother] is fixing a big meal for us." That is how we lived off the fat of the land.

Finally, the summer before my junior year at college, our three-year romance reached a decision point. Barbara quit talking to me. I would go her house and she would leave. I wound up talking to her sister, Penny. Several times I would throw rocks at her bedroom window just like in Romeo and Juliet.

That didn't impress her. I went to visit her at Lake Wenatchee where she was a camp counselor, and she rowed out to the middle of the lake to get away from me.

I don't know when she changed her mind. All I know is we got married on Thanksgiving weekend on Friday November 26, 1954 and had a one-weekend honeymoon before returning to college.

EXPLORATORY

In 1973 the Colville Confederated Tribes were just coming out of a long period of debating whether to terminate BIA supervision of our Rez or even liquidating its assets. The present Colville Business Council had changed from a termination to development majority during that time. They started searching for ideas on how to get started.

At a Council meeting discussing economic development Lucy Covington, Council Chairwoman and newly given the title of Roving Ambassador, looked at me before expressing the desires of the entire Tribal Council,

At the Open House for Dedication of the Tribal Building, September 19, 1974.

Left: Planning Committee Chairman Lucy Covington. (The Committee is in charge of the
planning for the Center at Chief Joseph Dam.

Right: Tribal Planner Wendell V. George, for
the Center at Chief Joseph Dam.

"Would you come help us develop the Reservation? We need your experience to get things going."

I was pleased for the offer but I had been building a career with Boeing for fifteen years and it wouldn't be easy to leave. But Lucy was persistent and she had already recruited Sherwin Broadhead by coaxing him to leave Washington, D.C. to become our Agency Superintendent. She was making a big change on our Reservation. It could be the start of something good.

So I made a counter offer, "What if I asked my bosses for a three-month leave of absence to come over and get you started?"

Lucy turned to the other thirteen members of her council and raised her eyebrows. Roy Seylor and George Muesy from Inchelium nodded their heads.

Joe Kohler, also of Inchelium and father of Dale, who was to be a long-term Councilman from Omak and one of my closest associates, said, "That would be great!"

Hank George [a second cousin] from Omak added facetiously, "Do we need another George?"

Mel Tonasket from Omak just grinned. The others acquiesced.

As I was traveling back to Seattle my rear tire kept going click-click. Darn rock caught in the tread. I knew it would bother me until the rock came out. I picked it up on the Reservation roads which were mostly gravel. It reminded me of a story my qqana grandma [fathers' side] told. She said people's lives are just like a rock caught in a car's tire. I don't know how she came up with that because she didn't drive and very seldom even rode in a car.

But her analogy was good. She said the pebble would gradually be worn down as it scrapped on the road. That was just like people's lives as they experienced hard knocks. The only way a rock could avoid that is to sink further into the tire tread which is to say, in peoples' case, to remove yourself from outside experiences. That would make your life very dull because you wouldn't "see the world" so to speak. Real adventurers would spin themselves out of the tire tread and explore what's beyond the road bed.

I guess I was a real adventurer. I had already proved that by moving my family all over the United States while working for Boeing after graduating from Washington State University with a Bachelor of Science degree in electrical engineering. We first moved to Seattle where I helped design the telemetry system for the BOMARC ground-to-air defense missile. I also worked on the Dyna-Soar Orbiter bomber and the Minuteman intercontinental missile. We then moved to Huntsville, Alabama, to work on the Saturn V booster vehicle for the Apollo Program. That turned into another move to Washington, D.C. to help NASA manage the Apollo Manned Space Program. It was pretty heady stuff until I moved back to Seattle and started working on weapons systems again, the B-1 bomber and two short assignments on an anti-submarine proposal and the Morgantown automatic [driverless] bus system.

The attraction of going back to the Tribe was to help people instead of building things to hurt them. I was tired of working on killing systems that we hoped to never use.

So that was it. In April of 1973 I started what was to be a 90-day leave of absence to work full-time for the Tribes. I had been commuting for over a year from my place in Newport Hills to Nespelem to help the Tribes on a part-time basis. Since the tribe didn't have any funds to pay me expenses I got a grant from the State [Part of the Jobs Now grant offered to tribes by Governor Evans].

It all started in 1969 while I was in Washington, D.C., working for Boeing on the Apollo Program. One day I decided to walk across the mall from my office in L'Enfant Plaza to the BIA Headquarters. Louie Bruce was the BIA Commissioner then and I took a chance that I would get to talk to him, if only briefly. His assistant was Sherwin Broadhead and, of course, Sherwin knew Lucy from our Council, so we hit it off well from the start. I did talk to Louie Bruce and later Sherwin told me Louie enjoyed the conversation.

From there I eventually moved back to Seattle with Boeing and began working with the Tribes.

One of my first involvements was with other urban Indians in the Governors Indian Advisory Committee, which Governor Evans created.

GOVERNOR DAN EVANS 1974

105

He told us to organize anyway we wanted and he would meet with us once a month in Olympia. Eventually, it was his assistant, James Dolliver [who later became a State Supreme Court judge] who met with us but we felt we had a voice into the State government.

We had three subcommittees: [1] Reservation tribes, [2] Non-Reservation tribes, and [3] Urban Indians. I talked too much and became Chairman of the Urban Indians. Ken Hansen of the Samish tribe was Chairman of the Non-Reservation. Mel Tonasket was Chairman of the Reservation tribes. The entire Committee elected a Chairman who acted as the spokesperson. Wayne Williams of the Tulalip tribe was chairman the first year I was there. I became Chairman the second year.

We would meet at least once a month to prepare for our meeting with the Governor. It was somewhat of a hardship on me because I had to take leave from Boeing to attend the meetings. One of our significant accomplishments was the disbursement of the one million dollar Jobs Now fund created by the Governor and the State Legislature. At that time that was a large amount of money. It was the first time the State actually became proactive to help tribes improve their economy. The State didn't put any strings on it except it was to be used to create jobs; we could use it anyway we liked. That was a problem in itself as it was the basis of a tremendous disagreement between all Indians. The Reservation tribes felt they should get the biggest share because they had more Indians, especially those in need and the Non-reservation and Urban Indians didn't have any infrastructure to build on. We finally arrived at a minimum base given to everyone of $50,000, which was enough to hire at least one person and provide him or her with an office and expenses. This plan established the appropriation floor but we still had to develop a formula for the greater needs of the larger population reservations. To reach as many people as possible we distributed the balance of the funds in proportion to population. It was a win-win and everyone was happy.

My 90-day leave of absence from Boeing eventually turned into a year, and one day a personnel representative called me, "Are you going to come back or shall we make this permanent?"

After talking it over with Barbara we decided to stay. Our boys were doing fine in school and we didn't want to make another change so soon. So I resigned from Boeing to stay on the Rez.

I was hoping this move would help our children learn about our ancestors. We bought a house in Coulee Dam that was big enough for our family, which had grown to eight after Rob was born in Bellevue on August 12, 1969. Rick and Mike were sophomores in high school; Kerry was in junior high, Matt in grade school, Kathy just starting school and Rob a preschooler.

In 1972 the tribe had only a handful of employees. Harry Owhi was the executive director with a couple of secretaries such as Judy Whetan to handle Council and administration correspondence. The enrollment officer was Eddie Palmanteer Jr. and the employment officer was Mel White. They ran the main tribal offices.

The Bureau of Indian Affairs [BIA] handled the major functions such as forestry management, realty, land operations, credit, range, and roads.

The tribe itself had no experience in developing or managing enterprises. It was a formidable job to create a culture of the tribe doing things for themselves.

The first breakthrough was the Indian Action Team [IAT] program that was an unusual innovation of the BIA. It was the result of three Indians, Lee Cook, Ernie Stevens, and Sandy McNaff, who were given free rein by Louis Bruce, the Mohawk Commissioner of Indian Affairs.

Contracts were awarded to tribes to train their members in the building trades. We got our contract first because Lucy Covington did some hard lobbying with the BIA. The idea was to develop a corps of trained people who could develop their reservation by starting or attracting new businesses. We eventually started our own construction company.

The Colville IAT was complete with a new building to house its activities and an adequate budget to hire instructors and perform the necessary administration when I came aboard.

My first task was to convince the Colville Business Council to invest in a business that would create jobs. Unemployment on the Rez was about 60 percent and the available jobs were seasonal, like farm labor and logging. So I put together a business plan and presented it to the Council.

"I would like to present to the Council an opportunity to start a post and pole plant. This fits our business plan of developing wood products. We can get $40,000 from a state grant if we match it in some way to provide ten percent of the cost of the project. I know of a used post peeler that we can get for $4,500. If we allocate $4,500 to buy the post peeler we have our matching so we can apply for the grant. For the size of that operation we could sell all the posts right on the Rez." The Council debated for quite a while. They had never invested in a business before. I have to give Joe Kohler, who was the chairman of the Land and Forestry Committee at the time, credit for helping me get it through the Council. He had a cattle operation in Inchelium and knew how to run a business.

I had assigned Ernie Clark, a young tribal member just out of college, to work on this project and he did a bang-up job. This was first time the Council invested money in a tribal enterprise. The BIA had run the only business they had, which were log sales. So I thought they would be more comfortable with this enterprise as it was closely related to logging.

Of course, the Council asked the BIA to evaluate our proposal. They said, "It will never work. It is too far away from the market!"

"We have looked at competing P&P plants and they are all close to the raw material source. They are not any closer to the market."

"What makes you think you can compete with existing post plants?"

"We have a big advantage because the tribe owns the resource. The other plants have to buy the raw material."

The raw material came from logs too small for commercial value as lumber. Also we could use the Lodge pole pine that wasn't good material for lumber.

Finally, Joe Kohler said, "How many people will it employ?"

"We will start out with about ten, but that number could grow to thirty or forty if we are successful."

"They would be year around jobs?"

"As much as lumber mills. We would stockpile the logs and peel, cure, and treat them all year."

"Sure would be nice to have that may people working all year. I wouldn't get so many complaints then. Anybody else have any thoughts?"

Another councilman asked, "Where would you put the plant?"

"Out on the flats in Nespelem Valley. We have a lot of tribal land there."

"When could you start?"

"As soon as we get the money. We can buy a used peeler to start with and go from there."

Joe said, "OK, let's see a show of hands. How many for it?"

Roy Seylor from Inchelium was the first to raise his hand. Then George Muesy, Dave Stensgar, and the others gradually did until all those present voted favorably.

Al Aubertin, Council Chairman from Keller who was attending the committee meeting said, "Looks like you got it. Good. We've been talking about this for several months now and I'm tired of hearing about it. Go to it."

So we purchased the post peeler, applied for and received the grant and started the business in Nespelem, the center of the Rez. Several years later, the plant was moved to Inchelium and a $2.5 million EDA grant helped expand the business to employ up to fifty people. It was a boon for Inchelium.

Our council consists of fourteen representatives elected from four districts Omak, Nespelem, Keller, and Inchelium. The only qualification for running for Council is to live in your district for one year proceeding the year you run and to be at least 21 years old. Also they were only paid $25 per diem on days they had business. That wasn't enough for a person with a family to support. So only retired people or persons with spouses who had an income would run for Council. If you worked for the tribe you had to resign your job before you could run. We had a lot of education to do before we could bring our reservation into modern times.

I was getting nowhere until we, along with several other tribes, created an Economic Development Board under the National Congress of American Indians [NCAI]. Sam Cagey, the venerable Chairman of the Lummi tribe, took the initiative after we explained our idea to him. He presented it and got it approved by the NCAI Reps during the convention at San Diego, California.

There were twelve members on the board: Lucy and I from the Colvilles, Mel Sampson from the Yakama tribe [Mel later became Chairman of the Yakama Tribal Council], and a member of the Seneca tribe [Stu Seneca] of New York, Seminoles from Florida [James Billie who later became their Chairman], Passomaquaddy from Kansas [Frank Battese], and several Southwest tribes. We met all over the country including Washington, D.C., introducing tribes to federal offices and opening up opportunities for them. I brought them all up to our reservation one year and toured it. It took two days in a van to drive across our 1.4 million-acre reservation. Except for Mel Sampson, because the Yakamas' is as big as ours, they were all impressed by our big trees.

An offshoot of this was the timber tribes who eventually created their own organization. But before that, BIA attorney Bill Veeder advised us to change a BIA regulation on timber management. Bill Veeder was a water rights attorney who helped us in many ways. He told us that the BIA was taking ten percent of our stumpage as a management fee to manage our own timber for us. This all went back to the BIA central office which balanced their budget, but didn't satisfy the federal government's trust responsibility to provide this service. We got on that one but it still took two years of hard negotiation. At first we thought we needed congressional action but found out that the BIA had the discretion to lower the ten percent fee to zero percent if it wanted. So we requested BIA officials to do so. They countered with the requirement that we spend all the funds on the Reservation on something related to forestry. We had no problem with that since our biggest business was forestry anyway.

This brought in an average of one million dollars annually that we didn't have before. A bonanza. Every year since then we have developed a budget, approved by the Council and BIA.

The first year, 1973, we added an Economic Development Administration [EDA] grant for timber stand improvement, which meant tree thinning. We put about 150 tribal people who didn't have jobs to work. It was a great opportunity but not free of problems. We didn't have anybody trained in management or supervision. With such a workforce, we needed organization. And, of course, everyone thought they were capable of being boss. As a result, we had a large turnover.

I was also manager of the Indian Action Team [IAT]. This was a truly innovative apprenticeship program in the building trades: carpentry, plumbing, electrical, graphic arts, and well drilling. By 1974 our budget had reached $764,745.

After a couple of years we found we were training the same group in all the trades. They just kept rotating through the programs. The BIA wanted to cancel our program and give the funds to a tribe that didn't have IAT.

We had a summit meeting with the BIA in Denver. I presented a pared-down trades training program and added computer programming, which no tribe in the country had in early 1974. They approved a larger budget instead of cutting us back. I quickly started recruiting for the computer programming instructor:

"Ralph, why don't you come to work for us and train our people in computer programming?" Ralph Van Brunt, was a tribal member and a computer programmer for Minneapolis-Honeywell. He eventually did agree to be our instructor. That solved only part of the problem. We used a standard IBM test to determine aptitude for computer programming. We thought we might have to limit our enrollment because everyone would want to enroll. We didn't have to worry because nobody passed the test. But Ralph and I were sure that many of them could learn to program. We enrolled about fifteen or twenty and hoped for the best. It turned out well; all of them learned something about programming, some more than others. All of them went on to better paying jobs. Some went on and graduated from college. This group is now the backbone of our tribe because some operate the IBM AS400 [Glo Simpson]; others have been on the Council, such as Mike Marchand or program managers like Dorothy [Cleveland] Hammer.

But parlaying the ten percent fee into an on-going business was the most difficult. The tendency was to just create jobs and not worry about making it a self-sustaining business. It was another Works Projects Administration [WPA] project like during The Depression. When the funding dried up, there would be no more jobs. I knew that our stumpage had good years and bad years; the fund wouldn't always be there. The BIA had data plotting the timber cut every year and showing major up and down cycles.

Then the Council created Colville Indian Tribal Enterprises [CITE] to explore economic development options. We had a charter but no funds. We had to go to the Council to fund our projects.

Our board was reviewing many options to determine what may be the best to develop for the Tribe. Our options were unlimited but we established, after discussions with the Council, that we would develop our natural resources first.

We first determined that the Reservation had 18,700 acres of agriculture land. Of that 4,500 acres could be used for orchards, grapes or hops.

I'm looking at my twenty-foot hop vines

We test-planted hops with seed we obtained from a hop grower in Yakima Valley. The plants grown in Kartar Valley did very well. We picked the hops and the quality tested good at the Yakima processing plant. A potential hop grower inspected Kartar Valley. He was looking to grow 250 acres of hops. Unfortunately hops were controlled by a consortium in Portland. The rules were that people bid on acreage. At that time the price was high and acreage limited. I also visited Coors brewery in Colorado to find out more about the barley they used in beer. They only used barley that was grown at 7,000 feet elevation.

We also test-planted grapes at several places around the Reservation. It was feasible to grow certain varieties depending on their winter hardiness. We did a comprehensive appraisal of a grape vineyard in conjunction with Dr. Walt Clore, horticulturist from the Washington State University [WSU] Extension Service at Prosser and two professors from WSU. The Bureau of Reclamation offered to develop an irrigation system for a 250-acre vineyard near the Timm Brothers ranch. The grape varieties used were Chardonnay, White Riesling, Cabernet Sauvignon and Merlot. The cash flow indicated the vineyard would be self-sufficient by the seventh year. I was able to get a grant and send William [Joaquin] Cleveland to get a viticulturist degree in California.

We worked with Blatt Brewery from Canada on a plan for them to partner with us. It was feasible but their upper management decided to expand their breweries instead.

I had been writing a Comprehensive Plan for the Tribe as the tribal planner before I became general manager of CITE. It was difficult because the Tribe and BIA did not have a good inventory of our resources.

Because we did not have a handle on our forest inventory, we could not be confident of the annual allowable cut. It was established at 120 million board feet, but there wasn't any real data to back that number up.

The BIA realty office did not have good maps, the roads department did not have good inventory, and the land operations had minimum soil type information.

Because of the Indian cattlemen, the range department managed the range units so they were not over-grazed but their data wasn't recorded.

So I worked with Art Wohl of the BIA Washington, D.C. office to fund a National Resource Information System [NARIS] program by the U.S. Geological Survey to develop up-to-date and state-of-the-art mapping. It was computerized and would provide enough information to do anything you wanted with the land. It was jointly managed with the BIA and was to be for the benefit of all tribes. Colville was one of the first and when it was proven, it was to be operated out of Denver, Colorado, as the central location. The main frame IBM 360 computer was to be eventually installed, but we were using Washington State University's IBM 360 on a time-share basis.

The idea was good but it took too long to develop. It was too much on the leading edge of technology. The limiting factor was the digitizing process. Software and hardware were not advanced enough to get the accuracy, and it was a very time consuming process. Raytheon was our prime contractor and they used the latest systems available. We had difficulty proving the benefits to the end users.

BIA forestry weren't interested at all. They didn't want to change the way they were doing things. They said you have to go out into the forest and count the trees. We weren't trying to change that. What was needed was a way to accumulate all the data and integrate it into a simulation model that could do "what-if" games. This way you could develop strategies for plans to react to drought, fires, economic down turns, bug-infestation and all the other things that you knew would happen. The Okanogan National Forest did develop a forest inventory system when the technology became available a few years later.

Without a good inventory it was difficult to identify what could be developed on the Rez. We received an EDA grant to perform a sawmill feasibility study. It had to use the inadequate BIA data that was available. As a result, the recommendation of the study was for a sawmill that would have an average log diameter of 17½ inches and would be provided 120 million board feet of logs. Neither was to happen in real life.

But the Council wasn't ready for a sawmill. It was too big of an investment. It would cost at least $10 million for a relatively small sawmill. The feasibility study sat on the shelf for several years.

Then in 1979 we had a bumper crop of stumpage. The price was high, and we harvested 130 million board feet of logs. This netted us $29 million for stumpage in one year that was several times normal. The tribe thought this was going to be normal from that point on. The clamor to raise per capita [annual payment to tribal members] was too much to resist. The Council caved and most of the funds were passed on to tribal members. The same thing happened to the $8 million left by the mining company that decided that molybdenum was not feasible to mine.

The Council did manage to put a little in a reserve fund but nothing went into development. So unemployment remained high, about 60 to 70 percent and the Rez was economically stagnant.

A year or two later the timber industry took a downturn. The national economy was in a mess because of the high interest rates of 18 to 22 percent. Nobody could afford to do anything. With no construction, the demand for lumber went to zero. The BIA was offering log sales units that were too large. Sawmills wanted smaller units so they didn't build up their inventory too fast. As a result, there were no bids on any of the sales units that year. Tribal income went to zero.

This put a scare into the Council that motivated them to act. They dusted off the old feasibility study and commissioned another to update it.

I had a consultant from the Forestry Department of the University of Washington, Dr. Barney Dowdle, who recommended that the Tribe sell more timber when the prices were high and less when they were low. The trend was easy to see because the BIA had a graph of total stumpage and prices for every year since logging started on the Rez. It was a curve that peaked every three or four years and, in between, hit a valley every three or four years. It was almost like clockwork. Barney's suggestion was too much for the Council. Chairman Al

Aubertin said, "I couldn't put all those loggers out of work. I used to be a logger myself and I know how I would feel."

Barney replied, "Give them a benefit package. Unemployment payment for the duration. This would be a cost but could easily be paid by the difference in the sales prices."

"Naw, I don't think they would want to just lay around and drink beer. They would want to do something!"

"They could get other jobs. You don't have to follow the state policy of cutting the unemployment benefits if you get another job."

"Really?"

"Yes, really. The state does that because they have limited funds. If you budget it properly your funds would be available."

"Sounds too complicated."

"At first, it looks that way but after you get a system set up it'll work smoothly."

The Council didn't agree with that plan but were amenable to modified versions of it later. Maybe this helped soften the resistance to a tribal sawmill, too.

The exotic was soon replaced by the mundane as we moved into the difficult job of transforming our reservation into a self-sustaining community. First we had to look at our resources and see what kind of economic development would be best for us. Then we could develop a plan to proceed.

One day I was setting quietly in my office at the Indian Action Team building when I got a call from Lucy Covington. She didn't mince words,

"You know that Casey's store burned down in Nespelem, right?"

"Yes, I do."

"It is the only store in this area and we need one. How soon can you put in a tribal store? I know you have been looking at the feasibility."

"Well, we are pretty far along. We have the wholesaler in Spokane doing a preliminary plan for us. We didn't have a deadline."

"Well, you do now and it has to be soon!"

"If we could use the old Council building, we could probably get a small store set up in about two weeks."

"OK, I'll get Council to approve the use of the old Council building and you get moving on the store. We'll expect it to open in two weeks. See you, then."

And she hung up. I listened to the dial tone for a few seconds before I realized what I had done. Two weeks! That's only fourteen days counting weekends!

I called Dwayne Butler into my office and said,

"Dwayne, you have been doing nothing but fooling around with that Army surplus program. How would you like a real assignment?"

"Like what?"

"As manager of the new tribal Trading Post. You have been working with our wholesaler anyway, so this is a natural transition for you."

"Yeah, I think I could do it. When do you want it? Next year, maybe?"

"No, Lucy just called and said we need it in two weeks."

"Two weeks! That's impossible."

"Lucy has a lot of confidence in us. She doesn't think it's impossible. You don't want me to call her back and say we can't do it, do you?"

"No, don't do that. I would hate to see a grown man cry. I'll call my buddy in Spokane and see what they can do."

We hustled for two weeks. We had to clean out the junk stored in the building and set up shelves and stock them. Luckily, a couple of Casey's long time employees, Lorraine Desautel and Bev Morin, were available. They were a big help. Miracle of miracles, we made our deadline.

From there I assigned Greg Wilder and his graphics class the duty of working with Garvey out of Spokane to build a steel Trading Post, 100,000 sq. ft. The tribe appropriated $150,000 for the project. This building still stands and the Trading Post still serves the community. The Tribe also contracted to build the tribal office building, which is still in operation today.

COLVILLE TRIBAL OFFICE

HOW HIGH CAN WE FLY?

"You're kidding, Dwayne. Do you really think I would go to the Council and propose that? They would laugh me out of the Council chambers."

"But think of the benefits. We would be the first tribe with an Air Force. We would put the Colville tribe on the map!"

"Your enthusiasm is infectious but I need a better plan than just arm-waving. What will be the cost to the tribe, how will we get it done and what are the economic benefits, not just the intangibles."

"It is just like I told you. No cost for the helicopters because they have been surplussed by the Army. All we have to do is transport them up here. They tell me the 'copters are already in running condition. I'll inspect them to make sure. We have plenty of funds in the Indian Action Team [IAT] travel budget."

"You haven't said anything about the economic benefits."

"First of all, it would provide fast travel to anywhere on the Rez. We would save a lot of driving time and even get into areas we can't drive to now."

"I like that. Our group studying Lake Rufus Woods could use it for a while. They go up and down that fifty-mile reservoir all the time. Most of it doesn't have road access."

"There you go. And that would only be a start. We could use it for surveying construction sites and maybe even rent them out to fire control during the fire season. They always use helicopters for their 'helitac' crew."

"OK, how will you transport them? By rail to Spokane or Wenatchee and then truck them to the Rez?"

"That's another thing I wanted to talk to you about."

"Oh, oh. Here comes the other shoe."

"You know I can fly. We've been all over together in a Cessna 175. Warm Springs, Pasco, etc. Did you know that Ed Marchand, your carpenter instructor, is also a pilot?"

"No, I didn't."

"Well, he is. My idea is for both of us to go down to the surplus depot in California. They will provide us with an experienced helicopter pilot who will check us out on the two helicopters. He said it would take about two weeks. Then if we pass muster with that old pilot down there, we will fly them back to the Rez."

"Wow, all that after a two-week training period? Dwayne, you're good but not that good!"

"Now wait a minute. I will not fly them unless I feel I can safely do it. And I would do no less for my cousin, Ed. I will not take any chances with him either."

"It's intriguing, Dwayne, but you know as well as I do that the Council is very conservative. They do not take chances, period. I think they will say no."

"But you'll ask them, right? I hear you putting together a winning presentation in your head, just like you always do."

"Come on, Dwayne, let's not pile it too high. This is a small office and we'll both suffocate."

"OK. I'll leave you to mull it over. Remember nothing ventured, nothing gained. Be a hero. See you later."

After he left I thought to myself, how do I get into these fixes? I was just sitting in my office at the IAT building trying to manage a bunch of mavericks. We had a good but undisciplined crew. Dwayne Butler served ten years in the Air Force with much of it spent trying to circumvent rules. He reminded me of a sergeant I met at Eglin Air Force Base when I worked for Boeing who operated the same way.

The idea had merit though. We needed something to motivate the tribe. This could be something to rally around. If he could only pull it off. Could he? If they had an accident, I would be held responsible not Dwayne. I better sleep on it.

I began the next day by reminiscing with Barbara about the Warm Springs trip. That story had been told by Dwayne and Council Chairman Mel Tonasket every chance they had. Dwayne's plan that time was for Mel and me to meet him at Owhi Lake. He would rent a Cessna 175 at Moses Lake and fly it up there. He used the paved road to the lake as a landing strip. It was straight for about a mile but not necessarily flat. We got in and Dwayne's wife, Joann, drove down to the turnoff to flag down any cars that come. We took off with the wing tips just missing the fences on both sides. I waved to Joann, not knowing if I would see her again.

We no sooner got in the air than Dwayne started looking at the map. He studied it for a while and asked Mel, who was sitting beside him, if he could figure out where we were. Mel looked at it and said it would be easier if he would turn the map right side up. I was sitting in the back and figured the smirk on their faces meant they knew something I didn't.

Everything went fine from there until we got to the lower Columbia River. I was dozing in the back noticing that we were barely staying up with the trucks on the highway. Dwayne said it was a strong head wind.

Shortly after that the engines cut out and Dwayne said, "Oh, oh," and Mel turned to look at me with that silly grin of his again. Then Dwayne reached over and switched to the wing tank.

Later Dwayne said we better gas up at The Dalles because his tank showed empty. He made one pass and landed. He filled up and took more than the capacity of the tank. He said he was glad he didn't have to make two passes because we would have run out of gas.

So I talked to the Council about getting two U.S. Army helicopters from the surplus depot. I didn't make a big deal out of it. I just said, "Oh, by the way, we have this opportunity to get these helicopters at no cost to the tribe"

I think all they heard was the no cost part. They didn't care what we did as long as it was no cost. I think Dwayne also primed big Al Aubertin, who was his cousin. Al had a lot of influence with the Council. Al didn't belabor the point he just said, "OK, as long as it doesn't cost anything."

So we were in. Dwayne and Ed flew down to California to learn about helicopters. I worried every minute they were gone. Every day or so Dwayne was to call and give me their progress. They spent a few days in ground school and then started flying around the base. At the end of two weeks they were ready. Dwayne was to call every day then and sooner if they had any problems.

The first day went fine as far as the flying but then I found out only one helicopter had a radio. So they were staying in sight of each other. They didn't know how fast the fuel consumption was so Dwayne called me the second day.

"Hello, Wendell, guess what."

My fear was that they wrecked but I said as calmly as I could, "You forgot your wallet and you want me to wire you some money."

"No, nothing like that, but I did have to make an emergency landing."

"What! Is everything OK? Where's Ed?"

114

"Ed's fine. I'm looking at him now. He is filling up his fuel tank in the middle of an Amoco service station just off I-5. The spectacle of two helicopters filling up here is too much. The traffic is backing up for miles."

"Don't you have to use high test petrol?"

"Yes. That is why it was an emergency. Amoco is the only gas station that has high test. It is their premium gas. When I saw this station I waved to Ed and we headed down. You should have seen the traffic stop for us!"

"Aren't they going to arrest you? Tell me how to get you out of jail. Where are you?"

"Naw, we'll take off before anyone can arrest us. Better go now. Ed's waving that we're all gassed up."

Then I didn't hear from him for a couple of days and was beginning to worry even more. Finally, Ed called me at home.

"Hello, Wendell, have you heard from Dwayne?"

"No, what did you do? Lose him? I thought you would be here by now and I was beginning to worry. When did you last see him?"

"We lost sight of each other this morning and I haven't seen him all day."

"Where are you now?"

"I landed in Almira. I thought it was getting too dark to make it home today."

"Good job, Ed. That was clear thinking. Want me to come out and get you?"

"No. My wife, Thelma, is here and she'll bring me home."

"You're going home to Omak?"

"Yes."

"Stop at my house in Coulee Dam. Maybe Dwayne will call by then."

"OK."

But when Ed and Thelma stopped, Dwayne still hadn't called. He didn't have a phone at Owhi, so I asked Ed if I should drive up to his place to see if he was home. Ed said, "No. He'll call when he is ready." He figured Dwayne was ahead of him enough to get there in the daylight.

The next day I found Dwayne had gone home and landed in front of his house, just to impress his family. He and Ed went out to Almira to get the second helicopter.

Later Dwayne took our police chief, Tim Wapato, and me for a ride over Lake Rufus Woods, just five miles from tribal headquarters. He hovered over the deepest part of the river and said, "You know when you lose the rotors on this thing it drops like a rock. Can you swim?" Tim and I looked at each other and said yes but not this far out from shore.

Our first opportunity to show off our tribal Air Force came when Interior Secretary Rogers Morton came visiting the Rez. This was the first time we had such a distinguished visitor. Ironically, he was to come by helicopter from the Spokane Rez. So we waited on the front lawn of tribal headquarters until the time he was to arrive. Dwayne was piloting my helicopter, and Gene Joseph was riding shot gun. Ed took some councilmen in the other one.

Gene brought his camera so he could take pictures for the memorable occasion. We flew towards the Spokane Rez, just circling over Lake Roosevelt, which connects the two reservations. The Secretary was late so we were in the air a while before we saw three helicopters coming at us. We escorted them in and made a grand landing in front of a sizable audience. After we were on the ground I asked Gene if he got some good pictures and he said, "No, I didn't."

"Why not?"

"I was too scared. I didn't even get the lens cap off."

"Well, better luck next time. You'll be an experienced flyer by then."

"There ain't going to be a next time."

Gene's concern made me realize that we could be in danger. Until then I had been enraptured by the green blanket of pine trees underneath us and our helicopter-to-helicopter approach to greeting the Secretary. Gene was thinking of his future, or maybe the lack of it, and I was just enjoying the moment. Who was the odd one? Probably me.

The helicopters were the talk of the Rez for several months and then it happened.

Ed was landing in front of our IAT building with several of our planners after coming back from Lake Rufus Woods when his rotor started oscillating. The 'copter went up and down a couple of times before it hit the ground and stayed permanently in a heap. Luckily everyone got out with just a few scratches, but the 'copter was totaled.

We now had only half of an Air Force.

I asked Dwayne to do more maintenance on the other one which he did. But a couple of months later he was landing at Owhi with Joann on the ground watching when his stabilizer rotor quit. He started rotating in a circle faster and faster. Luckily, he was close to the ground and just let it drop. He was unhurt but again the 'copter was totaled.

And our Air Force went to zero.

Dwayne talked about the crashes for a few weeks and then started searching for some more surplus helicopters. I said, "No way, Jose. I have less hair than when you started all this and what I do have has turned gray. We were lucky. Let's leave well enough alone, OK?"

"OK, boss, if you say so. It was sure fun while it lasted."

So that was the end of the Exploratory phase. We were now ready to enter the Implementation phase.

REFLECTIONS

Looking back I have mixed emotions. For example, some tribal members were against using atomic energy because they thought it was too dangerous. That may be true for electrical power plants but uranium enrichment plants have no history of being dangerous. The opportunity came to us when the Federal government announced they planned to close their three existing plants and privatize them.

I first became involved on December 8, 1972 when I met with the U.S. Atomic Energy Commissioner Dixie Lee Ray in Washington D.C. She then assigned Gil Cordova to our Advisory Board which included Bechtol Corporation, U.S. Army Corps of Engineers, BOR, State Nuclear Energy, EPA, BPA, and Representative's Mike McCormack and Thomas Foley's office.

In addition to economic development we wanted to commit the use of the Columbia River water to the tribes benefit and to reserve electrical power from the BPA. The plant would cost $1.5 billion with a 15 year pay-off and 15% return on investment. It would hire 5500 construction workers at peak and 1000 people for operation.

We were well on our way until the Feds decided against privatizing because the Japanese were aggressively pursuing it.

This activity did result in the opportunity for me to help Dixie Lee Ray campaign for Governor by taking her around the reservation. She won and gave tribes the recognition we deserve.

KARTAR VALLEY RANCH

"So you're leaving us now?"

"Yes, Lucy, I can't take it anymore. Every day I'm over at the Council chambers justifying my actions. I can't get my job done."

"Well, I know how it is. That's just the way we operate."

"I don't think it will change."

"Maybe not soon but eventually it will. It'll have to if we are going to survive."

116

Lucy had heard I'd decided to leave and came to my house at Coulee Dam to see if she could talk me out of it. She didn't tell me at the time but she was fatally ill. She passed away shortly after that. She lost her next election because her constituents knew she was too sick to carry on and wanted to give her a rest. She didn't look at it that way and would have preferred to stay on to the last.

I helped my folks develop their Kartar Valley ranch. Dad had retired in 1969 and moved there, going back home so to speak. We got a small, $5,000 grant from the BIA and put in a wheel-move irrigation system for 100 acres of alfalfa.

Dad on his own had a well drilled and found excellent water at 140 feet. We later found that the glacier that existed about 12,000 years ago pushed topsoil into the valley, mostly volcanic ash. There are virtually no rocks on the property. Soundings showed an underground lake in the valley about 220 feet down.

I consolidated ownership of all the allotments in our family by buying all of them out. Then in 1979 I sold the orchard that Tim Wapato and I owned and we moved to Kartar and expanded the operation to include cattle.

We lived in a 70-by-14-foot three-bedroom trailer house with a tip-out for two years. Two of our sons, Rick and Kerry, were at college but in the summer they returned to help on the ranch, very cozy.

Barbara & me June 1976

Barbara on Kartar

Our family spent a lot of time in the Kartar Valley riding horses. Dad started with a registered Appaloosa stallion while still at Wenatchee. He added several mares and before long we had our own registered Appaloosa herd. Mine was a mare we named Kartar. She was my favorite horse. We named her Kartar because she epitomized the spirit of the valley. She was the valley. She never left for the thirty-plus years of her life. But she had a mind of her own. She and I became one when we were together. We had some good times and some bad ones.

Barbara rode her quite often after Kartar made sure Barbara wouldn't fall off. At first Barbara didn't have a good seat in the saddle and Kartar wouldn't move. I recognized the worried look on the horse's face. She would do that with every new rider until she was sure they would be OK.

Kartar just tolerated me though. She didn't always agree with the way I handled cows. One time while we were separating yearlings she became frustrated with my lack of horsemanship. I would cut out one or two calves from the herd and drive them towards the holding pen. Everytime we approached the gate they would bolt before I could turn them in. After two or three tries she put her ears back and clamped down on the bit as we raced towards the pen. When we reached the gate she bumped them into the pen. She then trotted over to the fence, stopped and perked up her ears as much as to say "That's how you do it!"

But she did have her weaknesses. She liked to eat. One time I was feeding all the stock in the same area. The horses and cows separated themselves. But that wasn't enough for Kartar so she laid down sprattle legged and tried to cover all the alfalfa hay so the other horses couldn't get at it. I sure needed a camera then.

She could take a piece of spine cactus and work her mouth around the prickly needles until she could get the center, which she loved to eat.

One time we were stopped on top of the Omake Ridge looking at the beautiful Omak Lake scene below [at least I was, but she only saw different shades of gray]. Her ears twitched until I noticed. I said "What's the matter, Kartar?" and turned around to see three deer just a few yards behind us. That wasn't unusual but one of them was an Albino! Very unusual.

Another time we were coming back from an all day ride on the trail behind Leonard Condon's. She started twitching her ears again so I looked around but didn't see anything at first. Finally I saw a big four-point buck just a few yards up the hill from us. He was standing rigidly still and blended in with the brush. I thought, "You're OK, big buck. I don't have a rifle. But don't go downhill because Leonard does!"

I want to ride Loota today. You can't have all the fun." This was the umpteenth time our son, Matt, had asked. I was reluctant because Loota was a high-spirited gelding and I didn't want Matt to get hurt. Maybe too protective because he was eighteen or twenty years old and a very good athlete. Loota was actually "Outsider," named by Gabe Moses because he didn't mingle with other horses. Dad said Loota was the Indian word for outsider. He was sixteen or seventeen hands high with big feet but was five-gaited. His running walk was so smooth you could do it all day. When in shape he could go for miles without stopping. But he was trained as a Suicide Race horse. He had been in several races at the Omak Stampede. They kept him in shape by not overfeeding him. When I first tried to feed him oats he backed away like he thought I was trying to poison him. But he soon got over that. I naturally fed him too much and he got feisty. I had to be alert because he had bucked me off once.

So finally I relented. I said, "Matt, OK. I don't want to have all the fun, so you ride him today. Just make sure your cinch is tight but not too tight."

Matt no sooner got on when Loota started bucking. After about three jumps Matt flew off and then Loota really bucked. The saddle turned under his belly and he caught his back hoof on it and broke the cinch. He bucked himself out and just stood there shaking. Needless to say we were done riding for the day.

Matt did ride him often after that. We checked things carefully and didn't feed him oats to be on the safe side.

Rob, me, Rick, Matt with Loota

Implementation Phase

"SELF-DETERMINATION WITHOUT TERMINATION!"

Brad Patterson, President Nixon's special assistant for Indian Affairs said, "Alright, I hear you! We'll have the President give Congress a special message on Indian Affairs in his speech on July 8, 1970. He will promise administration support of "Indian Self-Determination" in no uncertain terms.

That is what many Indian leaders were working towards. It eventually became the prime recommendation of the Indian Policy Review Commission and resulted in the Indian Self-Determination and Education Act of 1975.

President Nixon began his message with, "*To the Congress of the United States:*

"The first Americans - the Indians - are the most deprived and most isolated minority group in our nation. On virtually every scale of measurement - employment, income, education, health - the condition of the Indian people ranks at the bottom.

"This condition is the heritage of centuries of injustice. From the time of their first contact with European settlers, the American Indians have been oppressed and brutalized, deprived of their ancestral lands and denied the opportunity to control their own destiny. Even the Federal programs which are intended to meet their needs have frequently proved to be ineffective and demeaning.

"But the story of the Indian in America is something more than the record of the white man's frequent aggression, broken agreements, intermittent remorse and prolonged failure. It is a record also of endurance, of survival, of adaptation and creativity in the face of overwhelming obstacles. It is a record of enormous contributions to this country - to its art and culture, to its strength and spirit, to its sense of history and its sense of purpose.

"It is long past time that the Indian policies of the Federal government began to recognize and build upon the capacities and insights of the Indian people. Both as a matter of justice and as a matter of enlightened social policy, we must begin to act on the basis of what the Indians themselves have long been telling us. The time has come to break decisively with the past and to create the conditions for a new era in which the Indian future is determined by Indian acts and Indian decisions."

Nixon concluded with, "In place of policies which oscillate between the deadly extremes of forced termination and constant paternalism, we suggest a policy in which the Federal government and the Indian community play complementary roles." In other words, he agreed with the Indians recommendation of self-determination without termination.

Notable Indian leaders like the Chairman of the Yakama Nation, Robert Jim, and the Chairman of the Lummi Tribe, Sam Cagey, had been lobbying for this with Brad Patterson and others for several years.

This was a major reversal from President Andrew Jackson's policy regarding Indians. He advocated for and signed the Indian Removal Act of 1830. During his time as President nearly seventy Indian treaties, many of them land sales, were ratified, which is more than any other administration. This resulted in 45,000 Indians being relocated west. His administration purchase 100 million acres of Indian land for about $68 million and 32 million acres of western land.

In all, the U.S. took about 1.9 billion acres [3.79 million square miles] of land from Indians living the continental North America.

COUNCILMAN GEORGE

At last! I had spent several frustrating years getting to this point. Looking back I'm sure my family thought I was crazy putting this much effort in something of questionable returns. Once it gets in your blood though there is nothing you can do but let it run its course. I was hooked.

I looked at the other new Council members; Vi Boyd from Inchelium, Nadene Naff from Keller, Mathew Dick Jr. from Nespelem and wondered if they felt the same way. Of course, I thought to myself, we are of one mind to "make a difference" on the Reservation. But naturally that is what every new councilman thinks.

My attention was brought back to the task at hand when the BIA Superintendent, George Davis, begin to swear us in.

Front Row, left to right: Yvonne Misiaszek, Mel Tonasket, Gerry Boyd, Violet Boyd.
Second Row, Don Peasley, Eddie Palmanteer Jr., Gene Joseph, Lou Stone, Mathew Dick Jr., Jude Stensgar.
Third Dow: Mike Somday, Dale Kohler, Joe Pakootas, Wendell George.

OATH OF OFFICE

I, Wendell George, do solemnly swear or affirm that as an Elected representative of the Confederated Tribes of the Colville Reservation and in performing the duties I am about to assume as a member of the Colville Business Council, I recognize and respect and will uphold and defend the Constitution of the Confederated Tribes of the Colville Reservation and to the extent applicable the United States Constitution; that I will work for the best interests of the Confederated Tribes and its members in all matters at all time without prejudice and partiality, that I am bound by and will follow the Council Code of Professional Responsibility and that at all times my conduct will comport with the standards of conduct and behavior befitting a tribal leader as set forth in the Council Code.

_____
Wendell George

State of Washington)
) ss
Colville Indian Reservation

SUBSCRIBED AND SWORN to before me, in the presence of the Colville Business Council, this 14the day of July, 1988.

_____
George M. Davis, Superintendent
Colville Agency

This started my four years of serving on the Tribal Council. It is a privilege because those who voted for you think you can help the tribe. You owe it to them to try. But there are the others who didn't vote for you or anyone else that are quick to criticize. I had run for Council once in 1979 for the Nespelem District when I lived in Coulee Dam. That was before the primary election was created and the Council positions were numbered. If you didn't have a big family it was difficult to win. Ten or fifteen people would run in the Nespelem District and split the votes. Some were obvious plants to take your potential support away. We could teach the Suyapenex some new tricks!

Then I moved to Kartar Valley, in the Omak District, and ran in 1983, 1984, and finally in 1986. It took me a while to get acquainted with the district. My constituents certainly knew what I stood for by that time. My campaign letter in the April 29, 1983, Tribal Tribune talked about one issue; the power revenues from Grand Coulee Dam:

"We have big hydroelectric projects on our land but the cheap power is sent to California and the aluminum companies are given preferential rates. BPA just announced another 27 percent increase. These rate increases will not stop until people quit using electricity or an alternative source is developed. Since electricity is now a necessity instead of a luxury we are not going to stop using it. The Tribe has people who could be working on solutions but they haven't been utilized. It is a complex technical issue and the present Council hasn't been able to handle it. And yet if these resources were developed it would benefit members both on and off the Reservation."

I followed with a Tribune article on July 31, 1984:

"Fortunately, there are people who are doing something about this problem. They are convinced that hydrogen can replace wood, coal, gas and electricity without insurmountable changes to our economy. Hydrogen burns clean without any pollution, leaving only oxygen and water-vapor. It is inexhaustible because of nature's way of cycling water [the main source of hydrogen] by evaporation from the earth to the atmosphere and returning to the earth by rain. Science fiction has predicted the next advancement of civilization. Was Jules Verne prophetic in 1870 when his Captain Nemo used hydrogen as a fuel in "20,000 Leagues Under the Sea?" More recently "Kitt," the talking super car, is powered by liquid hydrogen in TV's "Knightrider" ... Electricity can be generated by fuel cells, which use hydrogen and air for fuel. Each house or building could have its own fuel cell eliminating ugly distribution wires and reducing the cost of electricity....

What does this mean to us, as Colvilles? Our claim to half the Columbia River gives us enough water to be the key to the world's conversion to a hydrogen economy. Hydrogen can be generated by electrolysis at Grand Coulee and Chief Joseph dams using cheaper off-peak power and piped over long distances using proven gas and oil pipeline technology to the consumer and either burned directly or converted to electricity. There are four such electrolysis plants using hydro-power in the world today but none in the U.S.

"Just think: **a readily-available, inexpensive, pollution-free fuel** that the world dreams about! In addition to low fuel costs, we would have a major industry to provide jobs and higher per capitas from the power revenues."

My campaign letter for the 1984 election was a little different....**"Constitutional Revisions**

"Last year the Council refused to send a questionnaire to the membership polling them on what they wanted. This year the Council tried to ignore the one-man, one-vote issue, so I filed suit in tribal court. In my suit I suggested reservation-wide elections as an alternative to reducing the number of councilmen from Keller. If the court decides, it could go either way. The Council instead of meeting the issue head-on is trying to hide behind sovereign immunity to suit and a plea for dismissal. On February 15, 1984, I offered to withdraw my suit if the Council put reservation-wide elections* on the ballot for the membership to decide."

* Proposed Reservation-wide election process:

This election process would utilize the present primary system where the eligible candidates are elected by each district. In the Keller district two candidates with the highest votes and in the Inchelium, Nespelem, and Omak the two candidates with the highest votes in each of the two numbered positions would move on to the general election.

In the general election there would be a reservation-wide vote for all candidates that moved on from the primary election. The candidate with the highest number of votes in the Keller District and the candidate in each of the two numbered positions in the Inchelium, Nespelem, and Omak Districts with the highest number of votes would win the election.

I also lobbied the Council to add a primary to the Council election process. They were very reluctant at first but persistence pays off because on February 7, 1983, they passed resolution 1983-108 which provided for an amendment to the Tribal Election ordinance instituting a primary election in each district where only the top two vote getters would move on to the general election.

Later, they numbered each Council position so candidates would have to declare for which position they were running.

On January 9, 1984, Mathew Dick Jr. and I filed a civil complaint for one-man one-vote. Dale Kohler helped us with the legal brief.

Ironically on the same day the Council passed resolution 1984-3 which enabled tribal members to amend the Constitution by a petition of one-third of the eligible voters at the last election. This was another thing I was lobbying for.

In the April 27, 1984, Tribune it was announced that my lawsuit for one-man one-vote was dismissed without prejudice, meaning I could resubmit it later.

In the December 20, 1985, Tribune the Tribal Questionnaire was announced. The Council authorized that with resolution 1985-570. Betty Fry, Ralph Van Brunt, Councilman Richard Swan, and Councilwoman Mary Marchand and I had been working on that as a committee for months. In the January 31, 1986, Tribune the deadline for returning the questionnaire was announced as February 4, 1986.

Councilman Mike Somday said we received 486 questionnaires back with nine more unsigned, which we didn't use in the summary. This was more than received from the Mount Tolman questionnaire but still a low percentage. The answers showed a trend of support for development on the reservation.

My 1986 campaign went a little different than the others. I wrote a campaign letter, but that didn't have as much effect as what happened at an Omak District meeting just before the election. We had an unsightly garbage dump near our beautiful and scenic Omak Lake. Nobody liked that location so I wrote up a petition to ask the Council to move the dump and brought it to the district meeting. Over one hundred people signed it that night and the word spread throughout the district. I won by five votes, beating six-year incumbent, Norris Palmanteer.

After being elected to the Council in 1986 I spent four years of my life serving on the Tribal Council. Our terms are only two years but I was re-elected in 1988. During the time on the Council I wrote articles for our monthly Tribal Tribune entitled "Softly Speaking." Of the forty-eight articles I wrote, about half were devoted to Indian spirituality, history, or culture. The rest were about tribal activities and, unfortunately, included some on the fierce political infighting which greatly detracted from the welfare of the tribe. At that point I should have changed the name of my article to "Hard Rock Café." I became vicious, I am sorry to say. I called them as I saw them. I thought I could change the world of politics. Silly me.

The day I was sworn in, the Council was presented with a lawsuit by StockWest, the company operating our CIPP lumber mill. In 1984 the Tribes chartered both Colville Tribal Enterprise Corporation [CTEC] and Colville Indian Precision Pine [CIPP]. This marked the beginning of the Implementation Phase. On April 2, 1984, they contracted with StockWest for the design, construction, and management of a tribally-owned sawmill.

In addition, StockWest was to supervise the marketing and sales of forest products and off-species logs consistent with the allocation of timber resources by the Tribes. CIPP would be a subsidiary of CTEC.

By separate action the Council dedicated timber stumpage not to exceed 25 million board feet per annum to the sawmill. The mill would pay appraised stumpage value, plus an allowance for historical overbid, on a percentage basis for the preceding twenty-year period. Sixty people would be employed with the opening in July 1985.

Unfortunately many problems developed with StockWest. The quality of the mill design was inferior and the mill was inefficient with an obsolete design. The Tribes ended up suing StockWest to get out of the contract. The only mistake the Council made was not hiring a professional engineer like Mater to oversee the design and construction. The problems would have been discovered earlier and solved before it affected the mill operation. This became the source of many complaints by the tribal membership.

On September 16, 1986, shortly after being first elected to the Council I began writing articles for the Tribal Tribune about our economic development efforts. It was mainly a continuation of the comprehensive plan I published twelve years earlier.

I knew tribal members were reading my articles because I received a lot of feedback, mostly good. My cousin, Gloria [George] Hammond from Tahlequah, Oklahoma, told me during a phone call that she hung my articles on her refrigerator so her kids would read them. Her younger sister, Linda and her family, stayed in our mobile home at Kartar for a while after we moved into our log house.

I was elected chairman of the planning committee by the full Council. It was our job to write a strategic plan for development of the reservation. I wrote a Tribune article on September 16, 1986 that defined the criteria for the development. We ruled out anything that would impact our environment. Our highest priority was to provide jobs for our tribal members. This presented us with the additional task of training our people for whatever jobs we provided. Our IAT program gave us a head start on construction projects but many projects required other specialties. So our task then was to predict what kind of jobs will be available in the future. My next Tribune article on October 14, 1986, established ten priorities which we would develop through CTEC. These ranged from tourism to aquaculture. We then tracked each priority's progress. Some were already in motion such as tourism [Roosevelt Recreation Enterprise], hydroelectric development [power revenue claims], wood products [CIPP], retail trades [tribal stores], and Gaming [bingo enterprise].

The bingo enterprise was started in the Omak Community Center. Mathew Dick Jr. and I worked with the St. Joseph Church on a trial basis to establish feasibility. It was well received and profitable. We then wrote a resolution, which the Council approved, to use the $300,000 BIA grant to start the bingo enterprise. Mathew and I had been traveling around to the tribes in Minnesota, the Seminole reservation and others to learn about bingo. The Oklahoma tribes started a national organization which was the predecessor to the National Indian Gaming Association [NIGA]. We found an experienced bingo manager in Jerry Surveyor from Oklahoma and hired him. Bingo was profitable from day one.

Our biggest problem was where to hold the Bingo sessions. The basketball players were tolerant of our using the Community Center gym for a while but then started clamoring to get it back for their use. We looked at a number of locations to build a bingo hall but the Council couldn't agree on a location. It became a political issue [Oh, how we learn from the Suyapenex!] We finally compromised on the Highway 97 location near Okanogan where it still operates today.

Eight of the Council was involved in the startup of the Roosevelt Recreation Enterprise [RRE]. We flew to Lake Powell to visit their resort escorted by Bill Butts, the resort manager. It was a great and successful trip except for the trip down.

We were to change planes in Salt Lake City but our flight was cancelled. We were left stranded until the next day. Andy Joseph Sr. had a good idea to rent an eight passenger jet for the relatively short flight to Lake Powell. It was a little nerve wracking for me because I got claustrophobia sitting in a small tunnel-like airplane. Plus I was sitting backwards facing Nadine Naff. The other Council people were Mathew Dick Jr., Don Peasley, Dale Kohler, Vi Boyd, Andy Joseph Sr., and Jude Stensgar. After returning home we created Roosevelt Recreation Enterprises and hired Bill Butts as our general manager.

Our most successful lobbying was when we made a trip to Washington, D.C., on July 13, 1987. Dale Kohler wrote a very detailed and complete summary for the Tribal Tribune. [Appendix, *Pot-wan-na - Implementation* 1. Councilman's Corner.]

The issue was management of Lake Roosevelt. The Colville and Spokane Tribes own about one half of Lake Roosevelt according to a 1974 U.S. Solicitor's opinion. The tribes were not included in the 1946 management agreement by the Bureau of Reclamation [BOR], National Park Service [NPS], and BIA. This was typical for those times, but now we were exercising our prerogative. The tribes sent a contingent of eleven representatives of Council members and staff.

Since I was planning chairman, working on this issue, both tribes agreed that I be the spokesman. We met with the assistant secretaries and their staff, Congressmen Tom Foley and Sid Morrison and Senator Dan Evans. After some follow-up meetings we finally negotiated the new Five Party Agreement.

I mentioned in my Tribune letter of October 18, 1989, that the new Five-Party Agreement worked. Without it I'm sure the Feds would have ignored us again. We received $736,000 from the Bureau of Reclamation for debris cleanup on the lake.

Very few Council members expected me to win my second term because I was too outspoken. I didn't play the politics of the good ole boys. However the June 18, 1988, general election was a little easier for me because we had both a primary and numbered seats on the Council for the Inchelium, Nespelem, and Omak positions. This means that you have to choose who you are running against. You are not just another person in the crowd. Mel Tonasket and I won the general.

| W. George | PRIMARY | 186 | GENERAL | 304 |
| Tonasket | PRIMARY | 172 | GENERAL | 237 |

On December 21, 1989 at the Special Session of the Colville Business Council Chairman Jude Stensgar looked around the Council table and said, "That completes the vote for the amendment so let's move on to the main motion which is to dispense with the traditional opening prayer. Wendell you have the floor."

"I would like to add to Dale's previous statement that this is not a separation of church and state issue because it is commonly experienced in the Congress of the U.S.A. and other legislatures and it is a tradition with the Colville Reservation.

"Our own Congress has been doing this since the 1774 Continental Congress and 1789 when they started their regular Congress. It was brought in by Ben Franklin. They did it by recommending some chaplains. George Washington started it on April 3, 1789. The U.S. Congress has an opening prayer for every session. They bring in people that are designated to do the prayer. I don't think they have a lot of argument about who the people are that are designated. We designate people that are, to a lot of people, tribal elders. All of us at this table are, in one form or another, a tribal elder because we are leaders. This leading in the Indian tradition is especially important because of the fact that we are leading people in the spiritual and physical mode. It has nothing to do with the so-called separation of church and government." The traditional prayer was resumed.

I can't tell you that tribal members learned their politics from the Suyapenex or if it just comes naturally. Whatever it is seems to have been perfected. My second term became very political. One issue was our tribal credit department. Some of us wanted an outside audit because we were aware of abuse. Some tribal members were getting special favors like insufficient collateral accepted and no payment on their loans. The Council became split on this issue exactly at seven for the audit and seven against. This impasse carried over to many other issues. Since I was outspoken for the audit I became a political target.

This resulted in a false claim that I had violated the conditions of a grant I received before being elected to the Council. This grant was for a surveying enterprise that my dad sponsored because he had a state professional surveyor's license. My uncle, Pete, and others actually did the survey work for the Douglas County P.U.D. Since it was a BIA grant they made the claim that I violated the regulations because I didn't take out a loan for the project. I had approval from the Seattle First National Bank for a loan but the manager advised that we should not take out the loan until I needed to. Since the P.U.D. was paying as we submitted invoices and the grant guaranteed ability to meet payroll and other expenses we didn't need a loan. Although initiated by my opposition on the Council, the BIA brought the U.S. Attorney in and the political issue became a legal one. My fellow Council members and I appealed to the BIA Area Director by telephone. I asked why I wasn't notified of the issue before it became a legal problem. The BIA did not tell me there was a problem until the U.S. Attorney became involved. I could have taken the loan even though I didn't need it. I was brought to Spokane, fingerprinted and put on probation just as if I was guilty even though I hadn't been to court yet. I hired an attorney and we put up a defense that eventually caused the U.S. Attorney to drop the charges. I agreed if they paid my attorney charges [$8000] plus one dollar for admission of their mistake. That was the end of it. However, rumors spread throughout the reservation and I lost my next election.

No sooner did the grasshopper hit the water than a hungry rainbow gobbled it up. The hook set and I pulled it out of the small opening in the tangle of limbs and logs. Too bad it was only six inches long but he sure was a fighter, kinda like me. At last I began to calm down. I hadn't forgotten but I was starting to cope.

My depression was partly due to my damaged ego. But much of it was also due to my frustration because all the projects I had started probably would never be finished. I wouldn't be the only loser because these projects were all economic development for the Rez. It would have meant jobs for tribal members and income for the tribe.

Shortly after losing the election for Council in July 1990 I went into a deep depression. My friend, Mathew Dick Jr. told me I should do something like go fishing to take my mind off of it. So I went to my favorite spot at Owhi Lake just a couple of miles from where I was born. The fish weren't biting because it was late in the day and mid-July when the fish go deep. I made a few half-hearted casts and decided to go somewhere higher up in the mountains. That's how I wound up here at Frosty Meadows near the center of the Rez.

As I hunted for likely fishing holes I reviewed my four years on the Council planning committee concerning:

Oct. 86 – Possible garbage incinerator with Tulalip tribe.
Nov. 86 – Possible gun manufacture with BOR-O-LOY.
Dec. 86 – Creation of a tribal museum in Coulee Dam.
Mar. 87 – Offer to buy COMSAT Station at Brewster.
Apr. 87 – Served on Super Conducting Collider Committee.
Jan. 88 – Bingo Enterprise in Omak Community Center.
Mar. 88 – Exploration of economic development with CTEC.
Sept. 88 – Possible Computer Data Entry with Turtle Mt. tribe.
June. 89 - Served on Centennial Accord Committee.
Dec. 89 – Offer to buy Coulee Dam Shopping Center.
Apr. 90 – Lake Roosevelt Management Agreement.

Ahead the lights of the motel were twinkling through the early morning fog from the lake. Looming behind the small town of Polson, Montana, were the Glacier Mountains. The vivid green of the pines and firs brightened the day as I walked to the entrance.

Barbara and I had arrived late and we had to check into a motel a few blocks from the Salish Inn where the meeting was being held. Little did I know at the time that this semi-vacation we were taking would dominate my life for the next three years. We had driven here from our ranch in Kartar Valley, coming from one reservation, the Colville, and visiting another, the Flathead.

I was attending a meeting called by the BIA roads Division. Wayne Kensler, our BIA Roads Engineer, told me we may have a chance to have some input on the BIA road construction budget. We had a dire need to improve our roads so I went as a representative from our tribe's planning department.

All the Northwest tribes and many tribes from the West were there. It soon became a gripe session on how bad the roads were on our reservations.

Andrea [Smith] Alexandra from the Makah tribe brought the discussion home when she said, "We have been having these meetings for some time now. We all agree on how bad the roads are but that's where it stops. Nothing gets done from there."

I couldn't stand it anymore. We had been in this gripe session for hours rehashing old stories. I was a planner so I knew what had to be done.

"Andrea is right. The next step has never been taken. To take the next step we need to form a team or a committee with representatives from all the interested tribes and give them the responsibility to follow up with the BIA. Otherwise we will all go home thinking we have accomplished something when we haven't." Skip Curley, my new Navajo friend, said,

"Right on, Wendell. And to start that process I nominate you to be our leader, president or whatever we want to name it." Several people agreed and it was done. So I countered, "One person doesn't make an organization so I nominate Skip to be the vice-president." Everyone agreed. And then someone spoke from the back of the crowded room and nominated Andrea to be the secretary-treasurer. That also received unanimous approval.

After the meeting I said to Becky Rey, my assistant: "I must have talked too much to get elected president. I not sure what I got myself into." She agreed that I talked too much.

Our first order of business was to develop an organization. We decided on a man-to-man defense with the BIA so we set up twelve area representatives to work with the twelve BIA area offices. We later met in Denver with a Native American Rights Fund [NARF] attorney and finalized the charter.

Besides our executive committee we had tribal representatives from the Alaskan Natives, Metlakatla, Eastern Cherokee, Southern Ute, Oklahoma Cherokee, Comanche, Oneida, Turtle Mount Sioux, Rosebud Sioux, Assiniboine, Gros Ventre, Shoshone-Bannock, Navajo, Tohono 'Odham, and California tribes. We represented all 500 tribes.

From 1993 to 1996 we had monthly telecons, quarterly executive board meetings and summit meetings all over the U.S. including Denver, Col., Rapid City, S.D., Phoenix, Ariz., Washington, D.C., Green Bay, Wis., San Diego, Calif., Spokane, Wash., Lake Tahoe, Nev., Albuquerque, N.M., Las Vegas, Nev., and Port Angeles, Wash.

This team of a dozen or so Indians from various tribes had a lot in common such as tribal culture, poor living conditions on the reservations and endless tales of abuses by the federal government. I took every opportunity to learn about each tribe.

During one conversation I had with Skip Curley I casually mentioned that I learned about the Navajo from reading Tony Hillerman's books. I got a good reaction from Skip. He said, "Don't believe everything you read. He got a lot of our culture wrong. Many of us don't like his books."

I said, "Outsiders always misinterpret our culture. That's a given."

Later, I heard the Navajo delayed a movie that was to be made of one of Tony's books, "The Dark Wind." They didn't like Lou Diamond Phillips as Jim because he wasn't Navajo. It finally came out in 1991. PBS released three movies of Tony Hillerman's books, *Skinwalkers* [2002], *Coyote Waits* [2003], and *A Thief of Time* [2004]. Although no Navajos starred in them the cast was more acceptable. Adam Beach as Jim Chee, Wes Studi as Lt. Leaphorn, Alex Rice as Janet Pete, and Gary Farmer as Captain Largo. One of my favorites, Graham Greene, played Nakai, a character that wasn't in the books.

At the national meeting in Denver we demonstrated some of our culture. Nathan Winder showed us some of his Southern Ute using tobacco, which he pointed to the Four Directions and prayed for our well-being both as individuals and as tribes.

As president, I was moderator and keynote speaker. I opened up the meeting on March 14, 1994, with a speech in the Wenatchi Indian Language. I then translated it to English. I had been working with my Dad, who was proficient in several Indian languages. He helped me write my speech.

I said "La'm-Lampt', How-enchu-ten, hay-em-sto'-chum-nem [Thank you, Creator-God, for bringing us together]

"Kas-ho-en-tem, kee-tol-an chus'-h'ow-we [to solve the reservations' problems]."

I went on to encourage the delegates [there were about one hundred attending]. I ended with:

"P'antk-cawst'-keil [So be it, forever or Amen]."

I wrote this in Dad's version of phonetics because it doesn't require special knowledge of glottal pronunciation.

We made the Federal government aware of our problems all the way to Rodney Slater, the Federal Highways Administrator. The result was more and better distribution of several hundred million federal highway dollars to the reservations that needed it.

While this was happening I began working with Clay Antioquia, an Alaskan Native that was the present CTEC CEO, although I was part of the tribal planning organization. The reason I was in that fix was my main project was the co-generation project. Francis Somday, who was acting CEO before Clay came on board, asked me to write a proposal to the Department of Energy for this project. It was a competitive bid and Francis didn't give me a snowball's chance to win it. But that made me work even harder.

So after several months' work and an anxious waiting period we were notified that we won a $2.5 million grant including the matching we got from the BIA. Becky Rey worked with me on that and was a great help. Francis was ecstatic but he was in the transition of turning over his duties to Clay and was a short-timer. Clay was on a steep learning curve with all the tribes' activity so I was pretty much on my own.

It was Thursday June 13, 1996, and I was in Clay Antioquia's corner office overlooking Grand Coulee Dam. I was waiting for word from the ongoing Colville Tribal Enterprise Corp. Board meeting. Clay was in the meeting, which had been going on for a while. We were both anxious because the CTEC Board was to make a decision on the new Chief Executive Officer today. I was one of the candidates. The Chief Executive Officer is the head of CTEC, which at the time had up to 1400 employees, counting seasonal and part-time. The word "Chief" indicates that Indians did have some influence on the modern world.

It would have been a simple business decision but the tribal Council had to agree on the appointment, so it became a political process. That is what made it so unpredictable. It was worse for tribal members because they were scrutinized by personal dislikes and old previous battles within the tribe. Some things are never forgotten.

But I wasn't without resources. I made sure my support was firm. Although it probably didn't make any difference I had previously suggested to our council that Conrad Edwards be appointed to the CTEC Board. He not only was appointed but was now the chairman.

When Clay came from the board room to get me, I saw the big smile on his face. He was happy because he recommended me and had counseled me over the past year. He made sure I was familiar with all the CTEC operation, especially the gaming, which was new and growing tremendously. He appointed me acting manager of credit for several weeks [I think to see if I could manage people] as a trial and training effort. The manager, Sharon Holmdahl, was out on extended sick leave.

As we entered the board room some of the members couldn't contain their smiles. Conrad, speaking for the Board, said,

"Wendell, the Board has decided to appoint you the new Chief Executive Officer of CTEC. Congratulations!"

Then I went around and shook hands with all the board members. Everything was cool.

But, of course, that didn't last long. A number of problems were in the making and I was immediately confronted with them.

One was our slot machines. We had real slot machines which the State claimed were illegal. We were fighting a legal battle but, in the meantime, were running our gaming business with these machines. The Feds had allowed us to do that until the court decision. Unfortunately, our machines were old and were wearing out. We couldn't get replacements because of the legal question. We did quietly bootleg some but it was a battle. I was called on my car phone one night as I was driving home from Manson after a daylong series of meetings at our casino and was told that our replacements had been confiscated by the State. That meant I had to develop alternate sources, which I did, but how and who remains a secret that only Clay and I know.

Another immediate problem was the Council resolution, which delegated to CTEC the authority to borrow money for operating funds. Without this ability we had to go to the Council for every nickel and dime that we used. It was intolerable for a $100 million enterprise to operate that way. It was a situation of some of the Council wanting to micromanage, just like Dale Kohler wrote in his Tribune article on July 15, 1986:

"Constructive criticism and questioning is good and I am not for a moment suggesting that CTEC should be immune from this. I guess where I draw the line is when it is directly or indirectly suggested that this enterprise arm of the Colville Confederated Tribes be abolished. I presume those advocating this line of thought would have our tribal enterprises placed back underneath the Business Council. In my opinion, this would guarantee financial chaos and ultimate disaster for the Tribes."

I worked hard on this and was able to convince the majority of the Council that it was necessary. Clay had been working on that since he came on board and had no luck. He was amazed that I succeeded so fast.

Shortly after being appointed CEO, I remember traveling to Washington, D.C., with Councilman Richard Swan from the Inchelium District. He was civil to me but was disappointed with the Council passing the funding resolution. It was interesting that Richard supported me for the CEO appointment but now wanted to argue with me about my first major act of pushing the resolution through.

CTEC
Colville Tribal Enterprise Corporation

GROSS INCOME
Fiscal Years 1987-1996

NET INCOME
Fiscal Years 1987-1996

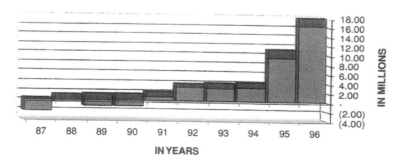

President and CEO
Letter to Tribal Member Shareholders

Dear Tribal Member:

Nineteen ninety-five to ninety-six were "turn-around" years for CTEC. The mill started making a consistent profit and the casinos at Mill Bay, Okanogan, and Coulee Dam turned in huge profits during their first full years of operation. The Board was reorganized again, this time to include three Council members in addition to two tribal members from the business community. In June 1996, I took over, from Clarence Antioquia, the duties for President and CEO. For the first time the entire top level management for CTEC are tribal members. This has helped mold us into a fast-responding management team in the last year and a half.

The strategy of CTEC management is to determine where we want to be in 5 or 10 years, establish a series of goals, which will help us achieve our vision, identify the obstacles, and then develop methods or action plans for getting us there.

Our vision of the future is being developed through the Holistic Management process adopted by the tribe. Our operating plan for this year (and for subsequent years) was, and will be, developed through a series of interactive meetings with the Colville Business Council and tribal staff. These have resulted in a teamwork effort to combine functions, improve efficiency, and reduce cost to assure that the tribe is getting the best product for the least cost.

The tool for assuring the best product is the goal setting. The same Holistic Management meetings were used to set the tribal goals. From these, we developed supporting CTEC goals that are specific and measurable. These are summarized in the introduction to this report.

Significant accomplishments for this period included:

Council approval of a ten million refinance package with Keybank. Six million was used to pay off higher interest rate loans with an Oregon Bank and four million was a credit line for operating expenses, especially for building up log inventory so the mill could continue in operation during spring breakup. This credit line was not needed for the mill this year because they had sufficient funds from their cash flow. But, in the future, this credit line will enable CTEC to cover short-term expenses of our enterprises without requesting funds from the Tribe.

This helps solve the obstacles of insufficient capital and the need for a business environment.

It helps meet the goals of self-sufficiency, diversify the reservation economy, and protecting tribal sovereignty.

Significant cost cutting measures were taken which not only increased the bottom line but also changed our image to "lean and mean".

As shown in the chart comparing the 95-96 financials CTEC's net income increased 83% (from $11.2 million to $20.5 million, including $1.7 million from Credit). Total revenues increased only 7% (from $102.6 million to 110 million including $2.7 million from Credit). This indicates CTEC increased the net income through better marketing and increased efficiency.

Gaming revenues were the major reason for the increase in revenues because the Gaming Division was in its first two years of full operation. The net revenues increased significantly in 1996 because of the cost control measures taken such as cutting back the workforce during the off season. Also a major factor was the exercise of the option to purchase the gaming machines instead of leasing them.

Some of our other enterprises did not fair so well. Roosevelt Recreation Enterprises (RRE), Keller Store, Wood Treatment Plant, CTRC, and Logging all recorded losses for the year. Corrective action plans have been developed for each of these enterprises and in the 1997 report will show much better results.

The main reason CTRC did not at least breakeven is the March 20, 1997 CBC resolution 1997-190 which required CTRC to reimburse tribal Administration the full discount amount, with no allowance for actual costs to market and to sell the logs. Included in the cost of production during the year ending September 30, 1996 is $1,199,335 for the discount payable to CCT on volumes removed in excess of 65 million board feet.

The 1997 fiscal year will reflect the results of many of the positive changes incorporated in 1996. This includes improved earnings, management systems, training programs and employee morale.

We have many dedicated employees at CTEC and I would like to thank them for their hard work. My priority is to make the Council, tribal members, and neighbors aware of your efforts to help our community grow economically.

Sincerely,

Wendell George

Wendell George, PE
President and CEO

1995-96 was the best year in the history of CTEC. The annual report indicates a continuing growth and was at the peak. It dramatically shows the size of our operation and the diversification of the enterprises. We had many irons in the fire which were intended to guarantee us a continuous income stream.

It was 1998, the second year of my tenure as CEO. I stood looking out of the big picture window of my corner office at the CTEC headquarters in Coulee Dam, Washington.

The view was majestic as it faced south and directly at the Grand Coulee Dam. But now the face of the dam was bare and quiet. A few years earlier tons of water poured over the eleven flood gates making a thunderous noise all spring and summer. I fondly remembered the sound and humidity when we lived in Coulee Dam twenty years earlier.

That was before they "optimized" the water flow to "maximize" the electrical output. Now the only time water flows over the gates is to help the salmon fingerlings go downstream in the spring and, in summer evenings for the visitors to watch the laser light show. The flow is very limited and makes little noise.

I was reflecting on my term as CEO of the tribal enterprises. I related to the water flow or rather the lack of it. I tried to move the corporation into major developments but for various reasons it didn't happen. I couldn't blame the tribal people because the projects were too big for them to comprehend. I was approaching development like I did at Boeing. Each project had a large payback but there is always some risk. We could minimize the risk with a thorough analysis but could not predict unforeseen events. These events could be good or bad so it could help us or hurt us.

For example the uranium enrichment plant that would have cost one or two billion dollars but would return millions in net income. The Japanese were especially interested either as buyers of the fuel or to own and operate a plant. They may have caused our Federal government to decide not to proceed because they didn't want foreign ownership.

While serving on the tribal Council I supported another project to get a block of power from the U.S. Corps of Engineers. It was summarized in a September 2, 1986, letter I wrote to Rodney Smikin, the contact for tribal members in the Seattle area. Some of the planning activities described in that letter were:

"Dale Kohler and I, along with Alan Stay from our Reservation Attorney's office, and Gary Passmore, our Hydrologist went to Portland in July to meet with the U.S. Army Corps of Engineers. We agreed on how to best approach getting a large block of power from raising the Chief Joseph Dam reservoir another four feet or so. We will apply to FERC for a license to study the problem. After receiving the license we will work jointly with the Corps to thoroughly analyze how the project will be accomplished. We will use their large Amdahl computer at Portland and revise their simulation model of all the Columbia River dams to determine the operating parameters of a four-foot reservoir level rise. At the same time, we will negotiate contracts with Tacoma, Seattle, or possibly even local PUDs for the sale of the power. This is how we'll finance the construction. It is a minimum risk approach. Finally, if the project is feasible we will apply to FERC for a construction license and proceed with it."

Unfortunately, after I left the Council this project died.

As CTEC CEO I proposed a gas-fired co-generation plant, which would have been another billion-dollar enterprise. This was feasible with minimum risk. I wrote a proposal for a Department of Energy [DOE] grant. It was a competitive bid and we were awarded $2.5 million including a match from the BIA. We designed it and had the contractors lined up and financing to be provided by selling private bonds. The natural gas for the fuel was to be brought down from Canada. We were working on establishing a right of way with the existing railway that went all the way to Wenatchee. The tribe wouldn't agree to the bonding. It was a major step and too complicated for them. It wasn't a new process because other tribes have done it but it was new to us. The tribal staff was too challenged to organize their budget and couldn't grasp such a large project.

Eventually, the balance of the BIA grant went to building health clinics on the Rez. The co-gen grant reverted back to the DOE. Now, the price of electricity and fuel has gone up. The market would be excellent for our project. But that was not to be.

I stood staring at Conrad Edwards, Chairman of the CTEC Board of Directors, after he finished telling me the board had voted to not renew my contract. They actually took it a little farther by buying out the last year of my existing three-year contract. The cost to them was six months' pay. They pay, I walk.

I looked at each of the board members –Conrad, Eddie Palmanteer Jr., Joann Leith, Debbie Oreiro, Robert Sandenine, and Jim Boyd – to see how much animosity there was. There was none in any of them. The only one who said anything further was Eddie, who commented that we seemed to always be on opposite sides of the politics. An understatement for sure, but I didn't hold any animosity either.

I said, "I know that you are doing what you have to do. The Council has spoken, that is, two or three of them have, so you have to jump to save your board positions. There is nothing else you can do." That conclusion came from their request that I not contact the Council on this issue.

The Wenatchee World published the news on July 5, 1998, with large headlines:

HEAD OF TRIBAL FIRMS FIRED

President of Colville Tribal Enterprises Corporation let go over "difference in philosophy." A July 3 press release from the Tribes said Wendell George's "at-will" contract as President and Chief Executive Officer of the Colville Tribal Enterprises Corporation was terminated June 26, in concurrence with the Colville Business Council, by CTEC's Board of Directors. George served for two years as head of the successful corporation that operates three casinos and other business ventures.

CTEC Board Chairman Conrad Edwards said the termination was the result of a "difference in philosophy and management style" in the direction of CTEC and its enterprises over the past several months, the release stated. He said the CTEC Board expressed appreciation for George's efforts in the growth and progress of the corporation over the past two years.

George, reached at his home Friday, said the decision was not a total surprise. "Some things have happened that gave early indication, but you never expect it until it happens. It's a disappointment that the Tribes and I couldn't stay together longer, but if they want to go in a different direction, that's their prerogative," he added, "I'm not going to look back. I'm looking forward."

George did not expand on what differences in philosophy caused his termination, other than to say the Tribes has a new group of leaders since he was hired two years ago, who seem to be looking more locally and less globally.

In the July 29 Omak Chronicle I pointed out, among other things, that, "The 1997 CTEC financial status report distributed by videotape and hard copy to each tribal household indicated significant progress. The tribe's auditor, LeMaster and Daniels, prepared these reports independent of CTEC so the data is authentic and valid.

"The report indicates that over the past four years CTEC has increased its net income more than 10 times from $2.7 million to $27.1 million. From 1996 to 1997 the net income almost doubled.

Good management was the key. There are many key managers within CTEC who contributed to this effort. I only hope they will stay with CTEC because the future of the tribes depends on it. Without their experience and knowledge, we will suffer."

Indian Dice

The dice in the picture are from Joanne Leith's family. They are made from deer antlers. The game, played by all our ancestors in the Northwest, normally used four dice with winning combinations not unlike the slot machines of today. A pair of lined faces wins four counters [sticks], a pair of dotted faces wins two counters, and four blanks wins four counters. If they crossed as shown in the picture, the player loses.

One of the most frustrating issues was how the Suyapenex defined "fairness". A fundamental trait of Indian culture is gambling. It is built-in. We have always had some form of it. When compared to the modern forms of gaming such as slot machines the only difference is the technological aids. Indians were not allowed to use computers.

According to Black's Law Dictionary a <u>SLOT MACHINE</u> is an apparatus by which a person depositing money therein may by chance get directly or indirectly money or articles of value worth either more or less than the money deposited.

	Slot Machine	**Indian Dice**
Player bet	Insert coins bills	Offer counter sticks
Player initiation	Press button/handle	Throw dice
Pre-determined	Combination of cherries or other symbols	Combination or lined, dotted, , or blank dice
Payout	coin or ticket	Take counter sticks

The U.S. Supreme Court ruled in favor of tribes on February 25, 1987 for the Cabazon case to operate large payout Bingo games.

This led to the creation of the Indian Gaming Regulatory Act in 1988 which defined three classes of gaming:

Class I – Traditional Indian gaming for ceremonies and exclusively regulated by tribes.

Class II – Bingo, pull tabs and punch boards including computer or other technological aids to be regulated by tribes with oversight by the National Indian Gaming Commission [NIGC].

Class III – All other forms of gaming specifically including machines. Lawful on Indian lands if authorized by tribe, NIGC, and permitted by the State.

On September 26, 1997 the U.S. District Court ruled in favor of tribes in the State of Washington for operating Class III gaming.

The ten year legal battle inhibited the economic development on our reservation. It was an attorney's paradise for they could argue the issue for all eternity. Our sovereignty was reduced even further.

POST CTEC - I never retired from an active life. I spent eleven years on the Wenatchee Valley College Board of Trustees and was honored to be chosen the 2002-2003 Trustee of the year of the 150-plus trustees in the community colleges. We have many tribal members attending WVC at Omak.

That wasn't enough, so I also joined the Paschal Sherman Indian School Board for seven years. During that time we built an $18 million new school. The design won some awards for its uniqueness, some of which is described in the epilogue. There are almost two hundred Indian children in this school, preschool to ninth grade.

And finally, I have spent the last six years as a member of the Omak School Board. We built a $21 million addition to the school, which includes a vocational center. There are about 350 tribal members in our Omak schools out of 1,500 total.

All these schools have many tribal members attending and I am doing my best to see that they are treated well. I am following through on my dad's commitment, made while he was a member of the Charter Council in 1938 by promoting education for our tribal members. I wonder if my grandma Kwa-ni [Christine George] would be happy with the results of her passion for education.

After I lost my CTEC job, people would sympathize with me and say, "Why don't you take time to 'smell the roses'?" It was a question posed to me with good intentions to get me back on my feet. I had all the tools to do that but I hadn't been using them lately. I was too busy competing in the physical world. So I took inventory.

Several years before, Barbara and I went to a workshop on Meditation in Seattle. Gene Joseph had introduced me to the Silva Method which was started by a Mexican-American, José Silva. It involved dedicating ourselves full-time for two weekends. A group of about ten of us learned how to go into deep meditation by that method. It was very effective.

While in meditation I could melt into a wall and see everything inside. But that was only the beginning. Our final test was to diagnose actual people's illness just by their personal description. I saw a man without a leg and another that had heart problems. I meditated and went through their bloodstream and noticed problems. I couldn't give it any technical name but I could describe the symptoms.

I seemed to have more aptitude for this than Barbara, but I think it was because she held back from completely immersing herself in the meditation. We had already gone through the Cursillo, which is a three-day retreat. We did several types of meditations: personal, group, praying, singing, laughing and generally enjoying the group's company. During the weekend we forgot all our troubles on the outside world. It was refreshing and very spiritual.

The common element in all these activities was, we enjoyed the moment. We lived in the NOW and lost our past and future. We concentrated on what we were doing and ignored the passage of time. We were basically suspended in time and completely occupied with our space and what we were doing.

Maturing Phase – 1996-2008

On a nice sunny day July 7, 2008, about fifty people collected together at the proposed site for the new Omak Casino.

I stopped to talk to Mike Marchand, Chairman of the Council. Unfortunately, he had just been defeated in his re-election bid. This would be one of his last official actions for the tribe. It was to be a ground-breaking ceremony for the $24 million project. All present and former Council members that were present took a silver-painted shovel and did the ground breaking. With pictures of course.

The new casino was to be built on Highway 97 just south of the tribal Community Center. It would be a 58,000 sq. ft. facility which would have 400-500 gaming machines, two restaurants, lounge area with a stage, gift shop, players' club, poker room, and table games. It was to be the first permanent, full-service gaming facility for the Tribe.

It would employ 250 people with a $4 million payroll and generate about $20 million in revenue.

The current Okanogan Bingo Casino would be remodeled to house bingo and a few gaming machines.

The expected opening of the new facility was to be the summer of 2009.

Then the unexpected happened. A skeleton was found during excavation and all work stopped to evaluate whether this was an ancient burial ground. It would take time to analyze. The Council directed that an alternative site be located. Another challenge for the Tribe to meet before moving into a mature enterprise.

In the years after we lost our slot machines and our competitive advantage with other tribal casinos. And then more recently we are experiencing a major world-wide economic downturn which started in 2008.
Later in 2009-10 the Tribes shut down both mills, gave back Seven Bays resort to the National Park Service [NPS], and are trying to sell Roosevelt Recreation. All is due to the recession that the world has slipped into. The outlook is dim for the short-term and the best we can hope for is a gradual improvement over the long run.

More than 400 people attended the September 9 dedication and grand opening of Wenatchi Hall, WVC's new three-story building that houses nursing, radiology and math classes, biology labs, student services and administrative offices. Named after the aboriginal tribe that once lived in the area, the college was honored by the response from members of the Colville Confederated Tribes who were on hand to dedicate the building as a "learning place of medicine" and bless it with cedar incense. "This is our way to make sure the spirit is right for this facility," said tribal member and former WVC trustee, Wendell George.

Wenatchi Hall dedication at the Wenatchee Valley College campus September 9, 2007.

UNIVERSITY OF WASHINGTON
School Of Medicine
June 7, 1986

THE
PICTURE
MAN

As is the microcosm, so is the macrocosm.
As is the atom, so is the universe.
As is the human body, so is the cosmic body.
As is the human mind, so is the cosmic mind.

Sages of India

My Dad tried to incorporate meaning into the process of giving Indian names to his off spring.

My Indian name is "Potwana" [a derivation of Patwankt] who was my qqana [Dad's side] grandmother's grandfather. It means "leader." I didn't receive it until I was a grown man and demonstrated leadership qualities. Robert Jim, Chairman of the Yakama Tribe in the early 70's and Lucy Covington, our long-time councilwoman started saying that, and it led to my dad, Moses, giving me the name. My grandmother came from the same tribe as Robert Jim.

Our children's Indian names are:

Mike - Shy-I-ken - My dad's uncle on his fathers' side.

Rick - Yumpt - Silent, quiet, never brags on himself. Or more recently his name is Takta - Doctor.

Kerry - Seese-Use - Able, capable.

Matt - Xest [huskt] - Good, steady, reliable, always available.

Kathy - Swinumtex [swen-noom-too] - Beautiful, pretty, handsome.

Rob - Slaxt - Friend, buddy, pal, partner.

When we were giving Rob his name he got a funny look on his face and I said, "What's wrong?"

"Nothing, it's just that most of my friends have been calling me that for a long time!"

"Well, that proves the name is accurate."

Each of our family is a good reader. We read for pleasure. It showed in our children's ability to do well in school. Five of them graduated from college with seven degrees among them. Rick is a medical doctor, Kerry is a computer engineer, Matt is a Certified Public Accountant [CPA], Kathy and Rob have business degrees. Mike, who is developmentally disabled, even went to college for one quarter at Wenatchee Valley College.

Rick graduated from the University of Chicago. He was able to go because he received a four-year scholarship from the tribe.

An interesting sidelight came up when Rick took a trip to Florida on October 30, 1978, and was voluntarily hypnotized. He supposedly had several incarnated experiences as a Native American, one as a lodge builder, another as a fisherman, and one named Wapiti. It "was intended to preserve Wapiti." We still don't fully understand the meaning of this.

After Chicago he spent a short time at Stanford, Arizona State, and Washington State University searching for a graduate major. His problem was that he had excellent aptitude for everything. He finally decided on medicine and graduated from the University of Washington Medical School. The following was printed in the Tribal Tribune,

Richard Louis George, the 29-year-old son of Wendell and Barbara George and grandson of Moses and Marie George graduated from the University Of Washington School Of Medicine on June 7, 1986, in a class of 168 who received their Doctorate of Medicine.

Dale Kohler, Colville Business Councilman, said that Rick is the first Colville tribal member to become a medical doctor.

Rick graduated from Coulee Dam's Lake Roosevelt High School in 1975. He received a four year scholarship to attend the University of Chicago, where he majored in psychology and graduated in 1979. He then studied business management at Arizona State University, biochemistry at Washington State University and attended Stanford before deciding to major in medicine in 1982.

On June 24, 1986, he will begin his internship at the University of Southern California's Medical Center in Los Angeles, California. He will be specializing in internal medicine.

Rick is also a sports enthusiast who likes to run for exercise. He has played in several Indian basketball tournaments with his brothers Matt and Kerry on the "Kartar Valley" team. He was chosen for the All Star team in the 1986 Phil Wak Wak Nespelem tournament. Rick now lives in Richland, Washington and works for the Veterans Clinic there.

When we first came back to the Rez we wound up living in Coulee Dam. Our older boys were just entering high school. My plan was to introduce my children to Reservation life and Indian culture.

139

Our son, Rick, had just transferred from Issaquah High School to Lake Roosevelt as a sophomore. At first he had a little trouble with the assistant basketball coach who was heard saying Rick was one of those Nespelem Indian ball players who knew nothing but "run and gun." Rick hadn't played ball in Nespelem and came from the 4-A Issaquah School, which played college-style ball. It turned out all right as the majority of the team were Indians just because of their ability. Besides Rick, that included Richard Whipple, Norris Palmanteer Jr., and Daryl Moulton. They had an excellent team that year. What was fun was the townspeople's support for their teams. Everyone turned out whether they had kids in school or not. Home games were packed and caravans of cars went to the out-of-town games. Rick's team didn't quite make it to the state tournament.

Mike didn't play many sports. He played "C" squad basketball and was a fairly good shot. His team and coach always cheered when he made a basket. Mike had many problems. The doctor told us when he was born he wouldn't live past about five years. Before he went to school he had several operations on his eyelids and nose. At first they didn't have special education classes, and he had a rough time in school. He had basic intelligence, because at one time he memorized all the parts of the human body from a picture in the encyclopedia. But later he had seizures and took medicine to prevent them. This led to a diagnosis of a bi-polar condition. He loved to play the guitar and sing. He liked the Beatles and others popular at the time. He married Josie at Christopher House in Wenatchee. Josie also has seizures. They stayed at the apartments near the Tribal Convalescent Center for a while. Melvin [Bugs] Toulou was their mentor. He did a tremendous job for their ego. He made them toe the mark too.

The high point was when Bugs set up a "concert" at the Nespelem Community Center. Several people performed including Bugs, of course. Many people from the Agency and tribal staff showed up for encouragement. For some reason Mike became bashful just before his turn, but he did manage to sing and play his song with Josie. They got a big hand. People still ask me about them although they had been in Wenatchee for a long time. Mike passed away March 12, 2012.

Kerry is the tallest, but he was a beanpole in high school so he didn't turn out for sports except for tennis, which he was good at. He did play Little League baseball and helped his Bellevue team win the city championship by knocking in the winning run -- excellent hand-to-eye coordination, just like the others boys. I had a hard time beating them at Ping-Pong [my boys would say "In your dreams!"].

Kerry wasn't sure of his major at first either, although he also got a scholarship from the Tribe. He first decided on Western Washington University because it was close to Mount Baker and he wanted to ski there. Unfortunately, [or maybe fortunately] there wasn't much snow that year so he transferred to Washington State University and took computer science. From there he blossomed, graduated, and went to work for Boeing on a space program. He did well at Boeing but he was inspired to take a sabbatical and went back to WSU for a year and took piano. He became an accomplished pianist. We still tease him because when he took piano lessons at age nine or ten he hated it. On the day of his lesson he would get up and say "This is the worst day of my life!"

Kerry now works for a French Company, Morphotrak, at their office in Tacoma, Washington. He is an expert in their large finger print identification program. His machine will compare and match up to 10,000 fingerprints a second. They have had contracts with many states in the U.S. and are now contracted to update the Federal Bureau of Investigation's system. He has spent a lot of time in France working on this. He has become fully immersed in the modern culture. It is work, work, and work. Many people are like that today and as the saying goes, they "don't take time to smell the roses." He intuitively knows this and has taken yoga classes in an attempt to balance his consciousness. Meditation is good and should be used by everyone. To be the most effective, though, it should be directed to a specific purpose in life.

Matt starred in football, basketball and baseball. Matt could accurately throw the football fifty yards, which he did a number of times in games. As a pitcher he was clocked at 88 mph and hit home runs. Because he starred in three sports he was Lake Roosevelt Raider of the Year in his senior year.

Matt's team was always the underdogs because they were so short. Matt at six-foot-one was their post. He was big and could jump, so he held his own with the taller players. They surprised everyone by making it to the State tournament in Tacoma and placing sixth. The opposing Cashmere coach said he was the best pure shooter in the state.

Matt originally received a degree in business and marketing from Eastern Washington University [EWU]. He then added an accounting degree and became a CPA and is now a business and tax consultant. He lives near Poulsbo in Western Washington. Before he went off to college Matt helped me with the cattle ranch. We worked hard and long. It meant "going back to the land." We harvested alfalfa and chased cows all over Kartar Valley. We were truly in touch with nature. I relived my Sxxapa Lahompt's life for a while. But we used modern techniques such as artificial insemination to improve herd quality.

Our only girl, Kathy, became a left-hander when her right side didn't work right. This limited her team sports. However, she loved riding horses and skiing. She was as good as the boys. She was my riding partner on the ranch for many years. Her love/hate relationship with her horse, Stockings, was something to watch: two stubborn beings. One time she came walking back to the corrals all dusty and dirty. I asked "What happened, Kathy?" She said, "Stockings bucked me off!" She went back and rode her horse until they had a meeting of the minds.

Kathy and Stockings

Kathy's EWU degree is in business with a specialty in management information systems [MIS]. She worked for the Tribe for over ten years but never in MIS. She managed several different tribal programs. Now she has decided she wants to be a registered nurse and is going back to school. She lives in Cheney, Washington.

Rob never used his EWU business degree. He has worked for both CIPP and Colville Indian Power and Veneer. Now he mostly works as a carpenter for such projects as the new PSIS and building private homes. He lives in Omak. Rob is the youngest of our children but he captured what none of the rest of us could claim, a championship. His mother and I were courtside witnesses:

The ball hit just inside the court boundaries to our right. I was sure that our son, Rob, couldn't return it but he did. That was just one of many returns that he and Cory Green, his doubles partner, made. They were unconscious.

The state high school tennis tournament at Yakima started on outdoor courts in beautiful sunshine. Rob and Cory easily defeated the Eastern Washington teams of Wapato and Sunnyside and made it into the final rounds. Then it started raining, which was very unusual for the Yakima area in May. It was decided to move the tournament indoors, which put Cory and Rob at a disadvantage as they had never played indoors. The teams they were to play, Vashon Island and Bainbridge Island, played year around, mostly indoors. The lightning was very tricky indoors with shadows that didn't exist outdoors and gave Cory and Rob a good excuse to lose with honor and dignity. But they wouldn't have any of that.

Barbara and I sat on the floor at the edge of the court, holding hands and praying for every shot. Barbara was a good tennis player at Wenatchee High School. Her high point was winning her mixed doubles match at the Spokane Regional tournament. They didn't have a state tournament in those days.

Rob and Cory decided the winter of their senior year to scrape off the snow on the outdoor courts and practice early in the season. It was paying off, because they were undefeated.

The last two matches went to match point against Cory and Rob but they managed to come back and win each time. It was a stunning victory for the doubles championship and resulted in their Okanogan High School winning first place in the tournament.

Barbara and I were thrilled and said a prayer of thanks for Rob and Cory afterward. They must have been in the "ZONE," which many athletes say is when the ball is in slow motion and you can see it very well. Author Eckhart Tolle calls it living in the NOW, meaning ignoring past or present and concentrating just on the moment. Superhuman feats can be accomplished in this mode.

ROB

It looks like we will need superhuman abilities to survive in our world as it evolves. The question is, have our ancestors prepared us for this? The previous story about Rob gives us a clue that maybe they have. The seventh generation is as far back as we can trace our ancestors. We are feeling the effects of actions or decisions that were made back then. According to Indian belief, all major decisions should consider the impact on seven generations down the line.

Success in sports has always been a priority in our family. This is something inherent in most Indian families. My uncle Bud [Emery Picard] was a trick rider. He and his son, Calvin, broke horses to ride. Calvin was a superstar at Chemawa in four sports: football, basketball, baseball, and track. He made the newspaper when he kicked the football in a game seventy yards, barefooted. That was in Salem, Oregon, where it rains a lot. He said his shoes were all muddy so he took them off to kick.

Most of our sons and daughter worked for the tribe during the summers. Fire Control was the main source of jobs. Kerry and Rick, were on the elite helitac crew. They rode a helicopter, which was usually the first to a fire. Kathy and Rob worked for the tribe and Okanogan Forest Service. Rob spent the most time on fire crews and even went to several fires off the Reservation to Montana and Oregon. Kathy cleared trails and manned a Fire Lookout Station.

As a family, we probably enjoyed fishing at Owhi Lake the most. Catching those big Eastern brook trout was fun. Later, when we moved to Kartar Valley we bought a boat and did a lot of water skiing. One year we had a family reunion with Barbara's family and went up Lake Roosevelt in a houseboat all the way to Kettle Falls camping, fishing, swimming, and water-skiing. It was fun but the close quarters caused some tension after six days together.

My family did make the transition into the "modern" world. They were models of success in the physical sense. But in doing so they lost much of their spiritual selves. We obviously pushed too hard for them to become successful in school and ignored their spiritual growth until they were adults. Now it will be very difficult for them but not impossible.

All of our offspring have a deep compassion for others. Rick and Kathy have been drawn to the health field to help those in need. Kerry has a deep, broader feel for life in general. He is like my friend John Dick who I observed while we were driving to Wenatchee on a business trip. John was driving when we ran into a flock of birds near Waterville. Some of them smashed against the windshield and were killed instantly. John slowed down and said "Oh my God, I am sorry!"

Kerry has developed his spiritual side in spite of our lack of effort. I offer a couple of observations to justify my conclusion.

First, I took him up hunting on the Omak Ridge above Kartar Valley when he was about twelve years old. I shot a deer and began dressing it out. He became green around the gills, but he did help. When we returned home he told me he would never do that again.

Another time, just a few years ago, I killed a rattlesnake in my shop at Kartar Valley. Again, he watched me do it and then said,

"Why did you have to kill it? He has a right to live too!"

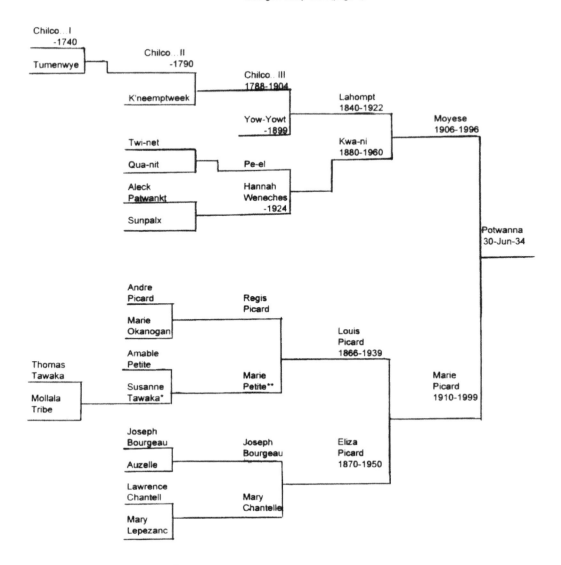

*Married Amable Petite on 12/27/1838 at Ft Vancouver
by Fr Blanchet
**Baptized 1/9/1840 at Paul's Mission on Williamette
by Fr Blanchet

Kathy - Colleen - Kerry - Jan - Matt - Mike - Rob - Olivia - Rick

Erin - Christyna - Andy - Wendell - Amy - Barbara - Brendyn
Brandon - Moses

Rick - Rob - Kathy - Kerry - Matt - Mike
Wendell - Barbara

REFLECTIONS

There are a lot of misconceptions about what will happen in 2012. The movie with the same name was about destruction of the world. Another movie, *Apocalypto,* tried to describe the "Age of the Jaguar" but did a gross injustice to the legacy of the Mayans. The scene that took place somewhere between 435-830 A.D. showed Mayan pyramids but ignored their significance. The Mayan natives were not ignorant aboriginals without any purpose in life but survival, as depicted in the movie. The movie showed Mayan priests that had a familiar ring of the terrorists of today who run in gangs intent only on killing. That describes our terrorists of today but not the true Mayans. It was more appropriate to the Aztecs who came later and understood very little of the Mayan culture. We cannot define our civilization by the acts of ancient terrorists.

To be fair, though, it would have been difficult, if not impossible, to fully disclose the deeper meaning of the Mayan culture in the movie.

For example, the Mayan symbol of the Hunab Ku means the life beyond the sun, or the galactic core. Its purpose is to give energy, both physical and psychic, through frequencies. In short, it is the Frequency Domain. The Chinese Yin-Yan symbol means the same.

The Mayan phrase Kuxan Suum means "The Road to the Sky Leading to the Umbilical Cord of the Universe." These invisible galactic life threads connect both the individual and the planet, through the sun, to the galactic core, Hunab Ku. These threads are the same as the luminous threads extended from the solar plexus described by the Medicine Man, Don Juan, in Carlos Castaneda's series of Yaqui Wisdom Books. In the Mayan texts, "Popul Vuh" and "The Annals of the Cakchiquels", the Yaquis were the first of the Mayan tribes to separate from the rest of the clans following entry into this world. The purpose of the Yaquis in so doing was to keep at least some of the original teachings of the Maya relatively pure and in a remote place.

According to 'Brian Swimme of the Holy Names College in Oakland, all this is incorporated into the Tzolkin of the Maya. This describes the following:

First, that human history is shaped in a large part by a galactic beam through which the Earth and Sun have been passing for the past 5,000 years, and that a great moment of transformation awaits us as we arrive at the beam's end in 2012;

Second, that the activities and worldviews of cultures follow the nature of the "galactic seasons," the code of which has been captured both mathematically and symbolically by the Maya.

Third, that each person has the power to connect directly – sensuously, sensually, electromagnetically – with the energy or information of this beam that emanates from the galactic core and can in this way awaken to one's true mind, higher mind, and deepest mind.

How do we know all this? Research and study are the first steps, but we must move our thought process to a new level. The seventh generation is in an excellent position to do exactly that. They have learned how to concentrate their thoughts to get new meaning out of old information. The process of going to college teaches you to think, if nothing else. It gives you the tools to think through complicated subjects. This is necessary now and will be even more necessary as our world moves faster and faster.

We wanted our offspring to be successful but we also wanted to put everything in perspective. The story of the American Indian is only one example of the collective attitude of the Western World. The migration of the Europeans to American resulted in an attitude of "me first and the h__with everyone else."

Lee Iacocca, former CEO of the Chrysler Corporation, is a case in point. He was a second-generation immigrant who rose from nothing to the top of one of the United States' largest businesses. This enabled Mr. Iacocca to view the Statue of Liberty from the front door, where she is receiving immigrant with open arms, a benevolent smile and a promise that the United States is truly a land of equal opportunity. It seems that all is needed is the ambition, ability and drive to go for it. This is true for everyone in the United States but the First Americans.

Our family has prepared ourselves physically and mentally for the coming changes in our world. My grandmother, Kwa-ni told my dad to get all the education he could to cope with the coming events. He not only prepared himself but he encouraged me and all our children and grandchildren to do the same. Each of us has followed our own path to enlightenment, but I am confident that we will all reach it in time. I may be the only one to clearly see what is in store for us in the future, but the others are ready for it whether consciously or unconsciously.

We, as Indians, see the Statue of Liberty from the back door where she has her arms around us in a choking bear-hug, a hypocritical smile and a promise that she can do more with our natural resources than we can. Yet our ancestors left a legacy in plant genetics which has developed into billion dollar crops like corn, potatoes and tobacco; native medical cures using quinine, cocaine and curare; heat-efficient, below-grade housing architecture; consumer uses of natural rubber including boots and even an early form of basketball. So

146

our system was working before Columbus and probably would have evolved with the times. But we were perturbated by the European culture and the resulting hybrid system left us in a social dependency.

This dependency is certainly not by choice. The system we have been forced into has limited our opportunities, sometimes by design and sometimes by omission. The rules are confusing to us because they are not uniformly applied. The jungle we live in only vaguely resembles our ancestors' spirit of democracy. It is called free enterprise but the 5,000-plus laws applicable only to Indians have redefined "freedom" for us. As the Americans to first practice democracy on this continent, the time has come for us to be teacher instead of student.

I have been concerned about the legacy my generation was leaving. The next generation is not aware of all the undercurrents that went on in both the dominant society and the Indian community. So I have summarized the situation up to about 1990. It went like this…

Indian democracy predates that of the United States even if only written history is used for comparison. The League of the Five [later Six] Nations was founded by Hiawatha about 1570 for the Iroquois. This League had a constitution that included initiative, referendum, recall, women's suffrage and a Bill of Rights. Ben Franklin was so impressed with this organization that he recommended in his Albany Plan of 1754, that the Colonies use it as a model. They finally, after debating whether the average citizen was ready to make decisions for himself, adopted many of the same features in the U.S. Constitution in 1789.

Other Indian Confederacies including the Creek, Cherokee, Delaware and my tribes, originally the Columbia Confederacy, and now expanded to the Colville Confederated Tribes, were also based on democratic principles. I made it a point to discuss this with my Indian colleagues whose tribes were members of the civilized tribes, Ernie Stevens Sr. of the Oneida, and Stu Seneca of the Seneca. Some of my cousins live in Oklahoma and married into the Cherokee tribe. We found many similarities about how our tribes operated.

The Columbia Confederacy was formed in the Pacific Northwest about 1829 by Half Sun, father of our notable Chief Moses. He was elected Chief of the Confederacy because of his demonstrated leadership abilities, not by his heritage, because he had none with the Sinkiuse, which was his adopted tribe. He was very sensitive to his peoples'needs and had a democratic approach to leadership because he always consulted his constituency before taking any action. This was a basic form of a referendum. He and Moses took all major issues to the "Council Fires" for a thorough discussion before a decision was made. Any member of the Tribe could bring an issue before the people for consideration; a basic form of the initiative. This group of people was also the "court" that decided on Bill of Rights issues. There was no way to "block" an issue from being heard as is so prevalent in all branches of government today, especially the judicial branch. After it was thoroughly discussed, a vote was taken and the majority ruled. Majority rule, of course, is another way of describing the one-man, one-vote principle. There was no imbalance in voting districts because each person voted for himself. It was democracy at its simplest and finest, and ironically, the Indian Way.

Under this truly democratic government our Confederacy, while not rich by most standards, was more than able to care for its own needs. As with most tribes, our Chief was a spokesman for his people, not a dictatorial ruler, as is commonly believed by Europeans who evolved from a monarchy. This was true because if a Chief didn't lead by being a good example and use logical reasoning he would soon lose the respect of his constituency. Since each member of the tribe made his own decision, he always had the choice of leaving the Band, either to start his own group or join another. In any event, individual freedom was foremost in the Indian culture.

Contrast this with Poland, who until 1788 used the liberum veto during their legislative [Seym] meetings which meant that a single dissenting vote would prevent any action from being taken on an issue. The potential for bribery or coercion by those with vested interests was infinite. Of course, this is how the Polish aristocracy stayed in power at the expense of the more numerous and poor farmers. It was a dictatorship in the guise of a democracy.

Sophisticated versions of this exist in the United States today. The BIA" "model constitution," which purported to follow the U.S. Constitution, was pushed on the tribes during the implementation of the 1934 Indian Reorganization Act. Unfortunately many tribes adopted it even though it is not the Indian Way or what is actually defined in the U.S. Constitution. It left out the key elements of initiative, referendum, recall, and a Bill of Rights. These omissions have been more devastating to our survival than anything else, including acts of aggression, disease, famine, theft and prejudice. Indians, as a group, have the resiliency to recover from direct attacks, as evidenced by history. Even slightly more subtle forms of genocide such as the Allotment Act, Reclamation Act, Homestead Act and termination of reservations have not been able to eliminate us. But genocide from within is a very real threat and has the potential to be the ultimate solution to the "Indian problem."

The seed was planted when the tribes eventually agreed to require a ¼ Indian blood quantum to be a member of the tribe. This was against all previous customs of Indian people. Our ancestors intermarried with other tribes before the reservation was created. The couple choose which tribe they wanted to join. The criteria for selection by the tribe or the individuals was whether they had beliefs and customs that suited them. That was more important than blood quantum. The initial tribal constitution created by the BIA on February 26, 1938 did not include a blood quantum limit. It wasn't until Amendment Three was incorporated on May 20, 1949 that a ¼ Indian blood requirement was added. Even then, all names on the June 1, 1937 census, which was used as the base role, were included as members. Many of those were members of other tribes but were considered members of the Colville Confederated Tribes and their descendants used their blood quantum to meet the ¼ requirement.

On May 9, 1959 Amendment Five was added which required ¼ blood quantum of the twelve Colville Confederated Tribes. This resulted in a lot of confusion because it was a total reversal of the original constitution and Amendment Three. From that point on other tribes could not be used to establish blood quantum.

Since there were only 300 plus full blood tribal members on the 1937 census we can't maintain our membership under the ¼ rule unless we inbreed or use blood quantum from other tribes. This will ultimately result in a steady decline in our enrollment.

The ¼ rule seems innocent and innocuous but it is an effective way to reduce our membership and eventually eliminate our tribe.

The story of my tribe is probably typical. The real or implied collusion of the federal government and individual tribal council members has become increasingly more apparent. The "model constitution" which was forced on us instituted four voting districts instead of voting by tribal affiliation. In 1945, just seven years after the tribal constitution was approved, our Colville Tribal Council, in one of their enlightened moods, tried to change the method of electing councilmen to a reservation-wide vote instead of by districts. This would have neutralized the large [2:1] voter imbalance in the districts. The council followed all the procedures, even ratification by a referendum vote of tribal members which wasn't required by the tribal constitution, but the BIA still rejected it. Their act of rejection itself ignored our presumed sovereignty status. Even worse, we were told it was rejected because it would be unfair to the smaller Bands. This was inconsistent because the BIA "model constitution" used by our tribe had replaced Bands with Districts.

At first, Council functions were mostly ceremonial because no one knew how to operate the government described in the tribal constitution. Members elected to the Council did not have the benefit of either Chief's training or, many times, a formal education so weren't prepared to meet this demanding challenge. By default, BIA personnel became the phantom government, which was disastrous as indicated by the cases our tribe subsequently won in Indian Claims Court and the Cobell case for BIA mismanagement of our reservation resources.

In this environment, the absence of the tools of democracy such as initiative, referendum and a bill of rights in tribal constitutions wasn't apparent. The Council didn't impose its will on the tribe, so members weren't motivated to search for corrective actions. Since there wasn't any industry on reservations, there was very little money and few jobs to fight over.

This changed when Lyndon Johnson became President in the sixties and launched his "Great Society" social and political reforms. Indians jumped aboard this bandwagon with rising hopes and increasing expectations that, by some miracle, industries and jobs would also be created by these training programs. Congress pumped billions into his War on Poverty which included Job Corps, Neighborhood Youth corps, Project Head Start, Community Action Program, Adult Vocational Training and the Housing and Urban Development. The scramble to get a piece of the record-high funding created a new skill called "Grantsmanship." A cult evolved which attacked the funding sources with the same vigor as the hunter did the buffalo.

But these programs encountered tremendous growing pains because such large volumes of money were being handled by inexperienced people, both in the government and in the Indian community. Insufficient planning went into the implementation because the training programs were treated as the end rather than a means to an end. All these programs were intended to provide training so Indians could either get jobs or start businesses in the private sector. But there was very little private sector on reservations and what existed didn't need the newly trained work force. The government had already learned that most Indians will not leave the reservation to find work. The Economic Development Agency tried to rectify this by helping build industrial parks that were intended to entice businesses to the reservations but these soon became white elephants because there were too few people who had the interest and ability to start new businesses on the reservation.

As Utopia began to wane, the 1970s brought the Indian self-determination era which changed the emphasis from training to contracting. The government gave Indian tribes contracts and technical support to perform various governmental functions, generally some type of service. But since they all depended on government funding, they weren't productive in the free market and did not have the inherent leverage to make them self-sustaining. So instead of becoming more independent and able to control and direct our own affairs we became even more dependent on the government. We simply moved from the "Fort" Indian begging for food at the entrance to the Fort to the more sophisticated "Agency" Indian begging for contracts. Without primary industries on reservations, the largest employer was still the BIA and a tribal staff which is at least partially funded by the government.

Then in 1983, Assistant Secretary of Interior James Watt, using Johnson's 1968 "Forgotten American" speech, described Indians as the example of the failures of socialism. He concluded that the socialist dependency is fostered by the Indian leaders to keep their own jobs which are funded by the government. This ignored the fact that the expressed purpose of these programs is to train Indians to operate their own affairs so the fault is in the design of the programs, not the performance of the Indians involved. If the programs are considered handouts, then they should be changed to correct the problem and to promote more independency by Indian tribes.

The emphasis on contracting has produced a certain level of independency on the part of Indians. However, these contracts usually only involves the delegation of a service delivery from Federal to tribal governments. The private sector, for the most part, still has not been included. Now we have to bring in private enterprise in such a manner that Indians are a part of the action. This means changing the government's contracting policy to include programs that will lead to new businesses. Through this approach Indians can gradually get the experience necessary to eventually become independent. A better job of planning is required to establish a business environment that will bring and hold new enterprises. Our Indian leaders must establish policies that encourage the creation of private enterprises, which usually means giving up their direct control. It has been proven that neither Federal nor tribal governments can successfully create and/or operate businesses. But to give up control is difficult for people because it takes skill in the art of delegation and an element of trust.

The millions of federal dollars flowing into the reservations have become a necessary habit and it is only natural for Indian leaders to fight to maintain this type of government handouts. This is certainly easier than facing the most difficult task of exploring new approaches to economic development on the reservation. Unfortunately, it has tempted many tribal councils to evolve into a totalitarian entity with unlimited powers. This is not the Indian Way.

Our offspring have seven college degrees among five of them. But too much education can be a drawback. The attitudes formed at college are those of the dominant culture. In addition to that the conscience formed from being too successful when compared to others with the same background creates an "I have to give something back" attitude. This is OK if properly directed, but it can result in a socialist state if not. That would be the result of a collective movement towards asking the government to require that everyone give something back instead of leaving it to individual choice. This is a very controversial issue and can result in a heated argument. A case in point is the discussion I had with three of our sons, Rick, Kerry, and Matt, a couple of years ago. I offer my best effort at reconstructing the conversation.

We were all sitting under the gazebo in our backyard in Omak having refreshments when I told of an argument I had with an American Association of Retired Persons [AARP] representative on their blog.

"Why is AARP against enabling the people to choose how their Social Security funds are invested?"

"Because the government knows how to invest better than most people."

"You know that for a fact?"

"Yes."

"What are your sources?"

"It's just a known fact."

"I don't know it and I can invest better than the government."

"You're the exception."

"Why should I be penalized because I am the exception? Give me the option."

"It is better for the majority."

"What is the majority?"

"More than half."

"OK, let's say 51 percent is the majority. So 49 percent of us are penalized to protect the other half. Is that right?"

"I wouldn't say penalized. It is more an act to help those less fortunate."

"So this super smart government will always be there to protect those unfortunate few?"

"That's the idea."

"Then why do major government offices such as my wife's Forest Service offer a retirement program similar, if not identical, to the 401K offered by private industry which allows many choices of investments?"

"Those are government workers and are assumed to be intelligent enough to make their own decisions."

"Just because they work for the government?"

"Not entirely, but partly."

"Private industry has many highly intelligent people and they make our economy work. Why aren't they considered intelligent enough to make their own decisions?"

"Some are, but not all."

"So you are saying one size fits all. If one person is lacking intelligence then we must all suffer for it. This looks like a "dummying down" process. None of us can rise above the dumbest one in our civilization."

"You are generalizing too much. It's not like that at all."

My boys surprised me by agreeing with this guy. It seems they all wanted to help those more unfortunate than they. I asked,

"Why don't you give money to charity then? That is a more direct way to help those less fortunate."

Their answer was that the government has much more funds to deal with and they can have more impact.

150

"Consider this. Our tax dollars go to the government who arbitrarily decide who they help. The system requires many government workers just to administer this which reduces the funds for those in need. They get whatever is left when the costs are deducted. Charities, even larger ones, are much more efficient. But you can improve on that by giving money directly to those who need it. Why not do that?"

Rick: "Most of my time is spent earning my pay. I don't have time to hunt for people to help."

Kerry: "Getting back to the Social Security issue why do you think it is socialistic to have the government decide how to invest the funds?"

"That is a good question. The investment part is only a small part of the issue. The bigger issue is why does the government have to control everything in our lives? To take a simpler case let's look at our ancestors when they were still nomads and lived in a pure Indian culture.

"The chief didn't take part of everyone's belongings so he could give it to someone he thought needed it. On the contrary, he gave his own to help his people. He was sometimes the poorest one in his tribe because he gave everything away. This attitude trickled down to everyone in the tribe. They each helped each other directly and voluntarily. There was no law that said they had to do it. It was true government by the people. The governing body had no power unless specifically given to them by the tribal members. It was the opposite of a dictatorship. If a chief became selfish he was soon replaced. The need for a governing body was only for warfare or problems putting the tribe at risk such as a famine. The rest of the time tribal members were pretty much on their own but tempered by their upbringing, which required them to do what was best for each member of the tribe. Independence was prime. Any law created would be a reduction of their independence."

Matt: "That sounds good but how do we apply that here? We have over 300 million people and to keep it from getting completely out of hand we have to have laws."

"At this point you're right. We are the victims of not having a good understanding of our U.S. Constitution. Part of the reason is it is not foremost in everyone's mind. The competitive nature of the predominant culture causes an attitude of doing things without considering the consequences down the road. Indians tried not to get in that fix by analyzing situations beforehand. When the U.S. Constitution was formed it was a poor imitation of Indian democracy. It left out referendum, initiative, recall, women's suffrage and almost everything key to a true democracy. The reason was, of course, is that the framers of the Constitution came from dictatorships and royalties, which was the opposite of democracy. They didn't understand it. Many still don't. They want the warm and fuzzy feeling that a benevolent government will take care of them. The Bill of Rights corrected some of this but it is piecemeal and the wording leaves a lot to be desired.

"Since our culture has grown out of a diverse mixture we do not have a benevolent government. Too many games are being played under the name of helping others. The AARP is a prime example. They are helping the government make new laws so they can stay in control and make more money. The shill I was talking to was actually part of the AARP staff assigned to minimize the effects of criticizing the governments' Social Security program. AARP is big business but in partnership with the government so they can both stay in power.

Kerry: "But we have many illiterate people and they don't understand any of this. Who's going to help them?"

"In a perfect world they would need some smart people who didn't have an axe to grind. But in this world of everybody climbing over each other to get ahead isn't a perfect world. Your question goes back to the Jefferson/Hamilton debate when framing the Constitution. Hamilton said nobody should be allowed to vote if they were illiterate. Jefferson said everyone should be allowed to vote. In practice only land owners could vote at first and no women were allowed to vote until 1920. I can only answer your question by saying we need a paradigm shift in collective attitude before we can actually help everyone. This means we have to be honest with ourselves and with others. Sound impossible? Maybe, but I have confidence our next generation will take major steps in that direction."

Andy, Moses, and Amy

Sometime in 1999 Barbara and I were sitting at the kitchen table at our log house in Kartar Valley reminiscing about things that happened over the last few years.

It all started when our youngest son, Rob, and Becki had our grandson, Moses, on January 27, 1999. He was named after my dad, which was a big responsibility for him to carry. We were living at our Kartar Valley ranch at the time and Rob and Becki were at the HUD housing in Nespelem. Although they were dirt-poor, there was a lot of love at first. Moses had three older half-sisters Jessika, Taylor, and Mariah, age's six to nine.

Things quickly became more complicated when Becki called us one day and said she was pregnant with twins. She was desperate. There was no way for her to care for them, as she was overwhelmed already. She was in the process of getting an abortion and wanted to alert us.

It didn't take Barbara and me long to decide to tell Becki not to get an abortion. We told her we would take care of her and the twins. That was a big step but we didn't flinch. To us abortion is the most horrifying thing that could happen to a human being.

Consciousness starts at conception and the human spirit becomes more and more aware of its environment as he or she grows.

She moved out to the ranch with us before the twins were born. The girls were sent to Paschal Sherman Indian School in Omak on a school bus. Every day I would drive them out to the bus stop that was about a half-mile away.

The twins came early at about three-and-a-half months before they were due. Becki went to the hospital in Spokane via a helicopter from Omak. Rob, Barbara, and I followed in our car but arrived just after they were born on November 19, 1999. Moses, who was about ten months old then, came with us. The twins were in incubators and on life support for some time after that. Andy would forget to breathe on occasion and Amy had asthma. When we brought them home our house was filled with life support equipment and baby things. It couldn't get any homier than that.

We were experiencing, all over again, the emotional [Yellow] quadrant of the Medicine Wheel. This quadrant is where you can experience and expand your family love, which is a basis for extending the love beyond to everyone. It was an on-the-ground experience of what we had been talking about for almost twenty years during our numerous Cursillos. It was where the theory came into a proven fact. Our understanding of life and all its peripherals were coming together.

Moses, Rob's oldest boy, is a chip off the ol' block. He showed his colors just a month before his tenth birthday. His Amateur Athletic Union [AAU] basketball team was having a fund-raiser on Saturday, January 3, 2009 so they could buy uniforms. Pledges were made either as a lump sum or donations per basket made. Stevens Gym in Omak was full of spectators, mostly parents, grandparents or siblings. Of course, the twins, Andy and Amy, were there to see their brother.

But Moses worried about it so much the night before that he started getting sick in his stomach. He didn't want to go and even took his basketball pictures of his previous teams off his wall. On Saturday morning he threw up. We knew this would happen, so we didn't pledge any donations per basket but just a lump sum. We didn't want to put pressure on him to make baskets. I made him go in spite of all this. He asked his grandma to tell me not to be so hard on him, but she acquiesced to me.

Once he got on the floor he was a little better but still nervous. Luckily, he was early in the contest at the No. Four position. He would have been a nervous wreck if he had to wait very long, as there were forty or fifty contestants.

As soon as he started shooting, which was a lay-in, he just concentrated on what he was doing. He shut out the crowd and made thirteen of fifteen shots. The last shot was from the top of the key which was out of his range, because he couldn't reach the basket. As you might suspect he was first for the fourth grade boys. He was only one less than the sixth grade boys. He was at a higher level of consciousness and, just like his dad and his Sxxapa, he was in the "ZONE."

Andy did well in his first third grade basketball game. He drove towards the basket on dribble drives and made eight points out of the team's 24. They won against Pateros. Both Moses and Andy have to be encouraged to take more shots. They prefer to pass off.

Amy can catch and throw any ball but she doesn't want to turn out for a team. She would rather watch her brothers. She is a little bashful so we don't force her. She did go to karate class with her brothers and got a white belt. Moses also got a white belt but Andy went on with his cousin, Brandon, to get his yellow belt. Brandon continued with it.

This high priority on athletics kept us all in good physical condition and, what some may not realize, it maximized our ability to learn. As a result, our children were all good students.

This is not unlike our ancestors who also had high esteem for physical conditioning. The methods were different of course because of the different times. They rode horses, walked, ran and endured hardships in outdoor environments. Today we control and moderate our environment with gymnasiums and covered ball parks, but we don't spare the physical conditioning necessary to excel at football, basketball, baseball, tennis and the many other games we play. The intensity is still there.

I am convinced that Moses and his siblings, Andy and Amy, the community-famous preemie twins, are probably Indigo children. I suspect their cousins Erin, Brandon and Christyna are, too, but I don't know them as well. This term refers to children with a high level of psychic powers. According to psychic Nancy Ann Tappe, ninety-five percent of the children born in the last ten years have this energy pattern. This trend was actually predicted earlier by Edgar Cayce. They are in three groups: The Indigos, who are about seven to twenty-five years old now; the Crystals, who are zero to sixteen years old, and the Rainbows, who just started being born about the year 2000. The Indigos have a warrior spirit and want to quash everything that is wrong today. The Crystals have large penetrating eyes and are happy, delightful, and forgiving.

These lightworkers are pointing to where humanity is heading. And, finally, there are the Rainbows, who are avatars and all about service. They are at their spiritual peak. This is a global trend, so these children will help bring in a new consciousness.

The Indigo, Crystal, and Rainbow children are leading us into the next world just like the mystery of the Kokopelli.

153

It is just in time, too, because Dr. Walter Russell wrote about 1940 that it takes a certain number of enlightened citizens on our planet to raise the level of all civilization. He said during his time there were too few of these to make a difference. But since then there have been increasing numbers brought to earth to help us.

According to Jane Roberts in her 1975 book, *Adventures in Consciousness*, there are what she called "Speakers," both on earth and in spirit, that teach what our life on earth is all about. Shakespeare and Blake were such persons.

And according to Ruth Montgomery in her 1979 book, *Stranger Among Us* there are also what she called "Walk-ins," who take over a willing person's body to preserve the present knowledge of science and industry and to awaken people's awareness of their inner self and life after death. They teach others how to tune into the wisdom of the ages through telepathy and inner knowledge. She wrote: "The future is NOW!" and "As we think, we become".

She also wrote that American Indians are a psychic race. They sing the song of Thanksgiving to the Creator. I found that is personified in the Hopi "Song of Creation." She said that Indians hold each day as a previous epitome of one's entire life.

As we sat pondering the waves on Omak Lake I asked my seven-year-old grandson, Moses, to throw a rock into the water. I didn't want him to try to skip it like he usually did but just lob it so it fell naturally. He did and we watched silently as the rock entered the water with a splash, creating waves that radiated outwardly in concentric circles. I said, "Let's imagine that rock is a stone person."

"OK, I can do that."

"Now, let's say you are that stone person. The concentric waves you created are all your thoughts, good and bad, which sometimes turn into action. You are responsible for those thoughts. Now throw another rock close to the first one."

"Why, Poppa?"

"To show how you will create lots of splashes in your life and the waves that come from those splashes will disturb the peace of all your family and friends. See how the waves overlap? The second rock is another stone person. The waves from each rock affects the waves of the other just like your thoughts affect other people. Sometimes it is a reinforcing thought and other times a negative thought."

"How can it be two different things?"

"It depends what you put in your circle because it will touch the circle of others. You have to live in a way that allows the good that comes from your circle to send a piece of that goodness to others. The splash that comes from anger or jealousy will send those feelings to others' circles. You are responsible for both."

Moses then began to realize that each person creates the inner peace or discord that flows out into the world. Each person radiates the feelings and thoughts that he holds inside, whether he speaks them or not. Whatever is splashing around inside each person is spilling out into the world, creating beauty or discord with all other circles of life. To punctuate the point I asked, "Can you create world peace if you are filled with inner conflict, hatred, doubt, or anger?"

"No."

"Good, Moses! You are a quick learner, Grandson. Just remember that whatever you focus on will grow and expand."

Moses was typical of the eighth generation and they came in waves. Each wave consisted of dedicated people with a mission. Their mission was the same but their methods were different. It was not unlike the commandos of World War II. They were all prepared for their mission and confident that they would achieve it.

The people in the first wave were determined to make major changes in the way the world works. These were the Indigo children. They had a warrior spirit but were not warriors. They were relentless in their efforts to instill honor as the primary trait that people respected. It was only honorable to help people not hurt them. But the help was not offered as a substitute for doing things for yourself. What the Indigos changed was the system. No more doing things for you. Each individual was to be held responsible for his own actions. Indigo children can sense dishonesty. They know when they are being lied to, patronized and manipulated. Their collective purpose is to usher us into a new world of integrity. They can't conform to dysfunctional situations at home, work or school.

What made the Indigos capable of achieving this was their direct communication with the Universal Mind of the Creator-God or Haweyenchuten. This is the first direction of the Medicine Wheel. They tuned themselves into the psychic messages being sent from the core of the universe. Their understanding of the messages was clear and uncluttered. It was like former astronaut Edgar Mitchell who once remarked, "I feel almost as if I'm operating under orders...Just when I think all is lost, I put my foot down over an abyss – and something comes up to hit it, just in time."

The primary direction they took was to decentralize government. To do that they had to help people and nations change their hearts and minds. One motto that evolved was, "Let there be peace and let it begin with me." Each person had to transform. But the effect wouldn't be noticed until a certain threshold was reached. The few could influence the many. This is in line with the old axiom that ten percent of the people do ninety percent of the work.

The belief is that individuals, once they are convinced of a need for change, can generate solutions from their own commitment and creativity. The larger movement is self-inspiring because it supports their efforts and gives them information but there is no paternal organization to direct or contain their efforts. They moved as one because they each had the same mind-set.

The next wave was the Crystals whose common traits were that they were happy, delightful, forgiving and wise beyond their years. They brought unconditional love to the community. This is the second direction of the Medicine Wheel. Their benevolent emotions spread to everyone. Their family extended to the whole world. The emphasis on the individual established by the Indigos helped the Crystals create a peaceful collective attitude.

The Rainbows were the third wave. They are avatars [Hindu meaning God's coming to bodily form]. They are all about service. They are entirely fearless of everybody. They are at their spiritual peak and are here on Earth only to give. They are the offspring of the Crystal children. This is the third direction of the Medicine Wheel, where each of us does a self-analysis to determine where we are in life and where we want to go. We then make changes in our lives to accomplish our goal. The changes will be learning to live by spiritual laws.

The Rainbows continue to develop the telepathic abilities given them by their Crystal parents. They are truly in direct contact with Noah's Rainbow. This makes them much more aware of their intuitive thoughts and feelings. They don't rely as much on the spoken or written word. Communication will be faster, more direct and more honest because it will be mind to mind. Their psychic abilities will grow.

I am becoming more and more aware of these Indigo children.

Our grandchildren are the eighth generation from our collective memory starting point. As such, they are the start of a new cycle of human evolution. As the saying goes they have a whole world of opportunity before them.

While on the Council I wrote articles for the Tribal Tribune which became the basis of my talks with students in both the Paschal Sherman Indian School [PSIS] and the Omak schools. For many years, even before I was on the Council, I would talk to students at St. Mary's/PSIS. At first my cousins, Anita Cheer and her daughter, Karen Sam, both teachers at the St. Mary's school would invite me to visit their class, which was usually the fourth grade. The class would write me invitations and then thank you notes. They were precious to me so I would hang them up in my Council office. One time when I went in the Koxit George building [named after my grandfather] the kids were pretty noisy until Karen introduced me and one boy said, "Oh! You're him." He meant the one they wrote letters to.

One of the first articles I wrote was on Indian Spirituality published on Friday, December 19, 1986. I related Indian Spirituality to Jean Auel's cave dwellers in her book, *Clan of the Cave Bear*. Their life was ruled by spiritual beliefs on how to live compatibly with nature. When they learned to talk they lost their "cosmic consciousness" and their relationship to nature. They began the life of physical emphasis that we now live in. The only way we can find the spiritual life again is through meditation, religion and study. To rediscover it we have the difficult task of overcoming the physical distractions.

Then I wrote on April 26, 1988, an article I called Indian Spirituality, Part II. The purpose of this article was to rekindle our Indian belief that we are one with nature, one with Creator-God [Hawenyenchuten]. Even though some families are doing a good job with their children, they are finding it more and more difficult to instill an "Indianness" in them because they are confronted daily with non-Indian activities, beliefs, and attitudes. I offer suggestions to help reprogram ourselves as Indians. In the old days Coyote stories were used to teach children tribal ways. These are still good for preschoolers. As children get older they need more, so I offered "Coyote Power" or Semyow Seesuse in the Wenatchee dialect. Coyote was the teacher of balance and the symbol of power, according to Michael Paul, a tribal elder. One story not told in the legends is the parallel of the near extinction and miraculous come-back of the Coyote and the Indian. Both have been hunted down and killed but not eliminated. They have a survival instinct and resiliency that is unbeatable. The key for survival is to find the balance of nature and to become one with it.

Along this line I made several presentations to the PSIS students. I showed them how to think like an Indian. To grab their attention I showed them a Bev Doolittle drawing of what at first glance looks like a forest scene. Upon closer inspection several faces of Indians show up. They were hidden among the trees. I pointed out that is us, as Indians, hidden among the multitudes. We have to look at life just right to see the Indian in us. One way to do this is to relate our life to the Medicine Wheel. The four winds are the same as the four directions of the Medicine Wheel except the wind indicates movement or something happening. Chapter Two of the Acts of the Apostles in the Bible mentions a strong driving wind which in Hebrew [Ru-Ah] means "spirit, breath or wind. In Greek the word is pneuma, which means power. Indian stories say the North wind is the strongest or most powerful in the physical world but each direction has a special meaning. South wind is supportive. East wind provides energy and West wind is the intellect. This is the same spirit that St. Paul says is poured in and out of our hearts. Indians always try to talk from their hearts.

In my February 17, 1990, article I discussed tribal members Sheila and Bill Timentwa's talk on what it is to be one with nature, trees and animals in the woods. The harmony that they described applies to families, countries and the earth as a whole. The European western culture has interrupted this harmony with their concepts of land ownership and their driving need to conquer and control the earth. Indian spiritualism is present when you "know" things are right and in harmony. Today it would be called intuition, but to be spiritual it must be based on spiritual not physical values. A few sample comparisons demonstrate the contrasts:

Indians tend to be group oriented and take pride in cooperation and harmony. On the other hand, the European western culture values individual competition. As a result, Indians sometimes do not do well in western schools because of their non-competitive nature.

Indians value modesty, dignity, personal autonomy and silence. Many of us have a low ego and tend to strive for anonymity. The needs of the group are considered over those of the individual. The European culture values individual accomplishments, giving free advice and constant action. As a result, Indians are sometimes mistakenly thought to be shy or backward.

Indians notably have patience and the ability to wait quietly. Sharing and generosity are also greatly valued. Indians are not status conscious in terms of material goods and lack an upward social mobility in society. Europeans, tend to act quickly and impatiently, value individual ownership and measure success by the accumulation of material goods. As a result, the European society may become impatient with Indians' comparative slowness and deliberateness. Indians are sometimes considered unsuccessful because of their lack of accumulated goods.

On March 10, 1990, I wrote about Native Americans in Canada who are three times more likely to die before age 35 than non-natives. Another survey of American teenagers showed non-Indians listing achievement, career choices and relationship as their concerns. Indians listed rejection, substance abuse and relationships.

Part of the reason for this contrast is Indians tend to be visual learners through demonstration not reading or verbal communication. Formal education relies more on the latter. Western schools have forced our children into their way of thinking. We have lost much of our language, customs and traditions. If they had "walked in our moccasins" they would have discovered a strong spirituality based on pure faith and intelligence built on intuition instead of logic. That is why we have a good percentage of our people highly skilled in art, music and the humanities.

On May 14, 1990, I wrote about how Indians have historically transformed the world. The glorified and heroic stories of the explorers, conquistadors, missionaries, colonists and cowboys are not true American history because they were written from a European viewpoint. In short, America is still being discovered.

Yet, none of this is described in American history books. We played decisive roles during the evolution of this society. Sometimes we were prime movers, sometimes we played equal roles with others and, of course, we played the well-publicized victims.

The gold and silver from the Americans did make capitalism possible in the rest of the world. Our mines, plantations and slaves also started the industrial revolution. Our cotton, rubber, dyes, and chemicals made this new system of production possible. Over thousands of years, our ancestors developed hundreds of varieties of corn, potatoes, beans, tomatoes, and peanuts that now feed the world. This includes popcorn, coke, chocolate, tobacco, coffee, maple syrup and cane sugar. We also discovered the curative powers of quinine, the anesthetizing ability of cocoa, and the potency of a thousand drugs, which are the basis of modern medicine and pharmacology. French sailors discovered that Indians cured scurvy with massive doses of vitamin C derived from pine bark and needles. Indians also used the bark of a poplar or willow tree to make a liquid for curing headaches and it was centuries later that it was found the active ingredient, salicin, closely resembles aspirin.

These drugs and agriculture made possible the population explosion of the last several centuries. We also had a form of democracy that has been haphazardly and inadequately adopted in many parts of the world. We were the true colonizers of America who cut the trails through the jungles and deserts, made the roads, and built the cities upon which modern America is based.

Three of our in-house grandkids, Moses, Andy, and Amy, started school so we spent a lot of time at the North and East Omak schools. Our daughter Kathy's kids, Erin and Brandon, are in middle and high Schools. This probably resulted in me running for the Omak School Board in 2005. I had already spent eleven years as a trustee for Wenatchee Valley College and seven years on the PSIS board.

I also worked with the Jesuit volunteers who were there at the tribe's request when the Catholic Church turned over the St. Mary's school to the tribe. The school was then named Paschal Sherman after Frank Wapato. Wapato got his name from the priests. They put names in a hat and the kids drew one out and became that name. Paschal Sherman was one of the elite graduates of St. Mary's school. He continued his education until he received a doctorate and worked in Washington, D.C., for many years. The Wapato family is also connected to my great-grandfather Chilcosahaskt who was a half-brother to Peter Wapato.

The articles I wrote were meant to give our kids encouragement that we as Indians had made a lot of contributions to the world. It is something that is not included in the history books.

So I naturally participated in the Native American Day on September 21, 2006, September 28, 2007, and September 22, 2011. The first time I concentrated on describing why we have Native American Day. The second time I tried to dovetail that into how our Indian culture is not necessarily compatible with the education system. Mostly because our culture has different learning styles than the school's teaching styles. The third and last time was a historical summary recognizing the contributions of Indians to the world.

NATIVE AMERICAN DAY   **September 22, 2011**

Tomorrow is Native American Day. What is Native American Day besides you don't have to go to school? Well, it is to recognize Indians. In the U.S. there are 562 tribes. Of course you live on or next to one of the biggest reservations in our state.

How many of you are Native Americans? OK, many but not all of you raised your hands. Well, you are wrong. All of you who were born and raised in America are Native Americans. We are all in this together.

How did all this start? Well, in 1968 California Governor Ronald Reagan established the fourth Friday in September as the American Indian Day.

The term American Indian means those whose ancestors met the European immigrants.

In 1998 California made the fourth Friday in September an official holiday called Native American Day. This is a little confusing because anyone born in the U.S. is a Native American. And that has contributed to American Indians becoming invisible.

In 1925 Zane Gray wrote a book called the *Vanishing American*, which was about American Indians disappearing.

Well, we are still here but maybe a better description would be the *Invisible American*. Let me tell you a story about that.

A few years ago I was on a business trip to Washington, D.C. As I was going through the airport concourse I noticed an athletic looking young man playing a video game. He was really involved. Later, for some reason, I was bumped up to first class, which was very unusual because the tribe doesn't travel first class.

Just before we took off the man I saw in the concourse took the seat next to me. I said, "Hello, I'm Wendell George from the Colville Tribe." He answered that he was Mark Rypien. He needed no introduction because I knew he was the All American quarterback from WSU and had just received the MVP award at the Super Bowl playing for the Washington Redskins. [For emphasis I put on my Washington Redskins cap]. He said he was going to Washington, D.C., to sign a contract. I later found out it was for $12 million.

I took the opportunity to ask him to not let them change the team name from Redskins. It was an honor to have that name because it recognized that Indians existed. Otherwise, we are ignored. The same applies to the Atlanta Braves baseball team. Stanford University changed their name from Indians to Cardinals. Part of the Vanishing American movement.

Even the Nespelem School changed from Savages to something else. When I went there we were proud to be called Savages even those who weren't Indian. We didn't win many games, but we usually won the Good Sportsmanship Award at tournaments so we weren't really Savages.

We might be invisible to some but we are in the background. And it is a very important background. We are the *backbone* of this country.

First, let's recognize that Indians were not limited to just the U.S. We populated all of North and South America and the islands in between.

We not only discovered the Americas before Columbus but we are America. But we are invisible.

Very few people realize the U.S. Constitution is based at least partly on Indian democracy. There was no democracy in the rest of the world before Columbus accidently landed on an island in the Caribbean.

Very few know the origin of medicines that are commonly used today. For example: Indians gave sailors in Montreal Vitamin C [bark of evergreen tree] to cure them of the scurvy. Europeans didn't recognize the significance until 200 years later.

The Incas in South America cured Malaria with quinine [Peruvian bark] in 1620. It was killing about two million people a year worldwide. A Noble prize was awarded to a European for the discovery of quinine in 1902 with no mention of the Incas. There are other medicines such as Iodine [from seaweed] and aspirin [from popular or willow trees] which were used by Indians before the rest of the world.

Many of today's foods and flavors came from the Americas. To mention a few: popcorn, peanuts, tomatoes, potatoes, zucchini, clams, 47 types of berries, maple syrup, fish and chips, and fried bread. Could we get along without French fries, corn chips, nachos, tortilla chips, jerky and dried meat?

But the totally invisible gift we are trying to give to the world is Spirituality. We have our Spirituality because we realize we are all part of nature from the smallest blade of grass to the largest galaxy.

REFLECTIONS

It was a beautiful sunny day on May 24, 1989, as it can only be in Portland, Oregon, that time of year. And I was attending the annual conference of Affiliated Tribes of Northwest Indians representing my tribe as a councilman from the Omak District.

After the usual opening prayer Chemawa Indian School officials asked if they should eliminate prayers like the States. The delegates supported prayer and said no.

But what I remember most is what Elmer Speedis, a Yakama elder, said. He gave a very enlightening speech on the difference between religions and spiritualism. He said spirituality is our personal belief in our Creator and religion is how we practice that belief.

My spirituality became alive and focused at the Cursillo I attended in the spring of 1986. The Cursillo is a three-day retreat organized by the Catholic Church but on the reservation run by Indians. We combined the Church and Indian Spirituality.

I give credit to Father Jake Morton for getting me into the Cursillo because he was my sponsor. He was to me what Father Lefty was to my grandfather, Lahompt.

The year 1986 was the turning point in my life. I won a seat on the tribal Council for the Omak District and I discovered what true spirituality was too. The point came home to me while attending that meeting in Portland.

Sir Julian Huxley and Pere Teilhard de Chardin described this spirituality evolution in people in the book, *The Phenomenon of Man*. They thought of the universe as being one gigantic evolutionary process. It is a process of becoming and attaining new levels. In addition, it is being led to cultural convergence. East and West merged together to form a unification of world thought. It is tied to the psychic energy that only the human being is capable of processing. Mankind facilitates exchange with the universe. Omega is the final state of the process of human convergence. The human is psychically tied to the earth, which becomes a true microcosm of the cosmos. The human has crossed the threshold of self-consciousness to a new mode of thought. The human personality trends towards more extreme individualism and more extensive participation in its own development. This new level will lead to new patterns of cooperation among individuals, cooperation for practical control, for enjoyment, for education and new knowledge. It will result in love, goodwill and full cooperation among people the world over.

The Hopi Indians predicted 200 years ago that the world could be destroyed if we collectively took the wrong path. If our technology continues to lead us down a materialistic path, the world could end.

But many of us do not believe that. A Mayan elder said, "The world will change for the better if we think with our heart rather than our head." Indians try to speak from the heart to be truthful and accurate.

If enough people do this a new world will emerge just like a butterfly from a cocoon. When we become spiritually aware, we will be totally in control of our destiny.

The Mayans [from the Yucatan in Mexico] say the world change predicted to happen on December 21, 2012 started in 2007 and will continue at least until 2015.

EPILOGUE

I sat contemplating the movie about 2012 while my wireless broadband router blinked on and off as it helped my computer communicate with unknown sources in cyberspace and provided my Internet connection. I am just one of many who log on the Internet. Three billion people out of a population of seven billion will be on line in 2011. By 2015 there will be five billion.

The blinking green lights remind me of the many episodes of Star Trek Voyager that I watched with my kids and grandkids.

It wasn't so much the stories that intrigued me but the projections of what could be our future. I could see it now,

"We are Borg. Our mission is to assimilate you. Resistance is futile!"

While chanting in unison the human-like creatures moved quickly and surrounded the real human. I used my mental remote control to turn off the TV. I had seen this episode many times before.

That TV series depicted a Borg that existed thousands of years in the future which were a highly advanced and aggressive network of humanoid drones that were part organic and part artificial life. A microchip implanted at birth improved the Borg mental and physical abilities. The chips linked the baby's brain to a collective consciousness that gave it seamless access to all knowledge assimilated by the Borg over thousands of years. The resulting drone was tuned into the collective consciousness but not aware of itself as a separate individual. Those Borg were ugly and machine-like. Their movements weren't smooth and their thinking process rather slow when compared to humans. We can do better than that.

For example, the 2008 Olympics opening ceremony showed the Chinese in a collective consciousness during the ceremonies in which their culture held them together psychically. How did the Chinese act with one mind?

By coherence of consciousness which is the greatest form of order known to nature. This order helps shape and creates order in the world. By a single act of wishing we create order.

The increasingly popular explanation for this is found in quantum physics where we operate as extremely small neurons. These neurons travel faster than light and enables every part of the universe to be in touch with every other part instantaneously. This causes human consciousness to be coherently organized and to control its effect [good or bad] on its environment. Does this sound like we are really a part of nature the way Indians believe?

Today this would be called the Internet of the Body where every neuron of the brain logs on at the same time and speaks to every other neuron simultaneously via the quantum process within. As we become more competent using this process we will have less and less need for the physical Internet. To efficiently carry this out we must block out our prejudices and ego hang-ups and try to see the world as it truly is. That is when the "team" really comes together.

The Maya understood that everything comes from and returns to the One Source which many call The Spirit. According to Indian belief everything has life or spirit.

Indian Spirituality is another way of saying "cosmic consciousness." To have cosmic consciousness is to know one's relationship to nature. This means maintaining a balance for everything you do in life. It also means analyzing how your actions will affect others before you act.

The Medicine Wheel is a powerful metaphor for the totality of life. All aspects of creation and consciousness, inclusive of the mineral, plant, animal, human and spirit realms are contained within the center and four directions of the Medicine Wheel. They overlap and interweave to form the whole. It is the center of the Medicine Wheel that we find the void, black hole, sacred zero, the chaos at the source of creation, containing all possibilities. Each of the elements - earth, water, fire, and air is guided and molded by the sacred life force energy contained within the void. It is the source of chi, which is the life force energy. Life could not exist without the life-force energy of the void, which is the catalyst for all the powers that are found within the 360 degrees of the Medicine Wheel.

At the entrance of the Paschal Sherman Indian School near Omak, Washington the Medicine Wheel is demonstrated by the Salmon Calendar. It shows the life cycle of the Salmon and how it is connected to the universe and all other creatures such as the Coyote. A plaque is mounted at the rear of the entrance which describes the movement of the Sun that passes through the Salmon silhouettes arranged in a Spiral and reflects the shadow of a Coyote on the opaque sheet behind it at exactly 10:40 AM every day the sun shines.

Salmon Calendar

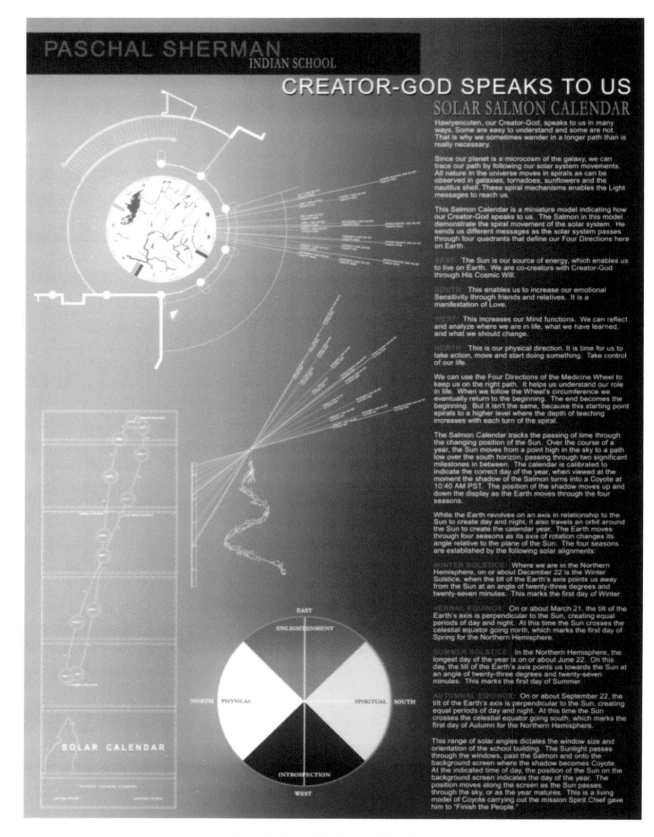

Description of Salmon Calendar

THE OMEGA POINT

The Mayan calendar is compatible to the 13/20 ratio that is the frequency of synchronization of the universe. This is how they achieved a telepathic unified human consciousness.

The radial quality of Fourth dimensional time makes it the universal synchronizing mechanism too. Time is the Fourth dimension according to Albert Einstein. As the universal factor of synchronizing, time is instantaneous and transcends light. This brings us to a new reality, the synchronic, which includes synchronicity as proposed by Carl Jung.

The velocity of time is instantaneously infinite and it transmits information from the core of stars.

The evolution of time is inseparable from consciousness and the converse is also true. Both time and consciousness are nonphysical Fourth dimensional factors, which coordinate the manifestation of the Third dimension. To do this they must work together. Consciousness of the Law of time is only possible through a profound act of self-reflection.

The Maya understood that the sun is the central source of energy and life within a solar system. They also understood that the planetary being is the source of life within the terrestrial environment. Then each respective being is linked back to the source of the next highest dimensions, or next respective frame of reference. The Maya called it the Kuxan Suum, which literally means "The road to the sky leading to the umbilical chord of the universe." This umbilical cord [or chord] is a resonant pathway, which connects you, the individual, through the center of the planet, through the heart of the sun, to the galactic core, or to the "Heart of all Things".

December 22, 2012, will be the dawning of consciousness, which is the Age of Aquarius and the next step of human consciousness. It is a collectively synchronized unification of galactic, solar and planetary levels of consciousness. This can be physically observed by the alignment of the galactic center [black hole] with the solar and planetary orbital planes of travel. The Great Convergence marks the attainment of critical mass within human consciousness. Thus effectively triggering the human collective imagination as an extension of planetary consciousness within the context of a galactic community.

This also relates to the harmonic ascension of planetary reality into the next highest octave. As the Hunab Ku mixes the matrices of realities into the fourth dimension of love, our civilization will transform into a multi-dimensional galactic culture founded on natural time, based on universal telepathy, and held together by art. Light technology is based on love, and can be used in right alignment with the source to create anything imaginable.

The illusion is that we exist in space and time. French priest and scientist Pierre Teilhard de Chardin believed the ultimate nature of reality can only be found through a collective spiritual awakening. He observed that human evolution trends toward greater complexity and concluded that the *ultimate in human consciousness was total connectivity with everything.*

He called the final stage, the Omega Point, which would be the collective spiritual birth of humanity as a whole.

The Alpha is the elementary material particles and their energies. Human beings evolved from these subatomic units to atoms, and then from atoms to inorganic and later, organic molecules, eventually to the first sub-cellular living units [self-replicating combinations of molecules] and then to cells, to multicellular individuals, to cepholized metazoan with brains to primitive humans, and now to civilized societies.

This process involves all the parts of the universe, which collapses in on itself to form organizational complexity. The result is a progressively more conscious mind. Humans are the only specie with full consciousness. The evolution of the mind uses both physical and psychic energy to increase the complexity of organized units.

Looking back we see this process enabled significant breakthroughs in consciousness and technology. The birth of agriculture about 11,000 years ago was a major turning point for mankind.

The invention of the wheel and written language between 4,000-3,000 B.C. advanced human technology.

The Industrial Revolution three hundred years ago was also a turning point.

Then thirty years ago we started the computer/information technology revolution.

Each period of the harmonic time wave is decreasing shorter in duration than the cycle which preceded it. Each respective period of the time wave is characterized by accelerated levels of new things happening faster and faster and in unprecedented, unpredictable ways. If this acceleration continues it will become mind-boggling.

For instance, we can expect a 400-day cycle in 2011/2012 when we will experience more transformation than in all the previous cycles combined.

Also a six-day cycle before the December 21, 2012, date will exhibit even more dramatic levels of hyper-accelerated transformations. There will be a point in our future when everything will be attracted like a Black Hole. The crossroads of 2012 will reflect the nature of a singularity.

According to Ray Kurzweil, author of *The Singularity is Near,* 2005, a mathematical singularity for $y = 1/x$ is when y approaches infinity as x approaches zero. A physical example of this is when a supernova explodes; it collapses to zero volume and infinite density. A singularity is created at its center. This is called a Black Hole and interrupts the fabric of space and time and becomes a new dimension.

In terms of human evolution, a singularity is created when the human has transformed every aspect of human life to infinity. At that point all combinations of life are happening at once.

In the last 135 minutes before we encounter this singularity, eighteen such transformations, comparable to the appearance of life and the invention of language, will be crossed. Thirteen of these evolutionary quantum leaps will be crossed in the last .0075 seconds of the Great Cycle.

This will be the end of the third dimensional existence. We will be totally conscious. We will realize the broadest sense of infinity. Your thoughts create your reality and they travel faster than the speed of light. We will be at the Omega point. The Coyote and Kokopelli missions are complete and **"The People are finished"**.

KOKOPELLI LEADING US INTO THE NEXT LIFE

APPENDIX

Chapter Five *Chilcosahaskt – Modern Times*

1. Heirs of Chilcosahaskt

Listed in probate case #51 documents	Tribal enrollment
	1st wife Ya-co-sit [died 1899]
George Saska from Alma	Son Koxit George [Lahompt] 1841-1922
Not listed ?	Daughter Achmeen [Margaret] 1840-1922
Not listed ?	Daughter Mary [died 5/8/1917]
Not listed ?	2nd wife Squen-hnmalx Suzanne 1840-6/23/1925
Joe Saska of Nesplin	Son Poker Joe 1852 1925
Elizabeth Long from Nesplin	Daughter Elizabeth 1885- 6/20/1940
Agatha Saska from Nesplin	Daughter Agatha 1865- 9/17/1950
Ossala[Lamai in Chinook] Saska	3rd wife Spo-ko-kalx [Rosalie] 1822-1919
Heirs of Mary not listed ?	Daughter Qui-hn-meetsa [Mary] died 1890
Cecil Antwine, Alma	Daughter Cecile born about 1860 or 1870

2. On October 19, 1914 the Superior Court ORDERED, ADJUDGED AND DECREED:

1. That the legal title to the land in question is held by the government of the United States of America under and by virtue of a certain trust patent issued October 22, 1896 under the Act of Congress of July 4, 1884, and such patent was the lawful patent and the only patent which under the proceedings had, and the laws governing the rights of Silico Saska, an Indian, at that time could be lawfully issued to him; that the United States of America holds and will continue to hold the title to the said property in trust for the benefit of the heirs of Silico Saska, deceased, until October 22, 1921.

2. That the action of the Commissioner of the General Land Office by its letter "B" in cancelling said trust patent and issuing the fee simple patent dated September 6, 1902 in lieu thereof was without the jurisdiction of the General Land Office and the said fee simple is null and void and all transfers had through the probate proceedings and all conveyance and transactions had with reference to the title of said property under and by virtue of the said fee simple patent and the title thereby conveyed are void and of no force and effect.

3. The heirs of said Silico Saska, deceased, are the owners of said property.

4. That Entiat Delta Orchards Company and all persons claiming through it have no title in or to said real property and the relief demanded in its complaint quieting the title to said real property is hereby denied.

Done in open court this 1st day of February, 1915 by J.T. Ronald, Judge.

The motion for a new trial was overruled and appeal was made to the Supreme Court of the State of Washington.

The case came on for hearing before that court en banc on January 14, 1918, whereupon an opinion was rendered by Judge Chadwick reversing the decree of the trial court, above set forth, and directing that a decree be entered in favor of the plaintiff [Entiat Delta Orchards Company].

No. 13167 JUDGMENT. Filed March 5, 1918.... that the judgment of the said Superior Court, be, and the same is hereby reversed with costs [The opinion of the Supreme Court can be found in 99 Washington Rep. page 84]; the petition for rehearing denied and that this clause be remitted to the said Superior Court for further proceedings in accordance herewith.

The Superior Court then followed directions from the Washington State Supreme Court and decreed that the Entiat Delta Orchards, a corporation, is the owner in fee simple of the said property.

The Court further decreed, as directed by the Supreme Court, that the identified heirs and unknown heirs, if any, of Silico Saska, deceased, also all other persona or parties unknown claiming any right, title, estate lien or interest in the said real estate and of each and every person claiming by, through or under said defendants or either of them are without right and title into the above described property and the whole thereof, and that the title of Delta Orchards in and to said property be and the same as hereby quiet in plaintiff. Done in open court, this 23rd day of April, 1918. J.T. Ronald, Judge.

Chapter Six *Lahompt – Entiat Valley*

1. A. Moses George interview with Gary Palmer November 19, 1990. "My Dad, Koxit George, died June 20, 1922 at the age of 90 or 92 perhaps older. The signing of the treaty of 1855 was told to me at the meal table."

   B. Vern Ray, PhD., anthropologist, Exhibit 4711 American Indian Ethnic history - Indians of the Northwest. "La-hoom [Entiat] was the fifth treaty signer. On page 21 the 14 Treaty signers are listed:

Name	Tribe
Kamaiakun	Yakima-Palus
Skloom	Yakima-Palus
Owhi	Kittitas
Te-cole-kun	Wenatchi
La-hoom	Entiat
Et, al.	

Ray Note: "The names are taken directly from the treaty; the tribal identification has been worked out from documentary and ethnographic information."

Chapter Nine *Moses*

1. The 1938 election results are shown below:

Nespelem:		Keller:	
Marcel Arcasa	77	Henry Covington	71
Moses George	76	Gus Whitelaw	54
Albert Orr	73		
Hiriam B. Runnels	63		
Inchelium:		Omak:	
Florence Quill	132	Joe Adolph	67
Peter J. Gunn	117	Lewis H. Runnels	64
Chas. A Hall	110	Daniel Samuel	55
Barney Rickard	85	Louie Smitakin	45

The losers for all Districts were:

Nespelem:

Pete Whitelaw
F. James O'Brien
Frank George
Antoine O'Brien
Ernest Orr
Nat Shrewsbury
Dick Armstrong

Omak:

John B. Cleveland
Alex Marchand

Inchelium:

Pete Noyes
Alex J. Covington
Louis Camille
Pete Lemery
Sidney Bills
Theo. Bourgeau

Keller:

Henry T. Nelson
Wm. F. Pooler

2. September 3, 1936 letter from Washington, D.C.

"The BIA cannot approve the Colville Constitution adopted at election on June 20, 1936, because powers are too broad for a non-IRA tribe. Thirty percent voter turnout and tribal voters voted to exclude itself from the provisions of the IRA.

"BECAUSE

Article VIII, Section 1 contains provisions whereby the Council has power 'to approve or veto any sale, disposition, lease or encumbrance of tribal lands or other assets; to employ legal counsel, the choice of counsel and fixing to fees to be subject to the approval of the Secretary of Interior.'

These powers can only be given to a tribe, which is under the Indian Reorganization Act.

The final Constitution approved by BIA February 26, 1938 and the majority of tribal members by a vote of 503 for, and 26 against with over 30% of voters voting. The section on Powers read:

Article V Section 1 a.

To confer with the Commissioner of Indian Affairs or his representative and recommend regarding the uses and disposition of tribal property."

Chapter Eleven, *Pot-wan-na – Implementation Phase*

1. The following is an edited version of the Tribes Lake Roosevelt issue described by Dale Kohler, Omak Councilman, in his article published on July 22, 1987 in the Tribal Tribune.

To The Omak District: WASHINGTON D. C. TRIP

Lake Roosevelt is the largest lake in the State of Washington. Created by the construction of Grand Coulee Dam in the 1930's it remains one of the largest undeveloped bodies of water within the 48 contiguous states. It is a continuing symbol of Franklin D. Roosevelt's depression era New Deal which provided employment and development opportunities for the Pacific Northwest. This project, however, holds a much darker legacy for the Colville and Spokane Reservations and their residents. They have gained little from it and experienced great disruption because of it.

In 1940 the United States Congress, in an act which provide for a number of things including the acquiring of Indian land for the Columbia Basin Project, recognized that the Colville and Spokane Tribes have paramount rights for hunting, fishing and boating on Lake Roosevelt in an area equal to one-quarter of the entire reservoir. This has never been defined. Later studies, however, show that the area encompassed by the two reservation boundaries is more like 48 per cent of the reservoir. In 1946 the Bureau of Reclamation, National Park Service and Bureau of Indian Affairs entered into an agreement, since known as the "Tripartite Agreement" which provided for the management of Lake Roosevelt. This agreement provided for a so called "Indian Zone". This 1946 agreement had no Indian input or participation.

In 1974 a major event for the two reservations occurred when the Solicitor for the department of Interior wrote an opinion which found that the above-mentioned 1940 Act, which provided for the taking of land within the two reservations for reservoir purposes, had not diminished the reservations and that their boundaries continued as they were prior to 1940.

This opinion also held that the Colville and Spokane Tribes continue to hold title to their portion of the riverbed of the former channel of the Columbia River [and, in the case of the Spokane Tribe, the bed of the original Spokane River covered by Lake Roosevelt]. It is this contention, which predates by many years the 1974 Solicitor Opinion, which forms the basis for the Colville claim known as 181-D which is now in the U.S. Court of Claims in Washington D.C..

In regard to the "Indian Zone", the Opinion held that the hunting, fishing and boating rights of the Tribes were exclusive of any rights of non-Indians and that they had the power to regulate these activities within this zone.

Because of the strong and unequivocal language in this opinion, the Secretary of Interior ordered that the federal agencies involved with Lake Roosevelt negotiate a new agreement which would include the Colville and Spokane Tribes in lake management.

The negotiation of a new Lake Roosevelt Management Agreement became a high priority in September of 1985. At that time strong objections were made to the issuance by the National Park Service of a concessions permit for the construction and operation of a hotel-marina development on Lake Roosevelt near Grand Coulee in an inlet known as Crescent Bay. The permit had been issued without any consultation whatever with the Tribes or assessment of potential impacts on reservation shorelines. The Colvilles later met with the developer of this proposed project and drafted an agreement. This agreement has never been finalized but the developers have not moved ahead because of their apparent inability to raise enough money for the project.

In October of 1985 attempts to negotiate a new Lake Roosevelt Management Agreement began. Involved in these negotiations were the Colville and Spokane Tribes plus the Bureau of Reclamation, National Park Service and Bureau of Indian Affairs. These discussions were conducted with local officials. It soon became apparent, where the Bureau of Reclamation and National Park service were concerned, that discussions on the local level would result in little progress. There was little willingness to have the Colville and Spokane Tribes as co-equals in any management arrangement for Lake Roosevelt.

In January of 1987 a letter signed by the Chairmen of the two reservations' tribal Councils was sent to the Secretary of Interior requesting a meeting. The meeting would be for the purpose of presenting the Tribes' proposal for developing a cooperative management agreement of Lake Roosevelt. The matter was referred by Secretary Hodel to Assistant Secretary of Indian Affairs, Ross Swimmer. It was through his office that a meeting in Washington D.C. with the two Assistant secretaries over the bureau of Reclamation and National Park Service along with Mr. Swimmer was arranged.

The meetings were held in Washington D.C. by the tribal representatives July 13th to 19th 1987.

Representing the Colville Reservation were Tribal Business Council Chairman, Mel Tonasket, Vice-Chairman, Andy Joseph; and tribal Councilman Wendell George, Don Peasley, and myself. Also part of the

Colville delegation were tribal attorney, Alan Stay, Colville Agency Superintendent, George Davis, BIA Environmental Protection specialist, John Rydzik and Tribal Hydrology Department Director, Gary Passmore. The Spokane Reservation was represented by their Tribal Council Chairman, Joe Flett and tribal Councilman, Glen Ford. It was agreed that Wendell George would serve as spokesman for the two reservations at all the meetings. The other members of the delegation would interject comments where appropriate.

That afternoon the meeting with the Assistant Secretaries and members of their staffs took place. There were at least 22 individuals in attendance. Chairman Mel Tonasket introduced the two delegations and made introductory comments after which Wendell George began the presentation. Copies of a draft of the proposed management agreement prepared by the Tribes were handed out. A series of charts with maps, etc. had been prepared by John Rydzik and Willie Womer which graphically described what the two tribes were proposing which Wendell referred to in his presentation. The presentation described the need for a new management agreement which would have the Colville and Spokane Reservations as co-equals with the Bureau of Reclamation [and possibly the Park Service] in making management decisions regarding the Lake. It was carefully explained that nothing in the proposed agreement would take away Reclamation's ability to continue to operate Grand Coulee Dam. Later in the presentation Alan Stay and others from both Tribes elaborated on some of the obstacles and frustrations the Tribes had experienced at the local level and why the meeting and the involvement of the Washington D.C. offices was necessary.

The Assistant Secretaries could only stay for one hour because they had been scheduled to meet with the Secretary of Interior on another matter. Other officials, however, remained and the discussion continued. The film entitled "The Price We Paid" was shown which details some of the disruption and hardship the Colvilles experienced when Grand Coulee Dam was built and reservation lands and town sites were flooded.

Before the Assistant Secretaries left it was agreed that they would have representatives assigned to work with the Tribes on drafting a new management agreement. It should be said here that Ross Swimmer was supportive of the Tribes' position and this support helped get the grudging go-ahead of the other two Assistant Secretaries [Reclamation first wanted to refer everything back to the local level!] to work with Washington D.C. involvement on a management agreement.

The next morning [July 16th] we began the day by meeting with aides from Congressmen Tom Foley and Sid Morrison's offices. Wendell again made the presentation and others in the delegation elaborated on various points. Gary Passmore talked about a meeting held with the Chamber of Commerce for the town of Davenport and Don Peasley described his meeting with the town of Wilbur's Chamber of Commerce. That afternoon we met with Congressman Sid Morrison. He was given a rundown via Wendell's presentation as to why we were in Washington D.C. and the importance of the management agreement to us. He said he would work with the congressional delegation on this matter. He was advised of the tribal houseboat enterprise being started on Lake Roosevelt and that $1.3 million had been committed to this project through this next years. He said he was very excited about the houseboat potential of the lake and observed that his form of recreation is a big thing in other parts of the country.

In the afternoon we met with Senator Dan Evans. Yvette Joseph and another aide were also present. Yvette had prepared a notebook with a narrative history and maps for the Senator and from his questions and comments we could see he had reviewed the material. Wendell again described the group's reasons for meeting with him and, again, other members of the delegation added to the discussion. The Senator expressed his support for moving ahead with the management agreement and indicated he would do as much as he could to help it along.

A lot of your money was spent sending us back to Washington D.C. I came home with a feeling that definite progress had been made. I thought you should know in some detail for what reason and how your money was used.

Until Next Time,
Dale L. Kohler, Councilman, Omak District

169

BIBLIOGRAPHY

1. Arguelles, Jose' PhD. – The Mayan Factor – 1987
2. Bauman, T. Lee M.D. – God at the Speed of Light – 2001
3. Castaneda, Carlos – The Teachings of Don Juan: A Yaqui Way of Knowledge – 1968
4. Chopra, Deepak M.D. – Quantum Healing – 1989
5. de Chardin, Teilhard S.J. – The Phenomenon of Man – 1959
6. Einstein, Albert – Theory of Special Relativity – 1905. Evolved into space-time – a four dimensional coordinate system of three space and one time by Minkowski – 1907
7. Kurzweil, Ray – The Singularity is Near – 2005
8. Roberts, Jane – Adventures in Consciousness – 1975
9. Russell, Walter PhD. – The Wave Lies in the Secret of Creation – reprinted in 1995
10. Tober, Jan and Lee Carroll – The Indigo Children: The New kids have arrived – May 1, 1999
11. Tolle, Eckhart – The Power of Now – 1997
12. Waters, Frank – The Book of the Hopi – 1959
13. Wolf, Fred Alan PhD. – The Spiritual Universe - 1999

Made in the USA
San Bernardino, CA
11 July 2014